ZENOBIA.
(*Enlarged from a Coin.*)

DARF PUBLISHERS LIMITED
LONDON
1987

THE GRAND COLONNADE, PALMYRA.

AN ACCOUNT

OF

PALMYRA AND ZENOBIA

WITH

TRAVELS AND ADVENTURES

IN

BASHAN AND THE DESERT

BY

Dr. William Wright

Author of
"The Empire of the Hittites," "The Brontes in Ireland,"
&c.   &c.

WITH EIGHTY ILLUSTRATIONS
AND THIRTY-TWO FULL-PAGE ENGRAVINGS

DARF PUBLISHERS LIMITED
LONDON
1987

FIRST PUBLISHED 1895
NEW IMPRESSION 1987

ISBN 1 85077 155 3

Printed and bound in Great Britain
by A. Wheaton & Co. Ltd, Exeter, Devon

CONTENTS.

CHAPTER I.
The Bible regarding Solomon and Tadmor—Classic history and Zenobia—The great king and great queen—The glory and obscurity—Chronicles in stone—Two visits to Palmyra—Dangers—Companions..................................1-4

CHAPTER II.
Leaving Damascus—The Lebanons—City suburbs—Early fruit—King Abraham—Turkish road-making—Party separated—The fortress convent—Miraculous picture—Christian refuge—Syrian handcuffs—Máloula convent—Wonderful town—The scene—Syriac spoken...5-16

CHAPTER III.
Party of Kurds—Among the mountains—Yabroud—Ancient tombs—Handsome people—Famine—Bedawi raids—A weeping woman—English lady....17-23

CHAPTER IV.
Our party—Prince of dragomans—Gaudy guide—Desolate plain—Vaulting ambition—Ruined cities—The gleaners plundered............................24-30

CHAPTER V.
More ruins—Vapour bath—Ancient sanitarium—The Jân—Bustards and Bedawîn—Hazar-enan—The Stone Age—Schooling—Border Arabs—Guide and guards...31-39

CHAPTER VI.
Searching for 'Ain el-Wu'ul—Rickety escort—"Brandy Bob" and "Gipsy"—Gazelle traps—Wild stampede—Drunk and incapable—Encamping in the dark—The "princess" and her gift—Revolution in hair—The captive maiden—The captive mother's lullaby—Wa'al hunting—Desert Quakers—The fountain—Suleib children supremely beautiful........................40-53

CHAPTER VII.
Coursing hares on our way—Castle of Palmyra—Cyclopean horse—Strange birds—Arab camping-ground—Wonderful lizard—Approaching Palmyra—First sight of the ruins..54-62

xii CONTENTS.

CHAPTER VIII.

Among the ruins—Encampment—Temple of the King's Mother—Hadrian and Palmyra—Temple of the Sun—Temple described—Holy of Holies—Zenobia in her splendour—City of columns—Public edifices—Palace of Zenobia—Palmyra statues—Statues to Zenobia and her husband—Zenobia's name—Splendid city................63–73

CHAPTER IX.

Sir Richard Burton's advice—Scaling implements—Waggish mule and ladders—Tomb towers—Dreadful dilemma—Facing the difficulty—Selecting diggers—Eighty chosen—Attacking the towers—Digging and climbing—Sculptures—A tower described—Skulls and remains—Scarab of Tirhakah—An African romance—Entrapped in a tomb—Among the bones—Sheol—Struggle to escape—Rescued................74–94

CHAPTER X.

The tepid river—A swim in the sulphurous fount—Penetrating the cavern—Fount Ephca and altar—Bedawi bathers drowned—Water supply of the city—Various sources—Climb to the castle—View from the castle—Name Tadmor—Building of Tadmor—Growth of Palmyra—Roman influence—Meeting-place of merchants—Trade routes—Origin of columns and statues—Cost of adornments................95–108

CHAPTER XI.

Zenobia in history and romance—Roman influence—Relationship of Rome to Tadmor—Roman policy—Odainathus—Roman blunder—Meditated revenge—Capture of Valerian—Sapor defeated by Odainathus—Odainathus murdered................109–122

CHAPTER XII.

Zenobia's beauty and splendour—Claims kinship with Cleopatra—Supposed to be a Jewess—Statues to Zenobia and Odainathus—Zenobia's generals—The head of Zenobia—Zenobia's descent—Her appearance—Cassius Longinus—Zenobia's opportunity—Roman disasters—Zenobia's call to arms....123–138

CHAPTER XIII.

Zenobia prepares to meet the Romans—Her levies—Her camps—Drilling and discipline—Her armies march by three routes—Water—The great battle of Immae—The heroic queen—Roman strategy—The Romans victorious—Flight of the Orientals to Palmyra................139–150

CHAPTER XIV.

The dogged West and the chivalrous East—The water question—The siege of Palmyra—Incidents of the siege—The city in straits—Aurelian's letter to Zenobia, and her reply—Zenobia looking for succour................151–158

CONTENTS.   xiii

CHAPTER XV.

Zenobia fleeing for help—Desperate ride—Pursued—Seized at the Euphrates—Brought back a prisoner—In the presence of Aurelian—Palmyra capitulates—Execution of Longinus—Revolt at Palmyra—Return of Aurelian—His vengeance—Restoration of the temple—Aurelian's triumph—The captive queen—Zenobia in Italy—Decadence of Palmyra......................159–170

CHAPTER XVI.

Last day at Palmyra—Bedawi charge—An awkward reception—Interview with the spearmen—Return—Followed by the Bedawin—Encamped beside the enemy—Guards asleep—Arms removed—Uproar—Giving the Bedawin the slip—Escape and pursuit—Caravan attacked—Battle—Defeat of the peasants and plunder of the caravan—Turkish official sharing in the loot—Turkish justice. 171–188

CHAPTER XVII.

Fox-hunting—Turkish misrule—Blackmail—The Turkish caterpillar and the Bedawi locust—Marriage of the sheikh's daughter—Housebreaking—Disturbed night—Orientals and Damascus...189–193

CHAPTER XVIII.

Incident in my first visit to Palmyra—Collecting curios—Mummies and skulls—Archæological fever—The Greek image and umbrella handle—Fever cured—Long ride projected—Leaving the ruins—Way blocked—We charge—Very irregular army—Judgment on prudence—Desperate ride—Blood-mare and plebeian—Evading a camp—Discovered and pursued—Race for life—Successful ruse—Escape from pursuers..................................194–204

CHAPTER XIX.

The delightful dawn—A new danger—Unpleasant company—Fired on and slightly wounded—Retiring salute—Marvellous escape—Short halt at Karyetein—Pressing onward alone—People by the way—Vultures to the prey—Ladies and naked soldier—Samaritanism 205–214

CHAPTER XX.

Two horsemen—Challenge and counter-challenge—The dabbous and the shillelah—Peace and interview—Enemies become friends—Home in Damascus. 215–221

CHAPTER XXI.

ADVENTURES AMONG THE RUINS OF BASHAN.

Starting for Bashan—Companions—The ways of dragomans—Camel panic—The street called Straight—Crusaders—Cemeteries—Massacre—Graves—Colporteur's spurt and the result—Scenery—The plain—The 'Awaj not the Pharpar—Rivers of Damascus—Naaman's choice justified..............223–239

CHAPTER XXII.

The potters' caravan—Brag and cringe—The field of forays—Father of a tree, and Abu Muraj—Desert tactics—First sight of the Lejah—Billows of basalt—Reception at Burâk—Water famine—Gloom of the Lejah—Bashan architecture—People of Burâk—Caves and inscriptions—Shooting partridges—Cookery in the desert 240–257

CHAPTER XXIII.

Coasting the shore of the Lejah—Resemblance to a coast-line—Churning and butter—Coursing and capturing a Bedawi—Stalking bustards—The katha migration—Grouse eggs—Entering Musmeih—Ruins and inscriptions—Character of the ruins—Our following—The use of a joke—Losing our way—Mazes of lava—Cruising round promontories and headlands—People of Khubab waiting for a lord—An old acquaintance 258–273

CHAPTER XXIV.

Position of Khubab—Agricultural village—Industries—Opposition of the priest—Sunday at Khubab—General description—Hermon—Hauran towers—Deserted villages—Reception at Tibny—The widow and her son—Villages on the plain—Ezrá and Adra'at—Identification of Edrei, the city of Og—Og's kingdom—Underground Edrei—Conquest of Bashan and defeat of Og—Bible narrative and the topography—Limits of Og's kingdom—Ashtaroth—Argument of identification... 274–292

CHAPTER XXV.

Ezrá and its ancient church—Ruins described—Inhabitants of Ezrá—Leaving by a slippery path—More coast-lines—Busr el-Hariry and its inhabitants—Battle of Nejrân—Druzes and Christians—A strange lady—Her dwelling and influence and treasure—Her coin with Og's effigy—A diplomatic sheikh...293–301

CHAPTER XXVI.

Druze courtesy and hospitality—Bedawi women—Druze women with horns—Christian women—Tell Sheehân open-mouthed—Druze women by the water—Kanawât and scenery—Identification and history—Gideon's expedition—The Bashan sanitarium—Rambles among the ruins—The people—"Our lord, King Herod the Great"—Atil and scenery—A discovery at Atil—Roman road.. 302–323

CHAPTER XXVII.

Horses at Suweideh—Our old guide—Character of hospitality—Druze politics—Identification—Loading a donkey—Jebel Kuleib—Druze towns and people—St. George—Extinct volcanoes—The use of the towers—A splendid sheikh—Excitement among the Druzes—Preparing coffee—Cause of the excitement—Warlike speech—Another acquaintance—New ground—Remarkable ruins..324–340

CHAPTER XXVIII.

Melah es-Sarrâr and its towers and people—Agriculture—Other ruins beyond—Arab carriers of salt from the Jowf—The Salchah of the Bible and Castle of Sulkhâd—Castle on a crater—Bedawi battle—Feasting the victors—A wild scene—Men feeding—The women's share—Separated party—Bosra and ruins—Christian inscription—Signs of magnificence—Stormy night and sand-drift—The Turkish garrison and officers—Preparing for an attack—An officer's dormitory—State of siege—Christian spies—Attack and escape—Departure from Bosra—A furious Druze—Battle of Mezareeb—The city that gave Rome an emperor and the Druzes a prince....................341-364

CHAPTER XXIX.

Druzes in conclave—Questioned by Druze women—Sudden descent through a roof—Family at supper—The feast and foods—Druze religion—An uncanny old sheikh—Abrupt departure—Crossing the Lejah—Druze head-dress—Dama and its reported wonders—Resolved to know the worst—Amazon women and savage-looking men—Exploring in safety—Dangerous Arabs—Arable land in the Lejah—Remarkable Arab shepherds—Business and talk—Wandering in a maze—Steering by fixed points—Out on the level plain—Enormous flock of gazelles—Curiosity of the Christians at Buseir—Local industry—Vultures following the Mekka pilgrims—Cruelty to animals—Filthy and ferocious pilgrims—Loveless return home—Light on the sacred record—Our duty to the Druzes—The end.........................365-387

LIST OF ILLUSTRATIONS.

Grand Colonnade, Palmyra..*Frontispiece*	Triumphal Arch............................ 71
Maps—Empire of Zenobia; Routes to Palmyra.................................xx	Side Archway of Triumphal Arch.. 72
	Ceiling of Tomb Tower................. 74
Fountain, Damascus........................ 1	The Father of Ladders................ 75
Soffit Ornament of Temple Cell Door 4	Tomb Towers........................... 81, 85
Pilaster Ornament, Temple of Sun... 5	Palmyrene Figure......................... 88
Straight Street, Damascus.............. 7	Seal of Tirhakah.......................... 88
Saidenâya..11	Baalatga and 'Alliasha.................. 90
Frieze Ornament, Temple of Sun......17	Mortuary Vault............................ 92
Yabroud..18	Palmyrene Figure......................... 94
Yabroud Family.............................19	Soffit in Temple of Sun................. 95
Entablature of Grand Entrance, Temple of Sun............................24	Castle end of Great Colonnade....... 99
	Central part of Great Colonnade.104-5
Sudud's Vaulting Ambition............27	Palmyrene Figure..........................108
Palmyra Tesseræ............................30	Zenobia..109
Entablature of Grand Entrance Portico, Temple of Sun......................31	The Triumphal Arch....................113
	Coin of Valerian...........................122
Soffit of Cornice, Little Temple........40	Projecting Entablature, Temple of Sun...123
Soffit supported by Four Columns....53	
Basso Relievo on Pilaster, Temple of Sun..54	Doorway of Zenobia's Palace.........125
	Supposed Heads of Zenobia....129, 130
Triumphal Arch, with Castle in the distance..57	Coin of Zenobia............................139
	Grand Colonnade..........................143
Palmyra Ruins...............................59	Palmyrene Inscription..................150
Temple of the Sun..........................61	Entablature, Temple of Sun..........151
Fragment of a Temple.....................62	Roman Lamp................................158
Fallen Capital.................................63	Frieze in Temple of Sun.................159
Temple of the King's Mother..........64	Colonnade of Temple of Sun..........165
Upright of Side Door of Great Temple..65	Scroll and Capital of Pilaster, Temple of Sun...................................170
Ceiling of Holy of Holies, Temple of Sun..67	Frieze, Great Door of Temple Court.171
	Granite Monoliths........................173
Temple of the Sun, Eastern Side.....69	Palmyra Terra-Cotta Head............188

xviii LIST OF ILLUSTRATIONS.

Cornice Soffit of Tomb Tower.......189	Coin of Edrei..............................300
Bedawi Robbers.....................190–191	Folding Stone Door (Hauran).......302
Ceiling of Holy of Holies, Temple of Sun......................................193	Tell Sheehân...............................303
	Druze Tantur..............................305
Palmyrene Inscriptions................194	Temple at Suleim...................306–307
Tesseræ from Palmyra..................204	Temple of Kanawât......................308
Ceiling of Tomb Tower.................205	Druze Ladies of Lebanon..............309
Soffit of Side Door of Temple........214	Ruin at Kanawât.........................311
Square Entablature, Great Temple 215	Coin of Kanawât.........................314
Damascus..............................218–219	Gateway, Kanawât.......................316
Solitary Column..........................221	Peripteral Temple at Kanawât......319
Bab es-Shurki, Damascus..............222	Ruins at Kanawât........................321
Map—Sketch Route of Bashan.224–225	Carved Head, Kanawât................323
Runaway Camels in Desert............227	Doorway at Kanawât....................324
Villa on the Barada.....................236	Temple at Es-Suweideh..........326–327
The Barada and Merj...................237	Stone Door (Hauran)...................340
Coin of Aretas............................240	Coin of Bosra.............................341
Basalt Bed of the Lejah...............245	Lebanon Druzes..........................345
Lejah Partridges.........................256	Castle of Salchah..................346–347
Stone Window (Hauran)..............258	Bosra..350
Bedawin of the Hauran................261	Columns at Bosra........................351
Temple at Musmeih.....................265	Ruins of Bosra, Theatre and Castle 354–5
Interior of Temple......................266	Ruins of Bosra............................357
Coin of Philip the Tetrarch..........274	Bab el-Howa, Gate of the Wind.....360
Hermon...............................276–277	Shuhba, Roman Bath...................364
Hauran Watch Tower..................279	Coin of Philip............................365
Palmyra Mortuary Tower.............279	Druze Sheikhs at 'Ahiry...............367
Coin of Herod the Great..............293	The Hajj leaving Damascus..........381

PREFACE.

THIS Book was written partly in the saddle and partly in the tent, and almost wholly amid the scenes and adventures which it describes. It should therefore not be lacking in local colour.

The explorations and events recorded were incidents of a residence in Syria during nine stirring years, and companions in the dangers and enjoyments are still with us.

The work—some chapters of which have already appeared—has been edited in the fresh light of new inscriptions and fuller investigations, and aims at giving a picture, in outline only, of the living past and the living present under consideration. The East moves slowly, and few changes in light or shadow call for alteration in tone or setting consequent on delay in publication.

I am indebted to Dr. Mackinnon of Damascus, and Dr. Macphail of Edinburgh, for the use of recently taken photographs in Bashan; and I am under special obligations to the publishers for the creditable manner in which they have produced the Book on both sides of the Atlantic.

WILLIAM WRIGHT.

WOOLSTHORPE, NORWOOD.

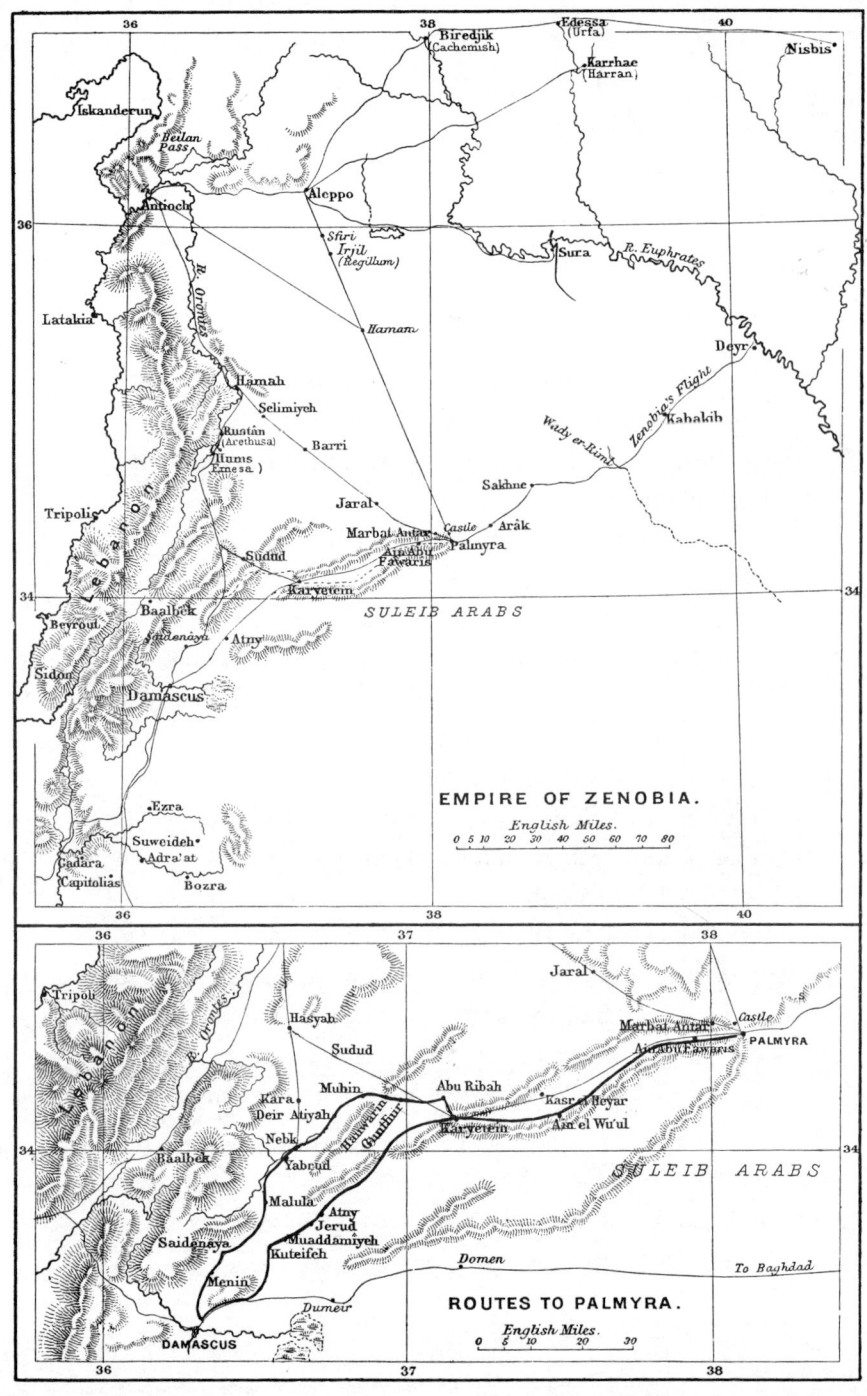

PALMYRA AND ZENOBIA.

CHAPTER I.

FOUNTAIN, DAMASCUS.

THE Bible tells us that Solomon built Tadmor in the wilderness, and classic authors inform us that Zenobia had her home there. History, sacred and secular, links the city inseparably with that magnificent King of Israel, unrivalled in wisdom and barbaric splendour, and with that desert queen and peerless woman, whose regal attributes and personal accomplishments were as remarkable as the brilliance of her reign. The city comes on the stage of history in the blaze of glory that surrounded the most wondrous of Oriental kings, and after many centuries of splendid obscurity, quits the stage of history in the meteoric glare that accompanied the most wondrous of Oriental queens.

And yet history, careful to preserve the remembrance of cities of which no vestige remains, has been so reticent about Tadmor, that the wonderful ruins, lately discovered, almost alone perpetuate her glory. Her chronicles are written in stone — in graceful villa and spacious palace, in massive mausoleum and mighty temple, in vistas of airy colonnades and crescents seen through triumphal arches, and in a thousand monuments of genius and taste, battered and hurled about as playthings of time, but conserving in every feature the blush and freshness of youth.

Like a shrinking beauty, Tadmor sits in solitary grandeur behind her own desert mountains; and those who would see her in her calm retreat must leave the beaten tracks of tourists, and cross " the great and terrible desert."

During ten years, I had seen many tourists arrive at Damascus, eager as devotees to gaze on this queen of ruins; but owing to the expense, danger, and general hardships of the journey, few of the multitude had been permitted to look upon her beauty. Of these few, fewer still had free leisure to become acquainted with all her charms.

I may consider myself the most fortunate of tourists, in that I twice succeeded in visiting Palmyra under the most favourable circumstances, and without stepping far out of the circle of my professional duties. I shall take my readers by my latest route, through a region seldom explored, and by an easy path, with water at regular intervals.

As my first trip to Palmyra was made in the ordinary prescribed manner, I shall get it out of the way as quickly as possible, and only refer to it again to illustrate or supplement my second. It consisted of long, weary marches, day and night, along the middle of an uninteresting plain, extending in an eastern direction, with mountains like walls running most of the way on either side. I left Damascus on the 20th March, 1872, and reached Palmyra in four days; but as the road was monotony itself, I came back to Damascus at one stretch, and my mare trotted into Damascus almost as fresh as she had trotted out of Palmyra. This long ride, which was beset with adventures, I shall describe further on.

From the time of my first trip to Palmyra, the people of Karyetein, where I spent a night, never ceased to urge me to establish a school among them, and I had promised to revisit them in the spring of 1874. During that spring the Bedawîn plundered the whole eastern borders of Syria. Caravan after caravan with Bagdad merchandise was swept off into the desert. The British Bagdad post, sacred in the most troublous circumstances, had been seven times plundered, the letters had been torn open and strewed over the plain, and the postman, without camel or clothes, left to perish, or find his way as he best could to human habitation. Spearmen, like swarms of locusts from the east, spread over Jebel Kalamoun, and having slain the shepherds, and stripped any men or women who fell in their way, drove before them all the flocks and herds of the region.

Feeble fanaticism held sway in the city, and absolute anarchy reigned in the rural districts; and so great was the terror of the peasantry, that, though they were actually starving, they could not move from their villages, except in large armed bodies, and even thus they sometimes fell a prey to the Ishmaelites.

In this state of the country, I had almost given up my promised visit, when two daring explorers, the Honourable C. F. P. Berkeley and wife, arrived in Damascus. Coolness and courage had carried them safely through Petra and Karak, and all the trans-Jordanic regions, where they were sometimes beset with savage and furious mobs. Their faces were set towards Tadmor, and the prospect of danger only gave a keener zest to the projected tour. A common interest drew us together, and I was able to avail myself of their escort and pleasant society, in return for topographical knowledge, and an acquaintance with the people and their ways. The season was already far advanced for making the journey to Palmyra, and so we resolved to start at once.

SOFFIT ORNAMENT OF TEMPLE CELL DOOR.

PILASTER ORNAMENT, TEMPLE OF THE SUN.

CHAPTER II.

ON the 25th May, 1874, we left Straight Street, Damascus, at nine o'clock A.M. As we passed out of the city, we saw green vegetables beginning to make their appearance in the markets, and jaundiced-looking apricots, ripened in the baths, were being eagerly purchased and greedily devoured by the famine-stricken people. A little beyond Bab Tûma, Thomas' Gate, where once stood St. Thomas' Church, the site of which is now unknown, we turned out of the straight road to Palmyra, into a shady lane to the left. We had planned our route through the highlands of Jebel Kalamoun, that we might visit the interesting towns and mission schools of that region, while escaping the great heat of the plains.

On most maps of Syria, the Anti-lebanon appears as a huge caterpillar, laid side by side and parallel with Mount Lebanon; but the Anti-lebanon consists of a series of mountain ranges, some of which run parallel with

Lebanon and sink into the great Hums plain, while some twist off in a more eastern direction, and shoot out into the desert. The most eastward and desertward of these ranges rises into Hermon at the one end, and sinks into Palmyra at the other; and the part of this latter range which lies north-east of Damascus is generally known as Jebel Kalamoun.

Our shady lane, through the orchards of Damascus, was overhung with great spreading walnuts, trellised with vines, and on either side were apricots beaded with new fruit, and thickets of pomegranate with scarlet blossoms bursting forth like handfuls of crumpled silk.

Half an hour from the city we crossed the Taura (Pharpar), a river of Damascus, a little below where a cotton manufactory was established with English machinery, and under English superintendence. The English workmen, however, found great difficulty in getting their wages, and they were kept in unhealthy lodgings, until three out of four died, and the survivor returned home broken in heart and constitution, and with experiences sufficient to deter others from being allured into similar service by the prospect of high wages.

Beyond the bridge, we met a party with a few sacks of new barley, artificially ripened, and carried on the backs of donkeys into the city; and we saw fields of barley pulled and left on its side to ripen, that it might be in time for the famine prices.

An hour from Damascus we passed through Burzeh, a Moslem village, where there is the sanctuary of

STRAIGHT STREET, DAMASCUS.
(*No. 21 on the left.*)

Abraham, and where the people still talk familiarly of "good King Ibrahîm," though the names of Sultan Selim and Salah ed-Dîn (Saladin) have already almost passed from local tradition. Here we struck into the mountains to the left by a pass up a gorge, parallel to the sublime gorge of the Barada, by which tourists enter Damascus, and much resembling it, but on a smaller scale.

Our road lay up a fine mountain torrent, through which our horses splashed and stumbled. Once a Damascus Moslem was riding up the same gorge, and he had his leg broken by the falling of his horse. When dying he left a sum of money to make a road through the pass, to prevent the repetition of such accidents as cost him his life. The money, after lying many years in the wrong place, was unearthed by an English engineer; but it found its way into Moslem hands once more, and in summer, when the pass was bone dry, a road was made along the bottom of the ravine. The fact of the Turks having made a road themselves was published in the papers, and people wondered. The road was made chiefly of dry dust, pressed down by the palms of the hands and the bare feet of the workmen and workwomen; and though it had been only one year made when we passed through, not a vestige of it remained.

In less than half an hour we issued from the gorge at Mâraba, a Moslem village, clinging to a bare rock overhanging the water. We turned up the western side of the ridge through which we had come, by a narrow valley full of fragrant walnuts, and white-stemmed poplars, and green corn as high up as the soil was watered, and no higher, calling to mind the words of the prophet, " And everything shall live whither the river cometh" (Ezek. xlvii. 9).

We lunched in a lovely green meadow, under the trees, near the village Et-Tell, and then continued our course in the track of the water past Menin. a village which, like Et-Tell, contains many remains of ancient buildings. This part of our route was charming. We had left the steaming city behind, and we were continually getting up out of the heated plain. Here and there we had pleasant shade, and everywhere the sparkling water murmured past us, and every vista and every eminence supplied pictures of blending landscapes, such as are rarely seen even in Syria.

Here our party was temporarily broken up. We had agreed to spend the first night at Mâloula, but my companions' guide had directed the tents to Saidenâya, and so I had to ride on alone, as I had arranged to visit the mission schools of Yabroud and Nebk on the following day.

I passed the fortress convent of Saidenâya, perched on a high rock, up which hewn steps lead to a small door, the only entrance. This convent contains a crowd of ignorant, idle women, and is famous for a picture painted by St. Luke, which distils a fluid very efficacious for eye complaints, and for replenishing the coffers of the convent. The picture was once stolen, but in the hands of the thief it became changed into flesh, and continues so to this day. I once tried hard to see this miraculous picture. I urged the cruelty of keeping a thing of flesh and blood so closely confined, and the advantages that might be expected from a little fresh air. I was also very liberal, and tried to bribe my

SAIDENÂYA.

hostess, who was not fair, but it was all in vain. I could not see it and live, and so I was spared the sight.

This miracle has attained to an antiquity respectable in these days. Nearly two hundred years ago, Henry Maundrell found the fame of the picture,[1] and the

[1] At a very early period the picture was supposed to represent the Virgin Mary. There is a Latin MS. in the Library of Trinity College,

reputation of the establishment, about the same as they are now. But they have a new miracle to boast of in the convent of Saidenâya.

In 1860, many Christians took refuge in the convent, and they were there for a time in a state of siege. There is no well in the convent, and only a cistern in which the rain-water from the roof is preserved. But, wonderful as it may seem, the water in the cistern swelled up to the brim, and overflowed in a stream all the time that the wicked Druzes hovered about the convent. Could I disbelieve the miracle when I was told of it by a lady who actually saw it take place, and pointed out to me the very spot? It is much to be regretted that this miracle took place in such an out-of-the-way convent; but even thus, I have no doubt, it will yet receive the fame it merits.

My path lay along the eastern side of the mountain range on which Saidenâya stands. The range has a sea-washed crest, showing in its length a clear tide-line. Though the mountains were bare and without vegetation, there were in several places little flocks of goats and sheep, attended by very small, half-naked shepherds, burnt

---

Dublin, consisting of a Guide Book to Palestine, written about 1350 A.D. The picture is thus referred to: "Ten miles from Damascus is the city of Saidenâya, in which is the venerate image of the glorious Virgin Mary, which was brought from Jerusalem. This blessed image was entirely converted into a fleshy substance, so that it ceases not night and day to emit a sacred oil, which the pilgrims who come there from every quarter carry away in little glass jars. No Saracen can live in this city; they always die within a year."

brown. The red plain had been scratched in several places, but the "thin ears blasted with the east wind" showed that, as on the six previous years, the crop of the region was about to be a complete failure.

In this solitary ride I met only one party of men. They were village recruits, who had been taken by conscription. Handcuffs in Syria are of a most primitive kind. A piece of a tree, eighteen inches long and eight inches in diameter, is split up; a place is hollowed out across the split, and the two wrists being placed in the groove, the two pieces are nailed together with large spikes. Each recruit had his hands nailed up, and the party was being driven into Damascus by one mounted dragoon. The sticks had been so unskilfully fitted that some of their wrists were bleeding, and the poor fellows were all lame and hungry. He would be a real benefactor who would supply Turkey with a few thousand pairs of civilized handcuffs.

In less than three hours I turned to the left, through a narrow cleft in the mountain, and then wound up and down its western side, till I reached the Greek Catholic convent of Máloula. About eight o'clock I reached the small iron portal, which opened to my first tap, and I found myself in a quadrangle with a two-storied range of rooms running all round it. Instead of nuns, as at Saidenâya, a great drove of mountain cows were housed in the court at night, and the place was kept by two agricultural monks and two "stout daughters of the plough."

My servant, who had preceded me, had my bed erected in an aerial cell, and the kindly old priest brought me a bottle of native wine, and what was better still, fresh eggs and milk.

It is only fair to state that the priest who honoured me with his company seemed to value more highly than I did this "wine of Helbon," which maintains in its neighbourhood the pre-eminence it held in the days of Ezekiel. In exact ratio as the contents of the bottle went down, the spirits of my entertainer rose, and till a very late hour he poured out stories of the place, natural and supernatural, until I was fairly driven into the land of dreams.

Next morning I was on the roof of the convent when the first shafts of rosy light shot over the eastern mountains. The upper convent stands near the edge of a fearful precipice, on a ledge of rock which seems driven wedge-like into a deep break in the mountain. Creeping close to the edge of the precipice, I looked over, and beneath me I saw the most picturesque town in Syria, perhaps the most remarkable in some respects in the world. The cliffs rise several hundred feet over the village, and the houses stick like swallows' nests one above the other about the bases of the cliffs. The flat roofs looked like the steps of a great ladder up the side of the mountain.

The Greek convent beneath, Mar Theckla, is wedged in under a huge ledge of impending mountain, and a door opens out of the living rock. The arch of the roof is supported by a slender column, which seems to mock the crushing weight above. The deep valley below is full of huge blocks that have fallen from the mountain, and the pendant cliffs are cracked and fissured, and seem ready to follow into the ravine. As I stood on a half-detached ledge that overhung the houses, I almost held my breath, lest the huge mass should plunge madly down among the human nests, bringing instant death to hundreds.

The scene was lovely as well as strange. Behind, the red hill curved around like a vast amphitheatre, and on either side the mountain cliffs stood up like the sides of a great portal. In front, the gardens opened out like a fan from the mouth of the gorge. These gardens, green with the many shades of walnut, and poplar, and bay, and cypress, and growing corn, terminated abruptly in a flat chocolate-coloured plain, around which rose tawny hills, in some places bleached white. Eagles soared and wild pigeons swarmed about the cliffs above; and the air beneath was full of swallows, which darted in and out under the projecting ledges; and there were several families of Syrian nuthatches — some of them rare specimens, even in Syria — which swung and sputtered about the brows of the cliffs.

The communication between the upper convent and the village is difficult. On either side of the wedge on which the convent stands, and against which the houses are stuck, there is a rent or deep fissure separating it from the mountain. I descended through the rent on the south-western side by a narrow path with stone steps cut in the rock. I found the people of Máloula as interesting as their village. They speak the ancient Syriac language, though most of them can also speak a little Arabic, but with a Syriac accent.

Máloula is the centre of a group of villages where the language of the conquering Arabs has not yet completed its triumph. In Bukha and Jub-'Adîn, neighbouring villages, the people are all Moslems, and all speak Syriac; so that while the religion of the prophet has prevailed, the language of the people has conquered the conquerors. In Máloula it is a drawn battle. Many of the people are still Christians, and most of them hold by their own old language. In all other villages in Syria the language of the Koran is the language of the people.

I ascended to the convent through the northern rent, in the bottom of which runs the stream of the village. The walls rose to a height of two hundred feet on either side, showing a very narrow strip of sky above. The cliffs are full of chambers, and closets opening off chambers, and there are hundreds of tombs all chiselled out of the solid rock. The village is of high antiquity, as the Greek inscriptions reach back to the first century of our era; and the rock-hewn chambers, which served for human habitations before the people learned from the swallows their present style of architecture, point doubtless to a very remote period.

FRIEZE ORNAMENT, TEMPLE OF THE SUN.

CHAPTER III.

HAVING thoroughly explored the village, and paid for my lodging as at an inn, I took leave of the simple-hearted old monk, and started for Yabroud. In a quarter of an hour I had got up out of the amphitheatre or basin, at the bottom of which Máloula stands, and just as I gained the level plateau I came on a party of very savage-looking men sitting round an artificial tank of stagnant water. They were clothed in black sheepskin coats, with the woolly side out, and they were armed with clubs and swords and skin-covered shields. They were a party of Kurds on their way to Damascus, and just such a party as constantly murder and rob solitary travellers. We measured each other's strength, and saluted formally.

A ride of three hours over swelling hills, with a range of slate-coloured mountains on the right, and a wide red plain stretching away to distant mountains on the left, brought us to a gorge in the mountain choked with vegetation. Beyond the gorge, high over the green, rose a curious conical hill, white as snow, called Ras el-Kowz.

At the base of this hill stands Yabroud, the Jambrouda which sent a bishop to the Council of Nice. The place still continues to be the residence of a bishop.

I entered the town past a beautiful fountain which pours its wealth of waters through the village and

YABROUD.

gardens, creating a little paradise among the parched hills. The sides of the gorge contain many ancient and unused tombs hewn in the rock. Some are high up in the face of the cliffs, and must have been difficult of access at all times, while others are level with the ground, and are spoken of as shops. In one of these some wild-looking gipsies were living as I passed, calling to mind the demoniac of Gergesa.

The first thing that strikes one on entering Yabroud is the appearance of the people. The men in this and the other villages about are as a rule tall, well-built, and

FAMILY OF YABROUD.

handsome. Even the Christians here have an air of independence about them such as one seldom meets with in Syrian Christians. The women are in still more striking contrast with their sisters elsewhere throughout the country. They are tall, red-cheeked, healthy, and comfortable looking, and though seldom beautiful, they have nothing of the gipsy appearance of the women in the south and east, nor of the sickly waxen complexion of Damascus beauties. They have a general resemblance to the women of Nazareth, but they have more stamina and less prudery than the maidens of the pitcher.

In ordinary times, as we passed along, we saw them standing at their doors, with big, rosy children in their arms, or grinding at the mill, or spinning woollen yarn with a spindle; and not unfrequently heard from them hearty ringing laughter, such as might resound from a harvest-field at home.

At the time of my visit, however, all cheeks were pale enough, and laughter and gladness had departed, and I started, on entering the mission school, at the pinched and hungry look of the children. There were thirty names on the roll, but only fifteen pupils in attendance. The explanation was brief and sad. Famine was in the district; five or six bad harvests had followed in succession. Madder root, which is largely cultivated in the district for dyeing purposes, had become almost unsaleable, owing to a German chemist having discovered a mineral substitute. Those who admired the brilliant aniline dyes, little thought that the new flash and fading colours in Persian rugs meant starvation among the mountains of Northern Syria.

The flocks of the villagers had been swept off by the Arabs, who had also intercepted their supplies; and the Turks insisted on having their taxes in full, though giving nothing in return.

I was assured that there were not ten bushels of wheat

in the village of three thousand inhabitants, and the people were living chiefly on wild roots and vegetables. Fifteen of the scholars were on the mountains and in the glens, competing with the goats and gazelles for something to drive away hunger. One-half of the children only went on these expeditions at a time, and the fifteen who were in the school were making a meal of bean bread and *hashish*, which consisted for the most part of mint from the stream and rhubarb (*rabbas*) from the mountain. They were like a flock of hungry kids feeding on clover.

One hour beyond Yabroud, I entered Nebk, through the mouldering huts of Ibrahîm Pasha's camp. The great Egyptian general, seeing the splendid appearance of the villagers, established his camp where the soldiers could have the best medicines — good air and good water. During his occupation of Syria, the villagers were safe from the Bedawîn. The Turks have learned nothing from his example, in the arts of either war or peace.

The village of Nebk crowns a high hill, or *nabk*, and is crowned itself by the residence of a Syrian Catholic bishop, whose chief business, like that of his mitred brother in Yabroud, seemed to be the suppression of education. Hunger was pinching also in Nebk, but the Protestants, having learned principles of thrift with the gospel, were all in circumstances of comfort. Fifty pupils were in the school, and though all were on short allowance, they had not the hide-bound, hunger-pinched appearance of the children of Yabroud.

Nebk had suffered severely from the two great enemies of the land,—the Bedawîn and the Turks.

On my previous visit, I entered the village just a few minutes before the Bedawîn made a *gazzo* up to the very entrance. They carried off a few camels laden with grain, and left the drivers without a garment. Great was the excitement in the village. People rushed to the roofs of their houses and screamed in concert, "He that has a sword, and he that has a gun, let him forth against the Arabs"; but while all screamed, none went forth, and the Bedawîn swept round the base of the hill and carried off their booty unmolested.

A short distance from the place, two miserable women were gathering brushwood for fuel. Every day they took their two donkeys out in the morning, and returned in the evening with their loads, which they sold and honestly maintained themselves and their animals. They had nothing in the world but the two donkeys, which were little larger than goats. The Bedawîn of romance would surely have spared such objects; but the Bedawîn of the desert rushed on the donkeys with a yell of joy, stripped the ragged garments from the women, beating them when they resisted, and left them barefooted, and without a fig-leaf, to find their way back in shame to the village. Never, perhaps, did romance take greater liberties with truth than when it threw a halo of chivalry round these cut-throats of the desert.

Next morning as I passed out among the high-walled gardens to visit the schools of Deir 'Atîyeh, I came suddenly upon a woman sitting by a little stream and wailing plaintively. Beside her was a little basket of cows' dung, which she had gathered for fuel. Her grief was not a surface exhibition to catch sympathy, as no one was near in the early morning. She told me her sad tale: her husband, returning with a load of grain from the Euphrates, had been speared by the Bedawîn, and she and her children were left destitute.

On emerging from the gardens, and reaching the desert once more, I saw a cavalier bearing down furiously upon me. At the distance of a mile, I recognized our lady companion whom I had left at Saidenâya two days previously. As I watched an English lady bounding over the desert on a splendid charger, whose neck of thunder swayed hither and thither to her silken touch, I could not help thinking how much Christianity, in its highest types, owes to its contact with Teutonic chivalry.

Deir 'Atîyeh was our rendezvous, and we all converged to the Protestant school. Thence we passed out of the village, and after skirting the gardens for some time, we turned into the desert eastward, in a direct line for Tadmor. We had soon to call a halt, for our muleteers were hugging the village, and hanging back, evidently with the object of making a short day, and putting us down at the first convenient resting-place, as they had done the first day.

ENTABLATURE OF GRAND ENTRANCE, TEMPLE OF THE SUN.

CHAPTER IV.

THE halt gave me an opportunity of estimating the magnitude and organization of our party. Two cavaliers stood out conspicuous from all the others. They were Gazâwy, the dragoman, the same who brought "Sheikh Stanley" through "Sinai and Palestine," and a Moslem sheikh, brought from Nebk as guide to the expedition.

Gazâwy was the prince of dragomans; his weakness, perhaps his strength, was to have everything of the best, and always ten times more than enough. The long line of laden mules carried, I believe, provisions for the party for twelve months. Booted and braced, he sat on a splendid horse, called the "Steam Engine," as if he were a part of the horse, and viewed the long cavalcade with a smile of pride on his kindly, weather-beaten·face.

Gazâwy's chief pride and glory that morning was his guide, chosen expressly on account of his radiant waistcoat. Half a mile from the village this guide lost the road, and led us astray, and fell back to the rear, where he could do no harm. When a village would rise into sight before us, he would suddenly gallop up and declare it was "Sudud," or some other town that he knew was on our way; but as we saw Sudud far down on the plain to the left, we called the guide "Sudud" for the rest of the journey, and groped our way by the aid of an incorrect map.

Our course during the day lay north-east over gently undulating ground. On our right was the bare northern shoulder of Kalamoun, which we were rounding, and to our left was the great plain which stretches away to Hums and Hamah. Green spots dotted the red expanse, and marked the sites of such towns as Kara, Hafr, and Sudud, the Zedad of Scripture, one of the border cities of the Land of Promise.

That plain once supported the flocks and hosts of the Hittites and the armies of the Seleucidæ, but under the beneficent rule of our Turkish allies, the sites of great cities are marked by lofty mounds and wretched huts, and the miserable inhabitants carry their provisions from the Euphrates. We met no travellers, for all who wished to escape the Bedawîn travelled under the protection of the darkness. Persian larks, hawks, vultures, and pin-tailed grouse, were the only tenants of that desolate region.

A little after mid-day "Sudud" spied two human beings creeping down from the mountain as if going to cross our path. He immediately gave the alarm, and as there were only two, and they were not likely to be Bedawîn, he charged direct at them, valiantly brandishing his rusty weapons, with all the awkwardness of a village horseman. Our bandit guard joined in the chase, which was picturesque and exciting, though ludicrous. "Sudud" kept in advance, and as he became convinced that there were no Bedawîn, and no ambuscade, he became more valorous. He would show that though he might not know the way, he was the hero of the party in the hour of danger.

But just as he was snatching his laurels, the fate of "vaulting ambition" befell him; for his horse, having had enough of it, stopped short at the edge of a dry river-bed, and "Sudud" shot over his head to the other side. All cheered, and called on "Sudud" to charge the enemy; but he once more retired to the rear, where he kept guard for the remainder of the day. The Bedawîn that we were going to annihilate turned out to be two gipsy tinsmiths who were stealing down the ravine to the village below, when the eagle eye of our "Sudud" discovered them.

We reached Muhîn before sunset, and pitched our camp beside a copious fountain. The water was warm and slightly sulphurous. Few Europeans had passed that way before, and the people of the village swarmed about us, more curious than civil. They were Moslems of the surly kind.

Muhîn stands on a little hill, and on the highest part, west of the houses, there are the remains of an ancient

SUDUD'S VAULTING AMBITION.

church. The building was about twenty paces long and sixteen paces broad, and from twenty-five to thirty feet high. The circular end of the church was towards the north-west, and from the middle of the side wall on either side, all round the circular end, there were pilasters with pedestals and Corinthian capitals. A piece had fallen out of the circular end, but there still remained seven pilasters on one side and five on the other intact. The church is still very perfect, and is unlike any other building I have seen in Syria. From the top we had a magnificent view of the whole country, from the Wall of Lebanon to the Gate of Palmyra, and we were able to take bearings, and mark out our line of march for the morrow.

About two o'clock in the morning we were startled by a horrid din in the village: every human being that could scream screamed; every dog barked to the utmost limit of his capacity; every horse that could make a clatter on the rocks galloped hither and thither. An alarm of Bedawîn had been given, and the people were gathering in their flocks for safety, and preparing to defend their threshing-floors. As we were close by the threshing-floors, we had a fair prospect of seeing play; but we kept our beds till morning, and by the time we were ready to rise the noise had all died away.

The Bedawîn, as we found out afterwards, made their attack, but not on Muhîn.

Every year the people of these regions go to the Hauran during the harvest. The men reap for wages, and their wives and daughters, Ruth-like, glean after them. This having been an unusually bad year, an unusual number of reapers and gleaners had gone to the Hauran.[1]

I here quote the sequel from the *Levant Herald* of 9th July, 1874: "These poor reapers had amassed 17,000 piasters, and were returning to their starving families. But the Arabs were informed of the easy prey they would find in these unarmed peasants. They waylaid them, and left them hardly a shred to cover their nakedness. The Arabs then swept on unopposed, under their leader Sheikh Dabbous; and making a circuit by Sudud, Hawarîn, and Karyetein, carried off all the stray flocks and donkeys that came in their way."

[1] I have seen scores of young Syrian women, from distant villages, gleaning in safety after the rough Bashan reapers.

PALMYRA TESSERAE BELONGING TO THE LATE M. WADDINGTON.

ENTABLATURE OF GRAND ENTRANCE PORTICO, TEMPLE OF THE SUN.

CHAPTER V.

THE next morning (May 28th, 1874) we sent our baggage animals and all impedimenta to Karyetein by the direct route, while we turned out of the way with a slender escort, to visit the wonderful hot baths on a distant mountain to the left.

We rode the first hour through high-walled gardens and flat fields to Hawarîn, a city famed in local tradition for its seven splendid churches.

We were surprised by the extent of the ruins of this place, and we had not allowed ourselves time to explore it as thoroughly as its importance deserved. I saw three large buildings, and the foundation of a fourth, called churches by the people. The largest and most perfect of these was a rectangular building, thirty paces long by twenty-five broad, and thirty feet high. The internal arrangements of the building consisted of a central hall, and three rooms on each side opening into the hall. The stones in the walls were large, but they seemed to have been rifled from other structures.

From the numerous foundations of houses, many of them of massive public buildings, there can be no doubt that Hawarîn marks the site of an important city; but the fragmentary Greek inscriptions which I found in my hurried search gave no key to the name of the place.

From Hawarîn we rode across a flat plain four hours to Gunthur. All the district showed signs of ancient cultivation, and were the people protected from the Bedawîn and the Turks, the flats would once more wave with golden grain. Little patches were cultivated here and there, but not of sufficient importance to tempt the hereditary robbers. Water, the great desideratum for cultivation, was abundant, though all the fountains and channels were choked up. At the water we found straggling flocks of pin-tailed grouse; and throughout the desert, wherever we came upon water, however small the quantity, we found grouse and snipe. We always approached little patches of desert marsh with expectation, and it required skill to bring down the brace of snipe which generally rose right and left.

At Gunthur we found, as usual, a few wretched huts on the site of what once had been an important town. The houses were cone-topped, and at a distance looked like cornstacks in a farmyard; but the illusion was dispelled when we entered the square, which was full of dung, in which a dozen naked children and a score of mangy dogs were disporting.

The huts were built round a court, so as to form a

rampart against the Bedawîn, but there were breaches which left the place unprotected, and about twelve days after we passed, the Giath and 'Amour Bedawîn came through the place, and swept it clean of the results of the late harvest.

At one corner of the court was the foundation of a very solid temple, twenty paces by fourteen, with two or three courses of the huge stones still in their places. A larger, more ornate, and more modern structure lay in ruins in the field a few hundred yards to the north-east. The peasants, who were gathering in their grain, told us that the flats about the village were often covered with water during the winter, and that the place was much frequented by wild geese, bustards, and wild boars. Grouse swarmed about the water, and there were some spur-winged plover in a meadow close by.

From Gunthur we started for Solomon's Baths, which we saw on the mountain, under the guidance of a kindly old African, who had lived long in that neighbourhood, a slave under many masters, and who was full of the traditions of the baths, and of Lady Belkis, the wife of Solomon, for whom the baths were erected!

In five minutes we passed a fine spring, slightly tepid and sulphurous. In half an hour we reached the base of a low mountain, and after ascending the mountain diagonally for about half an hour, we came to considerable ruins on its eastern summit. The only inhabitants of the ruins that we saw were a fox, a hare, and a covey of partridges.

The exact position of the place, which is called Abu Rebâh, is due north of Karyetein, a distance of three and a quarter hours, or about ten miles as the crow flies. Having made a general tour of the neighbourhood in quest of partridges, some of which I secured for dinner, our guide conducted us to the wonderful bath. He first pointed out to us, in the roof of a vault, an opening about a foot in diameter, the edges of which were soot-stained, and through which issued a hot vapour.

Descending from the roof, which was on a level with the foundations about, we passed through a low entrance into an arched vault eight or ten feet square. The walls and roof of the vault were scribbled over with Greek by the Browns, Joneses, and Robinsons of two thousand years ago. The literature was of the same serious character as that seen in many of our railway and other waiting-rooms at home. From this outer vault there was an opening twenty inches high into another similar vault, and through the opening there came hot puffs of sulphurous vapour. I crept through this hole, but I was instantly driven back by the intense heat. My servant then rushed in boldly, but he rushed out quite as quick, almost suffocated, and covered with perspiration from head to foot. It was a case of what·the Arabs call "head in ; tail out."

After this we explored more carefully the inner vault. In the centre of the floor there was an opening about the same size and exactly under that we saw in the roof. Steam came hissing from the hole as from the funnel of a ship, and we could hear a hissing and gurgling sound under the vault, as from water boiling over into the fire out of a great caldron. We threw stones into the furnace, and heard them descending to a great depth, but a piece of paper thrown in was instantly shot out by the current of the vapour.

Previous to our visit, Omar Bey, a Hungarian officer, had let down a brazen vessel into the orifice by a rope; but the vessel was snatched from the rope by the Jân, left by King Solomon to keep the water boiling! Our faithful guide lost his good opinion of us when we suggested that perhaps the fire had burned it off. Indeed, he ever afterwards looked upon us with that suspicion which is the reward of all who are foolish enough to think differently from their neighbours.

West of the bath, in the ravine, there is a large reservoir, the roof of which is supported on five rows of arches resting on buttresses of solid masonry. All traces of water are gone, but the cement on the walls remains white and firm, and is scrawled over with thousands of hieroglyphics, which are mostly the *wasm*, or tribe-marks, of the Bedawîn.

Judging from the foundations of the ruins, the houses appear to have been very small, and they were doubtless used as lodging-houses for invalids and others visiting the baths, for the only attraction to such a barren knoll was its heated vapour. Abu Rebâh must have been once an important sanitarium, and the bath has still a very high reputation for its healing powers. It is considered infallible in rheumatic complaints, and in the case of barrenness, and is much resorted to in the present day. Men are said to be carried to the bath confirmed invalids, and after spending a night in the vault, return home on their own feet.

In descending the mountain from the baths we started several very small whitish hares, and saw many holes of foxes and jackals. The ground was strewed with rock crystals, which glanced like diamonds in the sunlight. A low range of hills screened Karyetein from our view, but we had steered our course by a peak which we knew was in a line with the village. In the bright atmosphere the distance seemed as nothing, yet it was a most weary ride across a level plain, which was all seamed with footpaths, some of which had been trod by Abraham and his emigrants.

We passed several abandoned Bedawi encampments, but we saw no living thing in a ride of over three hours, except a few hares and bustards, and an occasional eagle hastening overhead to its prey. On reaching Karyetein, however, we learned that we must have passed under the very noses of the plundering Bedawîn, who were hovering about our path in the mountains.

My teacher, whom I had sent on with the baggage in the morning, had announced our approach in Karyetein, and a most cordial welcome was given us. The civil and military chiefs of the place turned out in their best to do us honour, and the people were profuse in their thanks for the school which we had come to establish among them.

The supposition that Karyetein is the Hazar-enan of Scripture (Num. xxxiv. 9, 10) is probably correct, but the identification of the place with the Greek town Koradæa is a mistake. Two Greek inscriptions (one on a long stone, now over the gateway of a Moslem house, and the other on the pedestal of a column in the sheikh's court) give the name of the place as Nazala.

The discovery of this name gave rise to a fresh examination of the Peutinger Itinerary, when it was found that the name reprinted "Nehala" was "Nazala" in the original. The name "Karyetein" is dual, and simply means "two towns," and one can see both the old and the new town. About a mile south-west of the present town, near the foot of a low mountain, there is a splendid fountain called "Ras el-'Ain." Around this fountain was built the old town, Hazar-enan ("the enclosure of fountains"). Close by the fountain — or fountains, for there are a number of them — there is a large artificial mound, on which are the massive foundations of a temple. The building was twenty-one paces long and sixteen broad, and some of the stones of the foundation were eight feet in length. On one of the largest stones there is a well-cut trident. A short distance north-east of the mound there is the base of a square building about forty-eight paces each way. The lower story of this building was vaulted, and the stones remain in their places, as they were too heavy to be removed to the new town, which is chiefly built of mud. It is not improbable that the inhabitants of the Fountain Village moved to a distance from the fountain to enjoy a quiet life, such fountains being the scene of constant strife.

At the fountain were flocks of grouse, and a few snipe, and I got a very small bittern, which, through the zeal of my companion, is now in the museum of the Protestant Syrian College, Beyrout. The ground was full of pottery, and, among other relics of antiquity, I picked up on the Tell two fine flint knives. We need not, however, rush into theories about the *stone*, *bronze*, and *iron* ages, for a famous sheikh of the Bedawîn, to whom I showed my treasures, assured me that such knives were still used by his people.

Karyetein contains about three hundred houses, and one-fifth of the inhabitants are Christians, chiefly Syrian Jacobites. The schoolmaster, for whom all had been petitioning and importuning, had arrived, and only one man in the place (the Christian priest) opposed the opening of the school.

In all places where a missionary opens a school in Syria he opens at least two; sometimes indeed all the sects open schools in self-defence. The opposing priest, under pressure of circumstances, and in a fine spirit of enterprise, opened a school himself; but as the work was not quite in his line, besides being hard, our teacher had all the pupils to himself in a few days, and Moslems and Christians learned to read the story of Christ's love and passion, sitting side by side. I hoped also to induce the Bedawîn to send their children to this school in the centre of the desert, but several blood feuds had first to be settled before such a thing was possible.

The people of Karyetein are a fine-looking race of men, — especially the princelings of the ruling family. They hunt and hawk, and are as good horsemen as the Bedawîn, and better shots. They resemble the Bedawîn, but have much more bone and sinew. Their independence has been developed thoroughly by resisting the encroachments of the Turks and the Bedawîn; but of late a Turkish garrison has been placed among them, and their acquiescence has been secured by giving them appointments of command and trust.

The civil and military chiefs are very great people in Karyetein, and we had to attend carefully to all the punctilios of receiving and returning visits. Long negotiations in the matter of guide and guards had to be conducted with as much diplomacy as might have sufficed for the cession of a duchy. It was at last arranged that we were to have an equal number of civil and military guards — that is, regular soldiers; and irregular mounted police.

The guide was a difficult question to decide; for each of the authorities had one to recommend, — "*the only one*" who knew the path to 'Ain el-Wu'ul, — and as it was understood that the protégé was to share his fee with his patron, our dragoman was placed in a delicate situation.

SOFFIT OF CORNICE IN LITTLE TEMPLE.

CHAPTER VI.

ALL things having been arranged, — for negotiations even in the desert come to an end, — we struck our tents, and started from Karyetein on the 30th of May, at four o'clock in the afternoon. Our object was to break the journey at 'Ain el-Wu'ul ("fountain of the Ibexes"), a reputed fountain in the mountains to the right, half way to Palmyra from Karyetein. The existence of this fountain was kept a secret, so that people might employ camels to carry water, and our innovation was looked upon with great disfavour.

Gazâwy compromised the matter by taking a few water-carriers, at a very high charge. Our cavalcade was led out across the river at the town mill, wobbled about through ploughed fields for a time, and at last turned Palmyra-ward into the desert.

We had now assumed the dimensions and character of an invading army. We were not stealing through the desert under cover of the darkness, but forcing our way where we pleased and at our leisure.

"Brandy Bob," a captain in the infantry, was commander-in-chief of our military escort. He rode a vicious mule, with only a halter, and without stirrups, carried a single-barrelled fowling-piece about eight feet long, and a bottle of brandy in each pocket, *à la* Gilpin. He had a habit of alighting abruptly, not always on his feet, but that may have been the mule's fault, or the brandy's. His soldiers were all mounted and equipped in the same unceremonious manner as himself.

Irregular police in Syria are a very irregular force indeed. Nominally in government service, they are ready to take a turn at throat-cutting for anybody who employs them, and they are the free-lances or government banditti of the country. If there is a prospect of plunder, they will join a Bedawi raid, and by their arms, such as they are, contribute to the victory.

On my first tour to Palmyra, our irregular escort proceeded to rob every individual they saw in the desert. Remonstrance on our part was of little avail, for our protectors replied that they had only agreed to take us safely to Palmyra, not to abstain from taking anything Allâh placed in their way. On the whole, we had such a guard as might have been safely trusted to make short work of any party weaker than themselves.

Faris, our gipsy guide, deserves a passing notice. He was a light, little man, with crimped hair, sallow complexion, coal-black eyes, which were always on one, and a stealthy, silent step, as if he were afraid of waking some one only slightly asleep. He always seemed drawing up his feet from behind, but he never let them get before him, lest they should let out some secret.

His mare was of the same gipsy cast, a marled grey. Her neck was hollowed down like a camel's where one expected a curve, and her under lip hung down and exposed the teeth, while her nose and upper lip were drawn back, and had a curious huffed appearance. Her legs were bent the wrong way, and her joints were in the wrong places, and she was so lean, and wizened, and dry, that she seemed to go nodding and dozing along without life or feeling. They were an uncanny-looking pair, and I could not look at them without an uneasy feeling, and much curiosity.

With "Brandy Bob" and "Gipsy" at our head, we swept along the desert in splendid style. In front were two little mountains, offsets from the range on the right. That to the left was called Khuderîyeh, and that on the right Bârady, and we made straight for the opening between them. We passed several gazelle-traps, near Karyetein. Little walls converge to a field from a great distance, increasing in height as they approach the field. The field is walled round, leaving gaps at intervals, outside of which there are deep pits. The gazelles, led on by curiosity, and guided by the little walls, march boldly into the field, and when they are startled, they rush out wildly in a panic, at the breaches, and tumble into the pits. Sometimes forty or fifty are taken out of a pit alive at one time.

The desert was tolerably smooth as far as the little mountains, when it became more broken and cut up, chiefly by the action of mountain torrents. The Arabs reported that in the mountain range to the right there were the remains of a great reservoir which once supplied water to Kasr el-Hiyar, the solitary ruin in the direct route between Karyetein and Palmyra.

That evening we had the finest sunset I had ever seen in the desert. The western horizon seemed literally ablaze. Soon the light blue veil of the mountains became tinted with violet and indigo, and finally settled into leaden death, and the wind came up cold as a Siberian winter.

We held on our course bravely till midnight, when our column became very unsteady, and began to wriggle about promiscuously over the desert. The cold was intense, and the bottle passed between our leaders more frequently than was consistent with their responsible positions, or than was expedient for safe and steady guiding. Suddenly we turned to the right, and marched straight against the mountain, which we had been approaching at an acute angle. We knew the fountain was in the range to the right, but thought it must be at least two hours farther on. Gipsy, however, spurned interference, and assumed all responsibility.

We soon got into a maze of rocks, and after half an hour's scrambling through them and over them, we came right against the precipitous side of the mountain. Gipsy went boldly at the mountain, with a few inarticulate words, when, suddenly, he came down on his head on a heap of stones, and the old horse turned and made a vignette over him. He lay in a bundle, motionless, where he fell, and when I asked what was the matter, he hiccoughed out, "It's a hare," as if he had got off to catch it.

"Brandy Bob's" bottle had done its work, and the guide was hopelessly drunk. Then commenced a scene never to be forgotten. No one knew exactly where we were, or where the well was, but we spread out across the rugged base of the mountain after midnight to look for a well of which we had only heard a report. Our horses staggered over precipices and scrambled out of ravines in the most marvellous manner; baggage animals followed wildly after the cavaliers, stumbling and rolling over rocks; the whole looked like a steeple-chase, or a wild stampede, everything magnified by the black shadows; and there was an appalling expenditure of nervous force, in the use of strong language.

We explored desperately for about an hour, which seemed an age; but as the moon was hurrying behind the mountain, and as we were only getting more hopelessly lost, we encamped for the night on a bare plateau at the base of the mountain.

The cold was as intense as had been the heat of the day; but we were soon in that happy land where the perplexities of the day are forgotten. The night, however, has perplexities as real and as distressing as those of the day, while they last, and so I dreamt of stumbling frantically over rocks, and of being in imminent danger of tumbling over precipices, until a little Bedawi girl pulled the door of my tent aside, and the sun, hot as a furnace, shone in upon me.

The little maiden we called the "Princess," and perhaps no princess, except in an Eastern tale, ever was the bearer of more joyful news or more acceptable gifts. She announced the lost fountain, and she bore in one hand a brazen vessel full of fresh milk, and with the other she led a snow-white lamb.

I remembered how African explorers, when hopelessly exhausted, had been ministered to by savage women, and I sighed for the pen of an African explorer, that I might celebrate the praises of this ministering angel of the desert and of the fountain. Our little angel was not of the white and shining kind; she was dark olive, and her only garment was a blue calico shirt, close fitting at the neck, and extending far down the leg. A blue fillet, wound round the head, left the hair free to stand up and enjoy the mountain breeze, and beneath the fillet it fell in uncombed plaits around her shoulders. These plaits were prolonged by bits of strings, made of camel's hair, down to below the waist.

Doubtless a revolution has since taken place in the disposition of Bedawi locks in the desert, for my companion presented the Princess with an ivory comb, a work of art which caused in the encampment no little speculation as to its use.

But we must not be diverted from describing our Princess, whose piercing timid black eyes shone brightly in deep, sooty sockets, and whose feet, which spurned the flint, gave a fine example of what Disraeli called "the high Syrian instep."

In a short conversation that I held with her, when paying for the luxuries which she brought us, I noticed that she pronounced the letter *j* soft, and otherwise spoke Arabic like a Syrian girl. I said, "You are not a Bedawi *bint* (girl)?" The Bedawîn who accompanied the maiden to see that their gifts were paid for were within ear-shot, and she replied loudly, "You do me too much honour in receiving my gifts; why should you pay for them?" and then in a low, but hurried manner, she told me she had been carried off by the Bedawîn from Rustan, a village on the Orontes, between Hums and Hamah.

The revelation was made with the swiftness of a lightning flash. The acting was exquisite, and the dramatic effect instantaneous and startling. I did not catch everything that was expressed, but the hurried and helpless appeal revealed the fact that our "Princess" was a little captive Syrian slave, and I resolved to rescue and restore her. My sense of pity as well as chivalrous instincts were awaked, and though I was in the land of the Bedawîn I did not despair of success.

The following nursery song, which I had often heard sung by Syrian mothers, came to my recollection. I had stumbled on the living drama in real life: —

THE LULLABY.[1]

    Sleep, baby, sleep! a sleep so sweet and mild,
    Sleep, my Arab boy, my little Bedawi child!
Aside to the   Once I was a happy girl,
grape sellers.   The Prince Abdullah's daughter,
    Playing with the village maids,
    Bringing wood and water.
    Suddenly the Bedawin
    Carried me away:
    Clothed me in an Arab robe,
    And here they make me stay.

    Sleep, baby, sleep! a sleep so sweet and mild,
    Sleep, my Arab boy, my little Bedawi child!
Aside.   Ye sellers of grapes, hear what I say!
    I had dressed in satin rich and gay;
    They took my costly robes away
    And dressed me in aba coarse and grey.
    I had lived on viands costly and rare,
    And now raw camel's flesh is my fare.

    Sleep, baby, sleep! a sleep so sweet and mild,
    Sleep, my Arab boy, my little Bedawi child!
Aside.   Oh! seller of grapes, I beg you hear!
    Go tell my mother and father dear,
    That you have seen me here to-day.
    Just by the church my parents live,
    The Bedawin stole me on Thursday eve.
    Let the people come and their sister save,
    Let them come with warriors bold and brave,
    Lest I die of grief and go to my grave.

I was only partially dressed in my tent, and to secure the return of the little captive to our camp later on, I

[1] This translation is, I believe, from the pen of Dr. Jessup, of Beyrout.

received back from her the money I had given her, promising to pay more for all when she had brought us an additional supply of milk. Whether the Bedawîn had heard what their captive had said, or had divined what was passing in my mind, they had taken in the situation completely, and before I was fully dressed, they had disappeared as secretly and noiselessly as they came. They departed without their money, and they left no trace behind them, nor could I get any information regarding them from the other people about the well.

The two Bedawîn who had accompanied the little "Princess" were clothed from head to foot in the skins of the *wa'al* (ibex) and gazelle. They seemed like ordinary Bedawîn — small, spare, dark men, with deep-set, restless eyes, and noses of the scimitar type. They belonged, however, to the Suleib Arabs, a unique tribe in the desert.

At a remote period this tribe was degraded from exercising the larger prerogatives of Bedawîn of the higher aristocracy. They do not make war on the weak, nor rob, except in a pilfering way, nor intermarry with any of the other tribes. Many wild stories relate the causes of their degradation, but that most common among the other Bedawîn is, that they ran away from the siege of Kerbela, leaving their friends to be butchered, "and the curse of Allâh still lies heavy upon them." As a part of their punishment, they were placed on the same footing with women, as unworthy to ride horses, and so they never ride anything but donkeys; but the Suleib donkeys (known as Bagdad donkeys) are the finest in the world, and will bring from twenty to forty pounds in Damascus. They are the large and beautiful white asses which reach England by Morocco.

The Suleib Arabs, unlike the other Ishmaelites of the desert, have their hand against no man, and no man's hand is against them. They live by the chase, and by the milk and wool of their flocks; and when they sell a donkey, its price supplies them with all they need from the outer world. On the declivities of 'Ain el-Wu'ul are still to be found *wu'ul*, or ibexes, which they hunt with great skill. Clothed in the skin of the *wa'al*, they follow them from rock to rock, on all-fours, until they shoot them at short range; and sometimes their disguise is so complete, that they even catch the gazelle and *wa'al* alive with their hands.

These Suleib Arabs take no part in forays; as one of them said to me, "Allâh has made enough for us all, and if we plunder one another, there will not be enough for us all." They will sit on the ground, impartial spectators of a battle, and when the fight is over they will nurse the wounded of both sides, like the Knights of the Geneva Cross. When one tribe is pursuing another, they will entertain with equal but limited hospitality both the pursued and pursuer; but nothing can wring from them any information as to the direction the fugitives have taken. These Arabs are to be found about the wells in the neighbourhood of 'Ain el-Wu'ul, and they are always of the same peaceful and hospitable character.

Our visitors informed us that the fountain was about a mile farther on among the mountains, and so, as soon as we had eaten their offerings, we moved our camp forward to the foot of the ravine below the fountain. We pitched on the site of a military camp where Omar Bey had stationed his soldiers when he wished to reduce the desert to subjection.

We should have had no difficulty whatever in finding the fountain; but our guide misled us, as I believe, on purpose. From the pass between the two little mountains we should have followed a beaten path, leading gently to the right to the lowest break in the mountain, about three hours ahead. On our return we rode from the fountain to Karyetein in ten and a half hours, so no one need ever again spend money in water-carriers on the road to Palmyra.

We ascended to the fountain through a gorge, the stones in the bottom of which were as slippery as ice. Every tribe that crosses the plain between Palmyra and Karyetein is obliged to pass up this gorge for water; and through the wear of ages the stones have become so polished that scarcely one of our animals went up to the water without a fall. The stones, however, were so smooth that none were injured by falling.

We discovered the fountain at the head of the gorge. It is a deep tank about twelve feet square, faced round with rough stones, and the water was about ten feet lower than the surface of the platform in which the tank was sunk, so that it had to be drawn up, and placed in hollow stones for the animals to drink.

The stones about the tank were squared, but not chiselled, and though we saw foundations of buildings, we could find no inscriptions. From between the high shoulders of the gorge, we had a good view of the broadest part of the plain that extends to Palmyra, and the Kasr el-Hiyar lay exactly north-west of the fountain, some six or eight miles distant.

The water in the tank was very green, but one ceases to be fastidious about the quality of water in the desert. Two cheerful little maidens were filling skins with the green fluid, and fourteen skins were lying about filled and festering in the sun. A number of camels were squatting at the troughs, waiting for some one to bring them water, and flocks of goats were pouring over the cliffs and converging on the fountain.

The little stagnant pond had attracted a great number of living things. Partridges scolded us from the rocks on every side, for interfering with their beverage; and myriads of linnets, of all kinds and colours, settled on the tall thistles, and awaited our departure; and eagles and vultures and red-beaked choughs soared over us at every altitude.

A little way over from the fountain was the Suleib encampment. It consisted of about a dozen tents — or rather a dozen long pieces of black haircloth, fastened down with stones at the side next the wind, and at the other side propped up with bits of sticks, and tied down with strings. Beneath the awnings thus formed women squatted, horribly tattooed, and filthy-looking; and one miserable creature, who was sick, lay on skins, with a skin filled with water for her pillow. The dirt of the tent was scarcely removed beyond the tent strings, and the odour, at least to us, was far from agreeable. Some of our irregular police were sitting in the tents, feasting on a half-roasted sheep that had been slain for them.

We saw none of the famous Suleib donkeys, and we learned with regret that a plague had swept many of them away, and that they had been obliged to sell a great many of what remained, during the Syrian famine. A few black and wretched substitutes stood nodding about the tents.

On our return to the fountain from Palmyra, we saw no trace of the Suleib, but three men were found dying of thirst at the fountain. They had made their way to the place, but were too weak to reach the water.

I was especially interested in the Suleib Arabs, as I thought they would not be afraid to send their children to one of our schools, in a border village, such as Karyetein, and I imagined that as they had no blood feuds or enemies among the Bedawîn, they might be employed to carry instruction and the light of the gospel to the other wanderers of the desert.

They, however, strongly objected to their children quitting the ways of their fathers; and I found, on consulting a Bedawi chief, that the blue-blooded Bedawîn held the Suleib in such contempt, that they would not on any account allow their children to be taught by them.

"We would let our children learn from Nasara (Christians), or Jews even; but that they should be taught by these low-souled, womanish Bedawîn — ask forgiveness from God for such a thought!"

Nothing in the Suleib camp made such an impression on us as the exquisite beauty of the children. Though unwashed and almost unclad, they appeared to me the most graceful and the sweetest little animals I had ever seen in the desert or elsewhere. In this opinion I do not stand alone. Lady Anne Blunt speaks of a Suleib family as follows: —

. . . "Two younger men, his relations, are exceedingly good looking, with delicately cut features, and the whitest of teeth. There is a boy, too, who is perfectly beautiful, with almond-shaped eyes, and a complexion like stained ivory. A little old woman not more than four feet high, and two girls of fourteen, the most lovely little creatures I ever saw, complete the family." — *Tribes of the Euphrates*, Vol. II. 109.

SOFFIT SUPPORTED BY FOUR COLUMNS.

BASSO RELIEVO ON PILASTER, TEMPLE OF THE SUN.

CHAPTER VII.

WE enjoyed a quiet day at 'Ain el-Wu'ul, much to our own satisfaction and that of our animals; and on the 1st of June, 1874, at four o'clock in the morning, we started on the last stage of our journey to Palmyra. The morning air was fresh and balmy, the peaks were tipped with amethyst, and purple shadows shot with gold lay heavy about the mountains, and as we streamed down from the plateau, we felt buoyant as the wavy atmosphere that danced and floated around us.

Five hares were started in the descent, and each became the subject of a fresh chase and general fusillade, and on the level plain one hare was actually run down and caught by a soldier on a one-eyed horse. That man was a mighty hunter, and his one-eyed horse was worthy of his rider. On our return through Karyetein, the sheikh's son presented me with a Persian greyhound. In the morning, a fox was seen creeping up the hill to the mountain, and instantly all our cavaliers started in pursuit with a desert yell.

The fox took in the situation and did his best, and he had nearly a mile of start. The hunters, from being an irregular crowd, soon found their places in the tail of the dust-comet that streamed up the hill. The head of the comet was the one-eyed horse, and there thundered in his track horses twice his size and ten times his value. In twenty minutes the greyhound had reached the fox, but did not know what to do with him. The question was soon settled by the rider of the cyclopean horse, who rushed in, seized reynard, and brought him back alive and in triumph, at his saddle-bow.

At five o'clock the Castle of Palmyra rose into view, and we felt delightfully independent of Gipsy, the guide. We had a weary ride before us, in which distance was felt, not seen. The way was monotony itself, for we had got almost back into the ordinary route of the tourist. In some places the ground was wavy, and then our column dipped and emerged like a boat among billows. At other places it was dead flat, and then we marched on, and on, and on for ever, leaving in our track a trail of dust. The mountain range on our right rose again from the break at the fountain, and stretched on in an unbroken ridge to opposite Palmyra, when it suddenly turned toward the city and shut in the plain.

Across the plain to the left, the edge of a highland, or step, like a mountain ridge, shut in the plain on the north; and this ridge also ran straight to Palmyra, and then turned off at right angles towards the Euphrates. Sometimes the monotony of our march was broken by a spurt after a hare, or a shot at a sand-grouse, and in crossing a *seil*, or the dry bed of a mountain torrent, I got two large grey birds, with big yellow eyes, called by the Bedawîn *darraji*, — perhaps a species of rock curlew.

We passed hundreds of places where Arabs had encamped, marked by stones left in circles, and by bones and ashes and graves. At one of these encampments I found beads of old Damascus manufacture, and a flint knife that had been recently used. The plain was a tawny brown, and the abundant grass and herbage of spring had been reduced to powder. A few spots were green in the distance, but when we came up to them, we only found the *el-kali* plant growing in greater abundance and perfection than elsewhere.

The plain, which runs between mountains, like the level bed of a narrow sea, from near Karyetein to Palmyra, varies in breadth from four to ten miles, and consists of good soil, which might be cultivated.

On my first return trip from Palmyra, I found it carpeted with grass and flowers to the fetlocks of the horses. One nowhere meets the desert sands of tradition till almost at the entrance to Palmyra.

About two hours from Palmyra, we were aroused out of a slumberous state by one of our soldiers firing off his rifle, and rushing about in an excited manner. We galloped up to him, and found that he had wounded a large lizard, thirty-nine inches long. It was horribly ugly as it writhed on the ground. It had a stuffed look, like

TRIUMPHAL ARCH, WITH CASTLE IN THE DISTANCE.

a Turkish officer, tightly belted, and bulging out on each side of the ligatures. The skin of this extraordinary monster is now in the museum of the Syrian Protestant College, Beyrout.

As we approached closer to Palmyra, the ruins on the hilltops came safely out of the mirage, and assumed their

PALMYRA RUINS.

permanent forms. Every hour new structures rose into view, and through the pass, to which we were hurrying, we could see the tops of the colonnades within. Perhaps there is no view of Palmyra which gives so much excitement as this. After the bare monotonous desert, we come gradually on a scene of enchantment, and though we have come expressly to see the scene, it breaks upon us as a surprise; not all at once, but increasing at every step — castle, and tower and temple, and serried lines of Corinthian capitals, seen in part, and in such a way as to suggest more, lead up with the most dramatic effect to the most splendid *dénouement*. The thrill of expectancy and delight is a rich reward for all our fatigue.

In the middle of the pass, with a path on either side, there is a rocky eminence, which was built over with tomb towers. Some of the towers are almost entire, and of others there only remain the foundations. On the right rises Jebel el-Mantar ("the Mountain of the lookout,") with the old wall running up its narrow ridge to the top, and its base sentinelled about with huge square towers. This mountain terminates suddenly in the plain, and the wall runs down its south-eastern side; and after passing through Abu Sahil, the vaulted cemetery, it draws a wide circuit round the southern side of the city.

On the left from the edge of the pass rises a chain of mountains, which screens Tadmor from the west, and runs away in the Dawara range towards the Euphrates. The wall took the course of the highest summits of this range, and after enclosing the castle, turned sharp in a south-easterly direction, and curved round the city till it met the wall coming up from the south-west. This wall, which can be easily traced, is no doubt that of the city in its palmiest days, and should always be kept in mind when estimating the greatness of the Palmyra of Zenobia.

On the north-east side the outer wall is about nine hundred yards beyond the modern Roman wall. Travellers generally express their disappointment at the smallness of Palmyra; but they form their estimate of its magnitude by the small oblong space enclosed within the Justinian wall, less than three miles long. While the city had no special claim to celebrity on account of its

THE TEMPLE OF THE SUN.

size, in that respect even it was not insignificant, as the old walls which we have pointed out were from ten to thirteen miles in circumference, and the enclosed space was closely packed with human habitations, many of them of the most splendid description.

As we swept through the pass, Tadmor lay beneath us; and its ruins, which seemed graceful and fantastic as frostwork on glass, stretched out for more than a mile before us, and ended in the massive Temple of the Sun.

On the left, the yellow mountains towered over it; and

on the right, green gardens of palm and olive surged around it. On the outer side, these gardens are girt by the desert, which stretches away to the horizon, smooth as the sea, and the yellow sands, which shimmer golden in the sunlight, are flecked by the silver sheen of extensive salt lakes.

FRAGMENT OF A TEMPLE.

FALLEN CAPITAL.

CHAPTER VIII.

WE hastened over prostrate columns, and along silent streets, till we reached the beautiful little temple called the "Temple of the King's Mother." Here we descended from our horses at half-past three o'clock P.M., having made the journey from 'Ain el-Wu'ul in about ten and a half hours' actual riding.

This little temple commands an excellent view of the ruins, and so we pitched our camp beside it, and my bed was spread within its once sacred fane. I had thus ample leisure by starlight and sunlight, to study what Miss Beaufort, in her pleasant book, called "a little gem of a temple, almost perfect in form," and which is still beautiful, though without the fluted columns which she attributed to it.

The temple was sixty feet long, including the portico, and about twenty-seven feet broad. Its projecting roof in front was supported by six columns with Corinthian capitals; and in the walls there were half columns and pilasters, so arranged as to break, by light and shadow, the monotony of a flat surface. Each column had a bracket, on which once stood a statue; and there are inscriptions on the faces of the brackets, one of which contains the names of Hadrian and Agrippa, and a date corresponding to 130 of the Christian era.

This dedication took place the same year in which Hadrian erected a temple to Jupiter at Jerusalem, and

THE TEMPLE OF THE KING'S MOTHER.

about nine years after the building of Hadrian's wall between the Tyne and Solway Firth.

In that year Hadrian visited Palmyra, and in an inscription he is called the "God Hadrian"; and Palmyra took to itself the name of the god, and was known for a time as "Hadrianopolis."

The door of our temple was nine and a half feet wide, and its jambs and lintels were monoliths, adorned with a tracing of the egg and dice pattern. There were windows on each side of the door, with bevelled and projecting stone frames, and there were similar windows in

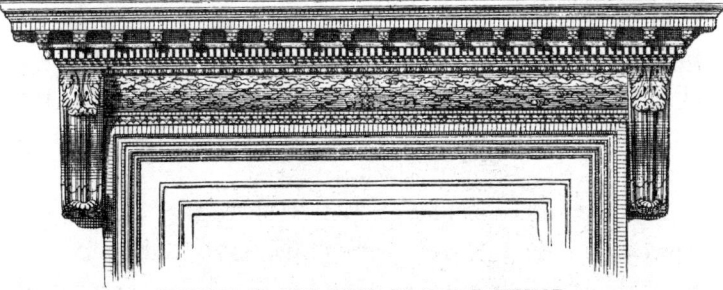

UPRIGHT OF SIDE DOOR OF GREAT TEMPLE.

each side wall of the temple. The whole edifice once stood on a raised platform; but the sand and ruins have silted up round it, taking away from its height, and giving it a slightly heavy look.

Half a score of similar temples lie prostrate among the ruins here and there, showing even in their fallen estate, by the grace and grandeur of their fragments, how much they surpassed this, which doubtless stands a solitary specimen to-day, owing to its having sacrificed airy beauty to solidity and strength.

Right in front of our little temple stood the great Temple of the Sun. Its northern wall rose before us to a height of seventy feet, and hid from our view all the glories within. The blank wall was broken by pilasters with carved capitals, which supported a solid projecting entablature, and there were windows between the pilasters which were all closed, except one, through which some of the superfluous dung of the village within was ejected.

The strong outer wall gave the temple something of the character of a fortress; and this was necessitated by the position of the city, surrounded as it was by the wild hordes of the desert, and subject to the sudden incursions of the Parthians from the east. The Moslems changed the temple into a real fort, by building up the windows, and raising a square tower over the splendid portico.

This magnificent old temple, I shall not attempt to describe in detail. It covered about six hundred and forty thousand square feet of ground, and in going round it you walk more than a mile. The entrance doorway, which was beautifully sculptured, was thirty-two feet high and sixteen feet wide, and its jambs and lintels were each single stones. Around the court, near the outer wall, were rows of columns, seventy feet high, to the number of three hundred and seventy-four, and these, like the other columns of Palmyra, had brackets for the statues of those whom the Tadmorenes delighted to honour. Within the spacious square enclosed by these colonnades stood a beautiful building on a raised platform, ascended by a flight of stone steps, and surrounded by a single row of fluted columns with Corinthian capitals in bronze.

This was the temple. Its length north and south was about forty paces, and its breadth nearly sixteen paces.

The entrance was in the western side, and at the other end there was what might be called the Holy of Holies. The ceiling in this *naos*, or innermost part of the temple, still remained entire, exhibiting the most lovely designs with zodiacal signs and the most perfect carving to be seen in Tadmor. Indeed, this temple is the chief triumph of the Tadmor artists; and at the time Zenobia used to

CEILING OF THE HOLY OF HOLIES, TEMPLE OF THE SUN.

grace its steps surrounded by her brilliant court, it must have been an object of surpassing splendour.

The great polished columns in the temple alone, if placed end to end, would have formed one column nearly six miles long; and the statues, if drawn up in form, would have presented about the same numbers as a regiment of the line. We can well understand how Aurelian spent such vast sums — three hundred pounds' weight of gold and eighteen hundred pounds' weight of silver, as well as the crown jewels of Zenobia — to repair this temple, which had been injured by his soldiers.

Let us look at the temple in its present state. As we approach it in front, we see, over the patched and broken walls, columns standing, and leaning about at every angle, as though the temple enclosure were a huge lumber-yard of columns. Around the outer wall is a deep ditch, and the entrance is reached by a raised causeway flagged with broad stones, among which I recognized a panelled stone door. The sheikh and a crowd of his people are sitting on stones in the gate. Camels and mules pass in and out, and women with jars of water on their heads, and babies on their shoulders, enter the enclosure. The men are tall, and, as it seems to me, have a Jewish cast of features. The women are coarse featured, but not very ugly, and they all blacken their eyebrows and blue their lips.

Within, we find the whole area of the temple filled with clay-daubed huts, so that we can only get an idea of the place by climbing over them. We pass on straight to the Holy of Holies, which we explore with our handkerchiefs held to our noses, for the inmost shrine is the cesspool of the community.

We hurry out to the fresh air; but it is not fresh, for all the offal and filth of the houses are flung out into the narrow lanes, and lie rotting in the sun. Wherever we go among these human dens there reek

TEMPLE OF THE SUN, EASTERN SIDE

filth and squalor, and the hot pestiferous atmosphere of an ill-kept stye. Such is now the state of that gorgeous temple which the proud Tadmorenes raised to their gods, which were no gods, and where they glorified one another in monuments of perishable stone.

Looking at the ruins of Tadmor, one wonders at the rage that must have existed for columns. Little houses had their tiers of little columns, and great houses had

TRIUMPHAL ARCH.

their tiers of correspondingly great columns. Public edifices for civil and religious uses had their quota of lofty columns. Little streets and public squares all had their rows of columns; and wherever you move, columns without number block your path. They lie, in some places, like trees swept together by a flood into heaps; at other places they protrude from the sand, or stand up in solitary grandeur, having no apparent connection with anything else.

The column mania found its fullest expression in the great colonnade of the principal street. This street intersected the city, running almost in a line between the Temple of the Sun and the Castle. The end next the temple commenced with a splendid triumphal arch, and after extending towards the mountain for about four thousand feet, terminated in what is now a maze of prostrate columns.

The triumphal arch consisted of a large central and two side arches, from which ran four rows of columns, forming a central broadway and sidewalks. About half way down the street, a little below the arcade which cuts the colonnade at right angles, there are four massive pedestals, on which probably stood equestrian or other statues of enormous magnitude; and near this spot, on both sides, are splendid ruins, which local tradition makes the palace of "Sitt Zeinab" (Lady Zenobia) and the judgment-hall.

SIDE ARCHWAY OF TRIUMPHAL ARCH.

Independent of the colonnades that branched off right and left, this one street, with its sidewalks, must have had about fifteen hundred columns. These columns were fifty-seven feet high, and were composed of three great drums, which supported Corinthian capitals and massive ornate entablatures. Between the second and third drum there was a section of a column inserted, with a protruding bracket for the reception of a bust or statue, and on the fronts of these brackets were inscriptions in Greek and Palmyrene, giving the names of the persons whose statues graced the pedestals.

On two columns side by side, near the central arcade, are two inscriptions of the greatest interest. The one records the dedication, by his generals, of "a statue to Septimius Odainathus, king of kings, and regretted by the whole city"; and the other is a dedication to his wife, "Septimia Zenobia, the illustrious and pious queen."

In the Palmyrene, under the Greek, we find Zenobia's Palmyrene name — Bath-Zabbai, the daughter of Zabbai.

Both statues were raised in the month of August A.D. 271, only a short time before the fall of the city.

What a splendid city Palmyra must have been in its palmy days, when the victorious hosts of Odainathus returned laden with the spoils of Oriental kings, and marched in glittering array through the long colonnades, beneath the statues of illustrious Palmyrans! Or when the fiery Bath-Zabbai flashed through those corridors in her gilded chariot, surrounded by her martial courtiers and fair companions! Or when, with bare arms and helmet on head, with all the pomp of real or mimic war, she sallied forth on her shining Arab to review and harangue her warriors on the sandy plain!

CEILING OF TOMB TOWER.

CHAPTER IX.

LET us pass on to the examination of the famous tombs, the most interesting objects in Palmyra, lest we be supposed to have also caught the column mania.

On my first visit to Palmyra, I arrived equipped for a thorough exploration of the tombs. Sir Richard Burton, who' had visited the ruins before me, urged me to take ladders and ropes and grappling-irons, for the ascent of the towers, which he had been unable to examine for lack of such appliances. In accordance with this advice, I made ample preparations. A trusty carpenter was employed to make three thirty-foot ladders; choice poplar trees were carefully split up and fitted with oak rounds from Bashan. Powerful hemp ropes were specially manufactured, and mighty grappling-irons were prepared. I sometimes thought if I could get up the ruin so as to fit on the grappling-irons, I might be able to dispense with them altogether; but then, what is the use of fol-

THE FATHER OF LADDERS.

lowing advice by halves? So I did as I was advised, that nothing might be wanting to enable me to reach those lofty resting-places of the dead, which all my predecessors had sighed in vain to ransack.

I had once had some skill in climbing to rooks' nests, but I was not then quite thirteen stone weight. I determined, however, that in this case the right hand should not forget its cunning, and for weeks before our departure for Palmyra I kept running up eighty-foot ladders like a hodman, and climbing the slack rope like a middy. A large grey mule was provided to carry the scaling-apparatus to Palmyra.

That mule was a wag. He would rush into the centre of a crowd, with the ladders on his back, stop suddenly, and, with the most comical expression on his countenance, wheel right round, and make a clean sweep of the party. And sometimes he would take a fancy to a cavalier, and go tilting after him, down the plain at full speed, evidently with intent to ram him down.

Remonstrance was unavailing, for a thirty-foot ladder reaches further than a whip; and with his load of ladders he would go point blank at the most wrathful horseman.

A Turkish soldier, who had got a punch in the back, rushed up valiantly to chastise "the father of ladders," as the mule was called; but before he reached the object of his wrath a sweep of the ladders unhorsed him, to the great amusement of all the spectators.

I advise future travellers who go by the old monotonous road, to take a mule laden with ladders, for ours gave us more than he cost in amusement; and the cry, "There is the father of ladders," was the most potent spell to drive away sleep, and save us from breaking our necks.

I shall never forget the consternation with which I first saw the tomb-towers. There they towered up to heaven, more than one hundred feet high, most of them horribly cracked and toppling over; even the stones seemed rotten. And was I to throw a grappling-hook over those lofty pinnacles, and commence slack-rope practice up those "bowing walls," which were only waiting for an excuse to fall?

Around the base of the mountains, on all sides, these huge towers of death lifted their heads aloft, grim and inaccessible. I was in a dreadful dilemma. If, on the one hand, I attempted to scale the towers, I was certain to break my neck; and if I failed, I was certain to become an object of ridicule to my party, who placed to my credit all the eccentricities and misdemeanours of the "father of ladders," and who had already some misgivings about my sanity.

What was to be done? I thought of pointing out the awkward questions that might be raised by my insurance company in case of an accident on the slack rope, or of explaining the irreparable loss my family and church would sustain should anything untoward happen; but I knew that I could not get the barbarians to comprehend what was meant by a company to insure people against dying, and pay them when they were dead, and I believed that they would look very lightly on what I considered a loss!

I kept my secret, and for three days explored everything that could be explored in Palmyra — interviewed the inhabitants from a missionary point of view, measured columns, stepped distances, explored cellars, bought antiques, copied inscriptions, and wrote copious notes, but never once went near the towers, all the time looking for some *Deus ex machinâ* to extricate me from my difficulty — some blood-thirsty *razzia* by the Bedawîn, or some other dreadful thing, which might render the exploration of the towers impossible. Every time my eye caught the ladders, or the towers, my heart sank within me.

"When are you going to do the towers?" said one of our party, sarcastically. The question could be put off no longer. Notice was given that forty men, with pickaxes, spades, and baskets, would be employed on the following morning, at six piasters for the day each. The following morning, before the sun had tipped the towers with gold, one hundred men were surging about our tent, drawn by the prospect of earning a shilling each. I began to pick out the strongest looking, and those who had the best tools, and to set them apart from the crowd; but suddenly the whole crowd would move across to join the chosen few. After an hour spent in vainly trying to make a selection, the crowd hit upon a solution. "Give us," said they, "three or four piasters apiece, and take us all." Eighty were easier taken than forty, and so we lessened the fee, and doubled the number of workmen.

It was the saddest sight I saw at Tadmor, the number of idle, able, hungry men, wanting employment, and willing to work, and the fields lying uncultivated. But did any enterprising man, with capital, attempt to utilize the resources of the place, the Turks would encourage him by taxing every tree he planted, and by holding him responsible for all arrears incurred before he was born while the place was unoccupied.

One old man, whom we were going to reject, held out his withered arms, and jumping off the ground, with a force that might have shaken out his few remaining teeth, shouted, "Let me go; let me earn three piasters; I can work as well as any of them."

The plucky old man got his three piasters, and was one of the most useful of the party.

We started for the invasion of the tombs, a motley but formidable band. Six men were told off to the ladders, two to the ropes, and the remainder, in companies of eight, were placed under the charge of our military guards. We were a noisy multitude, as we swarmed down through the ruins to disturb the bones of the haughty Palmyrans; and it was my last hope, that should the towers prove unscalable we might somehow take them by screaming, as the French took the Bastille.

We first proceeded to Abu Sahil, the most ancient cemetery, south of the entrance to Tadmor. Here were groups of towers, and the plain all round was full of mounds, which were supposed to mark the position of large excavated cave-tombs. According to local tradition, a camel passing over one of these had once suddenly disappeared, having fallen through the roof into the tomb.

TOMB TOWER.

Immense treasures, especially in works of art, were alleged to have been found in that tomb.

Our ten companies of eight were told off, under their military leaders, to drive shafts into the most promising mounds, and prizes were offered on a graduated scale to the first, second, third, etc., companies who should strike fresh tombs. The digging detachments commenced with a will, and we left them under the generalship of one European, supported by eight Turkish soldiers, and started for the towers. We began quietly with the smallest towers, and proceeded steadily to the largest, and in less than three hours of hard work, we had thoroughly explored them all. I stood on the top of every tower, and we had only twice recourse to the ladders; and even then I think we might have dispensed with them. The ropes were used for measuring, and the grappling-irons were not used at all.

I can now assure all those who sighed to explore the upper stories of the tomb-towers, and whose imaginations revelled in their undisturbed treasure, that the highest recesses had been ransacked before I scaled them, and that nothing remained but a few mutilated mummies and a great number of bones and skulls.

We brought away a number of skulls, choosing those that seemed most unlike each other, and one mummy very carefully wrapped up in many folds of cloth, of a texture and colour much resembling what is used in Palmyra at the present day. The bodies had all been embalmed, and all the skulls were full of olive stones broken.

We saw many pieces of broken statuary, but it was as a

PALMYRA AND ZENOBIA. 83

rule so stiff and conventional that we could not much blame the barbarian iconoclasts. The pieces were generally of a woman reclining on a couch, raised on her elbow, attended by a fawn, and receiving a cup from the hand of a slave who stood at the foot of the couch. So common was this type, with slight variations, that one would suppose the Tadmor belles never did anything but recline on couches, with a stereotyped simper on their faces, and receive sherbet from deferential slaves.

The towers were all of the same type, some of them being large and others small; some of them well finished, and others of undressed stones. I give two pictures of the most perfect of these monuments, and they may be used to correct Wood and Dawkins' plan of the same monuments, which are drawn somewhat out of proportion.

Great liberties have been taken by tourists with this monument. It is said to have been erected by *Gichos*, though the man had his name written up *Iamlichos*, twice, both in Greek and Palmyrene as plain as a signboard, so that he that runneth might read. The date,[1] also,

---

[1] Wood and Dawkins gave the date of this monument as 314 of the Seleucidæ era, corresponding to the second year of the Christian era; and, as far as I am aware, all who have written on Palmyra, except Waddington, have followed their reading. The inscription is written above the door, as well as on the table beneath the niche on the façade. Wood and Dawkins declare that inasmuch as the shape of the letters contradicted "a rule established by antiquaries," they "were careful in examining the date, which is very legible in both inscriptions." I have twice examined the date, and I have it in photograph, and it corresponds to 82 of the Christian era, not 2, as Wood and Dawkins assert.

is given eighty years too early, and theories in archæology, and on the ante-Roman refinement of the Palmyrans, have been founded on the mistake. The mausoleum is a marvel inside of beautiful carving and rich colours; but as it has often been described, we shall pass to another, and taller one, which has attracted less the attention of tourists, and which I explored very thoroughly.

Kasr eth-Thunîyeh is thirty-three and a half feet square at the base, and twenty-five feet eight inches square above the basement. Its height is one hundred and eleven feet, and it comprises six stories, reached by stone stairs now much broken down. It has also underground an immense vault, full of bones of wild animals and men, with pieces of mummy cloths, etc. Opposite the door, down the centre of the building, there is a long hall with a very beautiful panelled stone ceiling. In each side of the hall are four recesses in the wall, about the length and breadth of a large coffin. Shelves were placed in these recesses, leaving room for dead bodies to be run in between them. The upper stories were like the first, except that they were not so ornate, and contained more recesses in the sides, some of them as many as eight. My companion, Mr. Cotesworth, found by actual counting that there were places for four hundred and eighty bodies in this one tower. Any one with a steady head, who can jump across a chasm six or seven feet wide and one hundred feet deep, need not fear to reach the top of this monument, and he will be well rewarded for his pains.

TOMB TOWER

From the top of the tower he will get his best idea of the ruins and dimensions of Palmyra. In moister regions ivy and moss soon wrap ruins about so closely that they cannot be seen; but here every polished shaft lies where it fell, as clean as it left the hands of the workman, so that he will have a bird's-eye view of all the ruins, in their desolate grandeur; and even where the sand has covered the streets and foundations of houses, he will be able to trace the exact position which they occupied. He will be able, also, to trace the outer wall of Zenobia's Tadmor, and to conjecture the points at which the final struggle with Rome took place.

Having thoroughly *done* the towers, we returned to the diggers, and found that they had toiled with about the same success as ourselves. In nearly every place the barbarians and wild beasts had preceded us. The mummies had been torn from their cerements, and their bones scattered through the vaults. Skulls, mutilated statuary, consisting chiefly of reclining females with pine cones in their hands, coins, and clay tablets, with Palmyrene inscriptions, were our rewards.

One little terra-cotta scarab which I picked up with other tessaræ in a tomb-vault proved to be of more than ordinary interest. It resembled the Palmyra tablets in colour and form, and I was not at once aware of the importance of my find, but in looking over my collection in the tent, I saw that one of the little objects was Egyptian, and at a later period I became convinced that I had actually discovered a scarab of the renowned Tirhakah.   Tirhakah is twice mentioned in the Bible.[1]

Hezekiah and his people were hard pressed by Sennacherib, but the boastful Assyrian heard that Tirhakah, King of Ethiopia, had come to fight against him, and he returned to Nineveh, where he was slain by his own sons. These references in the Bible are of the most casual character, and I could hardly bring myself to believe that I had actually found at Palmyra a record of the mysterious Egyptian monarch who had flourished more than twenty-five hundred years before.

PALMYRENE FIGURE.

Being fully alive to the improbability of any relic of the great Tirhakah being found in a Palmyra tomb, and knowing how ready some at home would be to trip me up if I blundered, I did not proclaim my find publicly; but I sent the scarab to the British Museum by my friend, the Rev. Greville Chester, and the late Dr. Birch read the inscription as follows: —

" . . . of Amen, Tirhakah, he has given thee eternal life."

SEAL OF TIRHAKAH.

[1] 2 Kings xix. 9, and Isaiah xxxvii. 9.

PALMYRA AND ZENOBIA.

On May 4th, 1880, Dr. Birch read a paper on Tirhakah before the Society of Biblical Archæology, and referring to the scarab, said: "As the little object has much the same appearance as the other (Palmyra) objects, it is difficult to conceive how it came there, or if it is an indication that the conquests of Tirhakah extended as far as Palmyra." [1]

Tirhakah, who was a very powerful monarch, seems to have begun his reign about 688 B.C.

There is a very touching reference to his prosperity in an Egyptian inscription. At a very early age he left Ethiopia and proceeded northward, and he seems to have made his way to the throne while still a youth. His mother, who had remained behind in Ethiopia for a time, followed him north, and when she overtook him, she found him King of Upper and Lower Egypt. He extended his conquests to distant lands. Strabo says he penetrated as far as the Pillars of Hercules. A statue at Boulak mentions among his conquests, the Bedawîn, the Hittites, Aradus, the Phœnicians, the Assyrians, and Mesopotamia. The Temple of Thebes and the Fane of Mount Barkal and other Egyptian monuments attest the splendour of Tirhakah's reign.

One slab, discovered by us in an underground tomb, contained two figures, two feet three inches high, both holding up one bunch of grapes between them. It had also Palmyrene inscriptions [2] between the heads of the

[1] *Transactions*, Vol. VII. p. 208.
[2] The inscription between the heads of the figures reads thus:

statues and beneath their feet, and the drapery, like that of all the other figures, was of many folds and creases.

BAALATGA AND 'ALLIASHA.

On the lower corner of a somewhat similar slab I saw in very minute Greek the name of the establishment that supplied the ornament.

Crossing the Abu Sahil Cemetery, I noticed a hole made by a fox or a jackal, at the base of one of the mounds. I threw a stone into the hole, and heard it rolling down a considerable distance. The spirit of adventure was roused, and squeezing myself

---

"Images of Baalatga and 'Alliasha, children of Buna, son of Jashubi." The inscription below the figures reverses and amplifies the other: "In the month of Kanun [November], year 406 [94 A.D.]. These two likenesses are those of 'Alliasha and Baalatga, children of Buna, son of Jashubi, son of Belsazar, son of Hiram — Habal." The last word corresponds to our *Vale*, or *Requiescat in pace*. The tablet, which was too heavy for us to carry, was brought to Damascus by the Russian consul, to whom I am indebted for the photograph from which the engraving is taken. The engraved slab is now in St. Petersburg.

through the hole with some difficulty, and sliding down gently, I suddenly dropped seven or eight feet, into a pitch dark dungeon. I thought I had fallen a much greater distance; indeed, in the unknown darkness, I thought, in my descent, I was never going to reach the bottom.

Having recovered from the shock of the fall, I lighted a piece of magnesian wire, and found myself amply rewarded for my abrupt tumble, by the marvellous scene that met my view.

By the bright light I saw that I was in a low-browed vault, surrounded by the mouldering remains of one hundred and fifteen Palmyrans. The vault was sixty feet long by twenty-seven wide, and seven or eight feet high. There were nine recesses for bodies on either side, and five at the lower end. The recesses, in length and general dimensions, resembled the *loculi* in the tomb-towers which we had already explored; but they were cemented down the sides, and each had five shelves of hard-baked pottery fitted and cemented into them.

On these shelves the embalmed corpses of the Palmyrans were laid, the bodies having been rammed in head foremost, with their feet out. As I looked around this silent and awful resting-place of the dead, I could not help thinking that Isaiah may have had in view such a charnel-house when he described the commotion that would be caused by the arrival of the Chaldean monarch: "Hell [*sheol*] from beneath is moved for thee to meet thee at thy coming; it stirreth up the dead for thee" (Isa. xiv. 9).

My magnesian wire soon burned to the end, but before it was exhausted I had time to make the accompanying ground plan of the vault, on a piece of cigarette paper which I happened to have in my pocket.

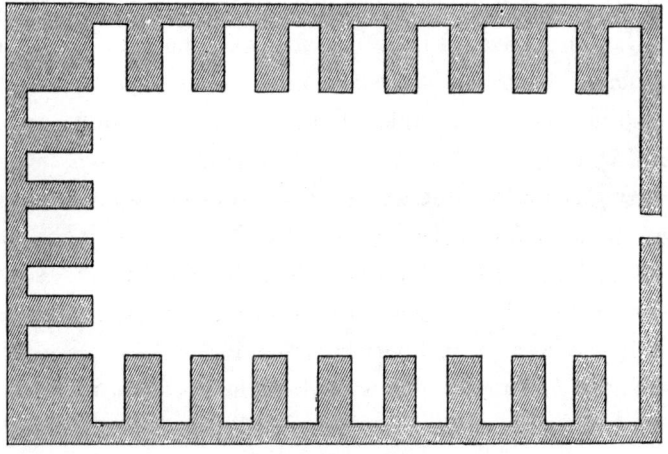

MORTUARY VAULT.

When the bright light went out, the darkness became palpable. I struck my few remaining matches, one after another, but they only served to disclose the denseness of the gloom. I was in a veritable trap of death. The hole through which I had descended was several feet beyond my reach. I had been a considerable time in the pit, but the minutes seemed hours, and it was clear that none of my party knew anything of my position. In the still darkness, I heard the beating of my own heart distinctly.

After a few minutes of bewilderment, it became apparent that I must depend on my own efforts to effect my escape from the awful charnel-house. I began at once to draw the pottery shelves from under the skeletons, to form a step by which to reach the hole at the top. It was not pleasant, in the darkness, to grope among the bony skeletons, sometimes putting my hands on a skull, and sometimes on the fleshless toes of a foot.

I tried to set up the longest tiles on their ends, laying others across, and propping up the structure with shin-bones and other fragments of skeletons; but the erection came down when I tried to mount it, and I found that it would be necessary to build up a solid mass of the tile shelves. The tiles were about an inch thick, and I knew that there were one hundred and fifteen, but some of them were so well cemented into their places that I could neither draw them out nor break them.

It soon became a struggle for life, and in the darkness I lost a good deal of time in finding the exact spot on which to place the tiles when I had succeeded in drawing them from under the fleshless skeletons.

In the midst of my operations, I heard footsteps overhead. I made all the noise I could, singing the Druze war-song, which carries a great burden of sound. I heard voices, and believed I was heard; but the sound of voices and of the footfalls died away.

I resumed my labours with a feeling of consternation. I do not think I was much troubled with superstitious feelings, but I worked so hard that the perspiration dropped from my face.

Suddenly, to my great joy, many voices and more

numerous footsteps returned. Some of the Palmyrans who had heard me underground declared with alarm that the dead were being disturbed, and that they were shouting for the "Sheikh Ibn el-Hamdan"; and some of my people, who had missed me, hearing the report, and recognizing a bit of my desert Druze song, came hurrying off to find me.

A rope with a grappling-iron was let down the hole. I put my foot on the hook, using it as a stirrup, and holding by the rope, I was, after a little trouble, drawn out once more into the light of day. I had been absent scarcely an hour, though the time of my detention in the darkness seemed an age.

PALMYRENE FIGURE.

SOFFIT IN TEMPLE OF THE SUN.

CHAPTER X.

I HAD spent eight hours among the tombs above ground, and one hour with the dead in the darkness. I was much in need of a bath, and one of the finest baths in the world was at hand.

We hurried to the fountain called Ephca, south of the entrance of the city, and plunged in. The water was warm, but not uncomfortably so, and one soon ceased to be distressed by the disagreeable smell of sulphur. It was a part of our plan to explore as far as possible this subterranean river, and so, leaving a guard at the entrance, I swam in with a candle. The river turned in somewhat to the right, under Jebel el-Mantar. Sometimes the roof rose fifteen or twenty feet above the water, and sometimes it was so close to the water as scarcely to leave me room to pass. The breadth varied from seven to twelve feet, and in several places where I dived to the bottom I estimated the depth to be from eight to ten feet.

As I proceeded, the water became sensibly warmer and

the air more difficult to breathe, and the flame of the candle grew smaller and smaller, and finally went out altogether. I estimate that I had penetrated between four and five hundred feet, and the cavern still continued broad and deep; but when the light went out, I was left in darkness that might be felt.

There is no resting-place after one leaves the entrance, as the water has scooped out and undermined the perpendicular sides, and the water is not buoyant; but as it is warm, one can stay in it a long time without receiving any harm. I floated out of the darkness, having received no harm except a few bumps, and having spent in the water about an hour and a quarter. I question, however, if it would be possible to penetrate into the cavern much further than I went, owing to the sulphurous atmosphere.

The aqueduct seems to be natural. The sides and roof are composed of a gravelly clay, which seems to be always falling in; and I saw no traces of man, except at the entrance, where there is some cutting in the rock to let the water out. An altar which stood at the mouth of the cavern gave it the name Fount Ephca. The date of the dedication of the altar was the 20th of October, 162 A.D. The grotto is much used as a bath still, and we seldom visited it without startling from their bath the nymphs of the village; and I am told that the Bedawîn are so fond of it that a number of them are drowned in it every year.

A considerable volume of water issues from the cavern and forms a little river. A slight steam rises from the water, and the stones are stained by the sulphur; but after passing over the sandy bed of the stream for a few hundred yards, the water loses much of its disagreeable taste. It is used chiefly for washing, and for irrigating the gardens; but it is also drunk, and considered wholesome by the natives.

The fountain of Ephca has been erroneously supposed to have been the principal source of the city's water supply. To the left of the entrance to Palmyra there are the ruins of an aqueduct of massive, well-dressed stones, which once brought water to the city proper. This was constructed to contain a volume of water eight feet high by four feet broad. Near the same place there passed into the city an underground aqueduct, which was conducted down the middle of the grand colonnade. It is first tapped, not far from the triumphal arch, at a depth of eight or ten feet below the pavement, and it flows out of the city north of the Great Temple, and is used for all purposes, especially for irrigation.

This water is drawn from a fountain called Abu el-Fawaris, which lies about five miles due west of the Castle of Tadmor. The water is good, but perceptibly impregnated with sulphur; and as all the channels have been choked up for hundreds of years, people busy themselves in conjecturing whence the Palmyrans got their water supply. There is no doubt that the Abu el-Fawaris fountain was their chief source; but the waters of Ephca were also utilized, and the houses had cisterns for rain-water, as we discovered in several places.

The Castle of Palmyra is perhaps the most conspicuous object in the neighbourhood, and well deserves a visit, not on its own account, but on account of the unparalleled view which it commands. We rode up the mountain to near the top, and when it became too steep for our horses, we left them with a guard and proceeded on foot. A deep ditch surrounds the castle, and partridges were sunning themselves about its edges.

We climbed up into the castle by the rough face of an almost perpendicular rock; but we saw the remains of a broken bridge across the ditch, which once gave easy access to the castle, and there are still marks of horses having been stabled within it.

The castle stands on the highest peak, on the highest summit, impregnable to any force in the desert; but the present structure is built of small stones quarried out of the ditch and rifled from the ruins, and is doubtless a late effort of the Moslems.

The castle is still entire, and the rooms, which were arched and cemented, are all in a good state of preservation. From its battlements we had an uninterrupted view on all sides. The Dawara range[1] of mountains, on which we stood, stretched away north-east to the Euphrates, and beyond as far as the Tigris; and near

---

[1] On some maps the mountain range north of Tadmor is called Jebel Amur. As it approaches the Euphrates it is called Jebel Bisshari; beyond the Euphrates it is called Jebel Abdularis; and as it stretches toward Mossul it has the name Jebel Sinjar. Dawara was the name by which the range was known to my guides at Palmyra.

CASTLE END OF THE GREAT COLONNADE.

the eastern base of the mountains we saw the village of Arak, with about fifteen huts and a Turkish garrison.

We could distinctly trace the old walls of Tadmor extending down the mountain, from outside the castle, in a south-eastern direction, and curving round the city. Away beyond, east and south, was the flat, yellow desert, patched and seamed with glistening salt. Far to the south, past the shoulder of Jebel el-Mantar, stood a solitary tower, called Kasr el-Hazûn; and on the horizon beyond, there appeared a low range of mountains, known as Jebel el-'Aleib. To the west, over a wavy highland of limestone hills, we could distinctly discern through the blue mists the lofty outline of Lebanon and the snows of the Cedar mountain.

What a watch-tower from which an enemy might be descried while he was yet several days' journey from the place! Beneath us, the city, half surrounded by its gardens, lay calm as a city of the dead, and supremely lovely even in desolation. As we stand on the battlements we see at a glance the appropriateness of its name. Tadmor in Syriac means "wonderful," and in Arabic "ruin." The Syriac and Arabic name still clings to the "wonderful ruin," while the Roman name Palmyra is absolutely unknown to the natives.

The name Tadmor has been supposed to mean in Hebrew "city of palm-trees," and it has been taken for granted that Palmyra is the Greek translation of the word; but the word Tadmor is not Hebrew, and the word Palmyra is not Greek. The meaning of the word should be sought for in the language of the people who frequented those fountains before the time of Solomon, for though he built Tadmor in the wilderness, he did not change its name.

The great king of Israel, having extended his kingdom by conquest to the north and east, "built Tadmor in the wilderness, and the store cities of Hamath." He found the important station Tadmor, in the desert, supplied with water, and forming the link between East and West, and he enlarged and fortified, and doubtless garrisoned it, the better to consolidate his empire and draw the wealth of the Indies into his little kingdom. Doubtless Tadmor was then, as now, an open and unsafe resting-place for the bearers of the commodities he so much desired; and he made it not only a strong outpost, but a secure haven.

As we have seen, the Bible [1] and local tradition unite in declaring that "Solomon built Tadmor in the wilderness"; but who built the Tadmor of Odainathus and Zenobia? Who polished and poised those columns now strewed on the plain before us? for not a vestige remains of the Tadmor of Solomon. As being the most remote, Tadmor was probably one of the first places wrested from the feeble successors of Solomon, and for

---

[1] Once and only once (2 Chron. viii. 4) is Tadmor mentioned in the Bible. The Tadmor in 2 Kings ix. 13 is Tamar in the Hebrew text, and is said to be "*in the land*," and is now identified as a ruin at Kurnub in the land of Juda. Every peasant talks familiarly of King Solomon, and yet there is not a Bible in the place, nor would the inhabitants accept a copy.

a thousand years it disappears from history, having become, in all probability, a "wonderful ruin" in the eyes of the savage hordes that encamped about its fountains. Palmyra, however, as the convenient half-way house between the commercial cities of Phœnicia and of the Seleucidæ on the Mediterranean, and the eastern realms about and beyond the Persian Gulf, rose into a wealthy and independent state. Secure in her surrounding desert, like sea-girt England, Palmyra, as the channel of East India merchandise, grew in wealth, but not in strength; and about half a century before the Christian era, she came on the stage of Roman history for the first time, when Mark Antony attempted to plunder her merchant princes.

For the next three hundred years, Tadmor continued to grow in wealth and power, and in the cultivation of all the arts of war and peace. Tadmor flourished, like Switzerland, a free republic, surrounded by mighty and despotic empires. Her architects and sculptors adorned her with edifices which excite the wonder of the world, and she became the congenial home of the greatest philosopher of his age, Longinus, the author of the "Treatise on the Sublime," and the prime minister of Zenobia.

Odainathus, one of her senators, rose to the proud position of holding the balance of power between Rome and Parthia, and of avenging the Roman arms, and wearing the Roman purple; and his widow, Zenobia, victorious over the Roman legions, reigned, Queen of the East, from the Nile to the Euphrates.

From the time of Mark Antony to the time of Aurelian the city had so grown in strength that the latter was unable to take it with his victorious armies, though only defended by the remnants of Zenobia's dispirited troops; and Tadmor did not surrender till Zenobia, who had escaped to raise fresh succour, was brought back a prisoner from the banks of the Euphrates.

The golden age of Tadmor's prosperity seems to have been from her first contact with the power of Rome, until she was finally crushed by that power; and her splendid edifices were the result of that wave of civilization which was put in motion by the Macedonian conqueror, and continued by the Romans. Like most of the splendid ruins of Syria, those of Palmyra date from the early centuries of our era. From the early part of the second century the relations between Rome and Palmyra became most intimate. Palmyra ministered to Roman luxury, and Rome became pledged for the safety and stability of the merchant city.

In all ages the wealth of India has flowed in a direct line to the centre of the world's power. The centre of the world's power had become fixed on the Seven Hills, and Pliny tells us that the city of Rome alone took annually one million *sestertii* of Indian merchandise. It is interesting to trace the routes across the desert along which, as by a magnet, Rome drew the riches of the East. One line passed through Gaza and Petra to Forath. A second, starting from Akka on the Mediterranean, ran across Galilee, north of Nazareth, crossed

CENTRAL PART

AT COLONNADE.

the Jordan below the lake of Gennesaret, and struck direct for the head of the Persian Gulf, past Bosra and Sulkhâd. The Roman road is still in many places uninjured, awaiting the European engineers to lay down the rails on the *shortest, safest,* and *cheapest* overland route to India.

The northern routes from Antioch through Aleppo and Karrhæ, or more northern still through Carchemish, Edessa, and Nisbis, were closed to commerce by centuries of turbulence. It was at Palmyra that the East and West joined hands in the mutual benefits of commerce. The Tadmorenes, like the English in our day, were the chief carriers and retailers of Indian merchandise, and Appian, the Roman historian, speaks of them with the same contempt as the first Napoleon spoke of the "*nation of shopkeepers.*" " They are merchants," said he, disdainfully, "who seek among the Persians the products of India and Arabia, and carry them to the Romans."

The Tadmorenes took a different view of the dignity of commerce, and many of the statues that sentinelled the long colonnades were placed there in honour of the successful leaders of caravans. Thus J. A. Zebeida was adjudged a statue in April 147 A.D., by the merchants who accompanied him with the caravan from Volgesia. Markos had a statue for organizing the caravan of which Zabdeathus was the conductor. Thaimarson was honoured with a place in the grand colonnade, on account of his having led a caravan from Karak for the liquidation of an ancient debt of three hundred dinars. And a statue was erected in the grand colonnade, in 257 A.D., by the senate and people in honour of Salmalath, for having conducted a caravan at his own expense. In several instances, also, we find tribes erecting statues to those whom they considered had merited well of them; so that the Bedawîn seem to have thrown in their lot with the merchants.

In those days, the Palmyrans held the monopoly of the overland route to India; and so long as they maintained a strict neutrality between Rome and Persia, they grew in wealth and in general luxury; and we learn from many of the inscriptions that the citizens lavished their wealth in beautifying their city. The inscriptions give us the best answer to the question, which has puzzled so many, "Who built the Tadmor of Zenobia?"

It has been generally supposed that Hadrian adorned Palmyra, but from the inscriptions we learn that the beautifying of the place was rather the work of the people and senate of the luxurious little republic.

The rule seems to have been that when wealthy citizens erected temples and colonnades in honour of the gods, and performed other public-spirited acts, their fellow-citizens honoured them with statues. Thus, from an inscription, we learn that one man erected six columns, with their architraves, and painted them, in honour of Shems and Alath (the Sun and a female deity worshipped by the Arabs), and his fellow-citizens erected a statue to him in March 129 A.D. Another citizen erected seven columns, with all their ornaments and brazen balustrades, and he was "statued" in March 179 A.D. And from the inscription, to which we have already referred, on the portico of the "Temple of the King's Mother," we learn that "the temple, with all its ornaments, was built by one Mala, called Agrippa, at his own expense." A statue was erected to Mala for his services during the visit of the "god Hadrian"; but he seems to have been a general benefactor, for it is recorded in the same inscription that "he gave oil to the inhabitants, the soldiers, and to strangers."

The small temples and the colonnades appear, from the inscriptions, to have been the gifts of private individuals; but such a work as the great Temple of the Sun must have proceeded from the senate and the republic. It is not unlikely that private donations may also have been used, and we find an inscription recording the dedication of a statue "by the senate and people to Ogga, who honoured himself by giving to the senate the sum of ten thousand drachmas."[1]

It would thus seem that the Tadmorenes could honour the gods, adorn the city, and have their vanity gratified by a statue, for an outlay of from £400 to £500. By the side of this statue stood another to Ogga, and the inscription significantly declared that "it was erected by the senate and people for love."

[1] The Attic drachma was worth $9\frac{3}{4}d.$, and the Aginetan, 1s. 1d.

The people of Tadmor, as the inscriptions declare, honoured and rewarded citizens who rendered distinguished service to the community, and in the bestowal of their favours they marked with special distinction their townsman Odainathus and his wife Zenobia.

PALMYRENE FIGURE.

ZENOBIA.
(From a Coin.)

CHAPTER XI.

THE history of Zenobia is linked inseparably, by fact and fiction, with Palmyra, and deserves at our hands a more detailed notice than we have given thus far. The very mention of Tadmor, as we have already said, recalls the names of Solomon and Zenobia, and both are associated in the Oriental mind with the wonderful ruin; but while Solomon is accredited with superhuman powers, the Sitt Zeinab, or Lady Zenobia, is renowned for her womanly graces and accomplishments, as well as for her vast learning and martial bearing.

In a bookless land, traditions are carefully preserved among a people who talk and listen, but do not read, and the wonderful story of the Sitt Zeinab is scarcely more mythical on the lips of the Palmyrans and Bedawîn, than is that of Zenobia Augusta in the pages of Trebellius Pollio, Zosimus, and Vopiscus.

In building up a slight history of Zenobia, and the dynasty of which she was the most distinguished ornament, I have three sources of information open to me, the Roman historians, the Palmyrene inscriptions, and the living traditions. Of the latter, I shall make sparing use, and only when it harmonizes with the two former.[1]

The Roman Empire came into contact with Britain and Palmyra about the same time. Twelve years before Julius Cæsar landed at Dover, Mark Antony, on a plundering expedition, made a raid on Palmyra. But the Palmyrans fled with their treasures beyond the Euphrates, and the Roman robber found the city denuded of its wealth. He also met a line of Palmyra archers, before whom his cavalry recoiled.

At this period Palmyra must have been an important place, for one of the great tomb-towers dates back to 9 A.D. Pliny defines the geographical and political position of Tadmor, as "situated in the midst of an almost impassable desert, and on the confines of two powerful and hostile kingdoms."

The definite history of Palmyra begins in the early days of the Christian era, although there is a great wealth of local tradition regarding Solomon and the Jân.

Palmyra owed its rise and splendour to a number

---

[1] For much of the traditions to which I attach weight, I am indebted to the late Lady Ellenborough, who spent a great deal of time at Palmyra, and busied herself in weaving together the local stories regarding the great desert queen. Chiefly from this source I derived my information regarding Zenobia's military camps, and the routes by which her armies marched to meet Aurelian. Lady Ellenborough's identifications were confirmed by an intelligent young Sheikh, who accompanied me to the traditional camping grounds.

PALMYRA AND ZENOBIA.

of causes, geographical, political, and personal. It was a buffer state between the Roman and Parthian spheres, and, as Mommsen says, "in every collision between the Romans and Parthians, the question was asked, what policy the Palmyrans would pursue." [1]

The wars between these rival powers contributed to the wealth and importance of the little neutral republic, which maintained its independence down to 130 A.D., when the Emperor Hadrian visited it, and gave it his own name, Hadrianopolis.

He did not conquer Palmyra, but he took it into a kind of client-relationship of mutual advantage. Seven years later, a law regulating the customs and dues of Palmyra was engraved upon a stone in the city, and this long inscription, recently discovered, throws much light on the life and industry of the place.

As interested and powerful protectors of the safest route to India, the Palmyrans were of vital service to the East as well as to the West, in keeping open the lines of commerce. As a mercantile community, and the guardians of merchandise, neutrality and peace were essential to the prosperity, and even to the existence, of the desert city; but the Roman legions crept slowly but surely closer to Tadmor. A Roman garrison was stationed at Danava, on the way to Damascus; Roman legions were on both banks of the Euphrates, as far down as Circesium; and Mesopotamia, which had been added to the Roman Empire by Severus, was occupied by imperial troops.

[1] *The Provinces of the Roman Empire*, Vol. II. 93.

Although the Roman power was firmly established on three sides of Palmyra, the relation of the little republic to the desert tribes was such that the Romans treated it with marked consideration.

Septimius Severus raised it to the position of a Roman colony, and a popularly elected senate managed its affairs. In drawing closer the bonds of relationship, the Romans did not impose irksome restrictions on the Palmyrans; and, unlike other peoples who had come within the Roman sphere, they were not limited to the two imperial languages, but used in public, as well as in private documents, their own language, side by side with the Greek. Palmyra also formed a customs district, in which the customs were collected, not on account of the state, but of the district.

As the bonds of union with Rome became closer, the Palmyrans began to add Roman names to their own Semitic names; but they seem to have taken whatever advantage they could derive from the Roman connection, and while growing in wealth and power, they maintained their independence, notwithstanding the veneer and nominal domination of Rome.

When war broke out between the Persians and Romans, Palmyra became a place of supreme importance to the imperial cause, and successive emperors visited it on their way eastward, and influential citizens received at their hands distinguished marks of imperial favour.

Septimius Severus, on one of his expeditions against the Parthians, visited Palmyra, and raised a distinguished

THE TRIUMPHAL ARCH.

citizen, named Odainathus, to the rank of senator; and the new senator assumed the name of his patron, and was known as Septimius Odainathus, the son of Hairan, the son of Wah-ballath, the son of Nassor.

This Septimius Odainathus was a powerful citizen, as well as a Roman favourite. He was, however, playing a double game, and being suspected of plotting a revolt against Roman authority, his assassination was procured by Rufinus, a Roman officer.

A crime is always a blunder; and Septimius Odainathus left behind him two sons, Hairan and Odainathus. Hairan, the elder, is mentioned as chief or headman of the Palmyrans, in an inscription dated 251 A.D. But the fame of the family centres round the younger brother, Odainathus. Both, however, contributed to the result; for while Odainathus led the men of action and the Bedawîn of the desert, Hairan guided the wealthy merchants and the aristocracy of the city.

Odainathus meditated revenge on the Romans for the murder of his father, but he bided his time and kept his own counsel. He spent his youth among the hardy spearmen, perfecting the instrument by which he hoped to throw off the yoke of the foreigner, and accustoming himself to the ways and wants of hardy warfare. His opportunity came, but not with so clear an issue as he meditated.

In the year 251 A.D., the emperor fell fighting against the Goths in Europe, and the Empire for a time seemed to have fallen to pieces. The West was in confusion, and the East was left to take care of itself, without any helping hand from Rome. Black Sea pirates ravaged the coasts of the Mediterranean. Sapor of Persia drove the Romans out of Mesopotamia, Armenia, Cappadocia, and Syria.

After a time of confusion, the Empire began to right itself, and Publius Licinius Valerianus ascended the throne of the Cæsars. He marched against the Persians, and drove them out of Cappadocia; but a terrible plague swept away a great part of his army, and delayed him in following up the enemy.

In 258 A.D., as Valerian passed through Palmyra, he raised Odainathus to the consular dignity; and the goldsmiths and silversmiths of the city marked the elevation of their fellow-citizen to the highest honorary title of the Empire, by an inscription which still tells the tale.

To the north-west of the city there is a space marked with black ashes, and the natives of Palmyra call it the "*Siaghah*," or silversmiths' quarter. There the workers in the precious metals carried on their craft, and formed probably one of the most powerful guilds of Palmyra. They used their influence in the elevation of Odainathus, who intended to succeed whether the Roman or the Persian proved victorious.

Sapor the Great was then at the zenith of his power. There had been a revival of the old Persian faith and Persian valour, and the Romans had fled before the hosts of Iran. After long delay, Valerian crossed the Euphrates at the close of 259, or the beginning of 260 A.D. A desperate and decisive battle was fought near Edessa. The

Romans were beaten, and the emperor was taken prisoner and carried into captivity. The disaster to the imperial cause at Edessa in the East was as great as the fall of Decius at the mouth of the Danube had been to the Empire in the West.

Sapor treated the unfortunate Valerian with savage cruelty. He boasted that on mounting his horse he always placed his foot on the neck of a Roman emperor; and when Valerian died, after enduring the most cruel indignities, he had him flayed, and his skin stuffed with straw, and preserved as a trophy in the national temple.

Sapor pressed his victory with ruthless vigour. Antioch and other cities and towns were sacked by his barbarian soldiery. Endless trains of captives thronged the routes to Persia, and were led like cattle to the water, once a day; and it is said that the Persians, in order to facilitate their passage of a deep ravine, filled it with their captives, and marched across on their throbbing bodies.

Odainathus, having watched the campaign, resolved to conciliate the victor. The whole East seemed at Sapor's feet, and Odainathus sent him congratulatory letters, rich presents, and an enormous train of dromedaries. But the haughty Sapor, flushed with victory, rejected the Palmyran's gift with scorn.

"Who is this Odainathus," asked the Persian, "that thus insolently presumes to write to his lord? Let him prostrate himself before our throne, with his hands bound behind him, or swift destruction shall be poured on his head, his race, and his country." So saying, he ordered the presents to be hurled into the river. (Patricius in Excerp. Leg. p. 24.)

Odainathus, who had meditated freedom from the golden yoke of Rome, had no desire to become the abject thrall of the arrogant Sapor. The city and the desert shared with him the feeling of resentment roused by the insolence of the barbarian, and as they perceived the common danger, they united all their powers to meet the impending blow.

Sapor had shown his teeth before he was ready to bite. He had met no opposition from the Empire after the overthrow of Valerian, and city after city, following the example of Antioch, opened its gates to the victorious Persians. But on reaching Pompeiopolis, on the coast of Cilicia, a stubborn resistance was offered, and Sapor was obliged to invest and besiege the city.

At this juncture an enterprising leader, known as Callistus or Ballista, turned the fortunes of the war by a bold stroke. Without any special authority, he got together the scattered Roman ships, sailed for the besieged city, and falling suddenly on the besiegers, slaughtered several thousands of them, and captured the royal *harîm*.

Sapor, on receiving the sudden check in Cilicia, hurried home to quell the little storm he had raised at Tadmor. Odainathus, accompanied by his beautiful and warlike wife, Zenobia, had already taken the field, and marched to intercept the returning foe. He had with him the sheikhs of the desert tribes with their swift cavalry, and the archers and spearmen of Tadmor, who had known their leader from childhood. The patriotic guilds of the city were there in their strength, under the eye of their distinguished fellow-citizen. The desert and town Arabs were united to drive back the barbarians, and save the beautiful city, the centre and source of their industry. In addition to the Orientals, Odainathus had collected the remnants of the shattered legions in that region, and he had under his command a disciplined Roman force eager to meet the Persians again, and wipe out the stain of defeat.

The army of Palmyra encountered the Persians to the west of the Euphrates, before they had crossed the river. A battle was fought, and Odainathus and Zenobia gained a decisive victory. The Bedawîn swept the Persian cavalry before them, and the gallant Tadmorenes and steady Romans completed the rout of the barbarians. Sapor fled with the remnant of his army beyond the Euphrates, hotly pursued by the man whose presents, a short time before, he had arrogantly thrown into the river.

According to Trebellius Pollio, Odainathus captured the king's treasures. He also captured the remainder of the king's wives who had not been seized by Callistus, and he caused Sapor to flee into his own country.

In the hour of victory the hand of Odainathus was stayed. A Roman general had thrown off the Roman yoke in Northern Syria, and an Oriental empire was being set up in the East, on the shattered foundation of the

Roman. Such an empire would have been fatal to the existence of Palmyra as a kingdom.

Odainathus grasped the situation. He saw an opportunity for collecting under his standard the scattered fragments of the Roman army, which, under his skilled generalship, he knew would carry him to victory; and so, recalling his forces from the pursuit of Sapor, he marched against the usurper.

The armies met at Emesa, in 261 A.D., where it is said that Callistus betrayed his master to Odainathus. Another account, by Zonaras, speaks of Callistus having been put to death by Odainathus. One thing is clear, that Odainathus was successful in his campaign against the usurper.

By his brilliant victories, Odainathus had become king of the East. The emperor had given him an exceptional position, without a parallel. He was not merely joint ruler, but "independent lieutenant of the emperor for the East."

Odainathus had gained the point at which he aimed. Valerian was a captive in the hands of Sapor, and his son Gallienus was just the kind of weak and frivolous emperor that suited the ambitious designs of the Palmyran.

According to Trebellius Pollio: "While Gallienus was idle, or only doing foolish and ridiculous things, Odainathus crushed Ballista (Callistus), a pretender to the Empire. He then immediately waged war on the Persians to avenge Valerian, which that emperor's son had neglected to do; occupied Nisibis and Carras, and sent the captive satraps to Gallienus to shame him.

"Persia being desolated, and all Mesopotamia being reduced to the Roman power, the conquering troops having marched to Ctesiphon, the king being fled, Odainathus was, with the approbation and applause of the Roman world, declared Augustus by the senate, and received as colleague in the Empire by Gallienus, and the money taken from the Persians was ordered to be coined in their joint names."

There are several Roman accounts of the events of this period, but they are somewhat confused. It is certain, however, that Odainathus cleared the Eastern field of all rival representatives of Western authority. Besides, he harassed the Persians, devastated their country, and plundered their cities, and on two occasions the Palmyra army besieged Ctesiphon, and won a great battle before the walls of the city. But though he pressed Sapor hard, he did not succeed in liberating the captive Valerian. Perhaps, like the worthless Gallienus, he was not anxious to see Valerian at liberty.

Whatever his feelings towards Valerian may have been, Odainathus vindicated the majesty of the Roman arms to the satisfaction of the Roman people. Odainathus had undoubtedly saved the Eastern Roman Empire from being overrun by Persian barbarians, but he saved it for himself; for while Persia was crippled, and the Roman Empire disorganized, he held the balance of power in his own hands.

Gallienus was supposed to be *suzerain*, but Odainathus was practically king. By 264 A.D., he had, in the name of Rome, and by the help of Roman soldiers, attained to supremacy from Armenia to Arabia; and while controlling the legions of Rome, he was able to rely on the fidelity and loyalty of the provinces that owned his sway.

When at the height of his victorious career, Odainathus was murdered in 266 or 267, at Emesa, by his nephew Maconius, whom he had punished for insubordination.

PROJECTING ENTABLATURE, TEMPLE OF THE SUN.

CHAPTER XII.

ODAINATHUS was famous for the brilliancy of his wars, but he was more famous still for the beauty and brilliance of his wife. He was a man of great ambition, courage, and success, but he is now remembered as the husband of Septimia Zenobia.

While Odainathus was engaged in driving the Goths out of Asia Minor, and clearing the eastern Roman provinces of usurpers and barbarian intruders, Zenobia ruled in Palmyra, and carried forward the conquest of Egypt. Odainathus was to some extent associated in the Roman sovereignty with Gallienus, and Zenobia shared in his honours; but she was enthroned a queen in the hearts of her people, and dowered with the charms that inspired to heroism. Aurelian, in a letter to the senate, which we shall quote further on, attributed the victories of Odainathus to the genius of his wife.

Zenobia claimed kinship with Cleopatra, but the claim was advanced on her conquest of Egypt, as if to strengthen her title to the throne of the Ptolemies. There may, however, have been some grounds for Zenobia's pretensions, or she would not have pressed them in the face of Roman historians, and scholars like Longinus, and her perfect command of the Egyptian tongue indicated a close connection with that country. On the other hand, had her claim been well founded, the historians would have eagerly emphasized the fact.

With less probability she was declared to be a Jewess, but her enlightened treatment of the Jews of Alexandria no doubt gave rise to the report. Had she been a Jewess, she would not have failed at Tadmor to claim descent from Solomon, the builder of the city, and she would not have allowed heathen symbols to appear on her coins.

Arab historians and romancers have traced the origin of the great queen of Tadmor, through a long pedigree of Bedawi sheikhs who belonged to the tribe of the Beni-Samayda, and who frequented the borders of Syria.

About the middle of the great colonnade which marks the *via recta* of Palmyra, statues were erected in August 271 A.D., to Odainathus and his widow. They were placed

[Translation. — The Statue of Septimius Odainathus, king of kings, regretted by the entire state. The Septimii, Zabda, General-in-chief, and Zabbai, General of Tadmor, Excellencies, have erected it to their Lord, in the month of Ab, 582 (=August, 271 A.D.).]

DOORWAY OF ZENOBIA'S PALACE.

PALMYRA AND ZENOBIA. 127

on brackets protruding from the columns, and on the fronts of the brackets there were inscriptions in Pal-

𐡣𐡓𐡌𐡉 𐡒𐡀𐡌𐡕𐡐𐡎 𐡉𐡋𐡓𐡉 𐡀𐡐𐡎𐡁𐡋𐡉 𐡉𐡍𐡔𐡋𐡐
𐡀 𐡋𐡐𐡌𐡄 𐡉𐡀 𐡐𐡉𐡀𐡎𐡐𐡁𐡋𐡎𐡀𐡔𐡋𐡓𐡎
𐡀𐡍𐡋𐡆𐡋𐡔𐡎𐡉𐡎𐡕𐡍𐡎𐡉𐡀𐡒𐡌𐡐𐡉𐡎𐡉𐡀𐡎𐡉
// 3333 𐡓𐡉𐡐𐡎 𐡋𐡎𐡉 𐡆𐡀𐡔𐡎𐡑 𐡐𐡉𐡔𐡓𐡕𐡎𐡋 𐡐𐡎𐡎𐡎𐡀

[*Translation.*—The Statue of Septimia, the daughter of Zabbai, the pious and just Queen. The Septimii Zabda, General-in-chief, and Zabbai, General of Tadmor, Excellencies, have erected it to their sovereign, in the month of Ab, the year 582 (=August, 271 A.D.).]

ϹΕΠΤΙΜΙΑΝΖΗΝΟΒΙΑΝΤΗΝΛΛΑΜ
ΠΡΟΤΑΤΗΝΕΥϹΕΒΗΒΑϹΙΛΙϹϹΑΝ
ϹΕΠΤΙΜΙΟΙΖΑΒΔΑϹΟΜΕΓΑϹϹΤΡΑ
ΤΗΛΑΤΗϹΚΑΙΖΑΒΒΑΙΟϹΟΕΝΘΑΔΕ
ϹΤΡΑΤΗΛΑΤΗϹΟΙΚΡΑΤΙϹΤΟΙΤΗΝ
ΔΕϹΠΟΙΝΑΝϹΤΟΥϹΒΠΦΜΗΝΕΙΛΩΩ (sic)

[*Translation.*— Septimia Zenobia, the illustrious and pious queen. The Septimii Zabdas, the great General, and Zabbai, the local General, Excellencies.
. . . their sovereign. The year 582 in the month of August.]

myrene and Greek. One inscription declared that Zabdas, commander-in-chief, and Zabbai, commander of Tadmor, erected the statue in honour of the lamented Odainathus, king of kings, their master. The other proclaimed that the same illustrious generals erected the statue in honour of Septimia Bath-Zabbai (in Greek, Zenobia), the pious and holy queen. The name "Bath-Zabbai" signifies literally the daughter of Zabbai, and she may have been the daughter of the commander-in-chief of Tadmor, who shared in the erection of the statue.

An important item in my Palmyra programme was to find the statue of Zenobia. I set about the work with earnest deliberation, first going up on a ladder to the

PZ-K

bracket on which the statue had been placed, and reading carefully the inscription in Greek and Palmyrene. Then we began to overturn the accumulation of sand at the base of the column where the statue must have fallen. To encourage the workers, I offered a *beshlik* for the discovery of a head. The head of Zenobia for five piasters, equal to one franc! And how the descendants of the proud Tadmorenes delved in the *débris* of the beautiful city for the head of the illustrious queen that once ruled the East, and set at defiance the Romans! The diggers strained every nerve and muscle to secure the reward; in fact, I believe a syndicate was formed on the spot, so that each of the five diggers might receive one piaster dividend, should the prize be secured!

I had mounted the ladder to examine the inscription to the late lamented Odainathus, when I was startled by a tremendous yell that burst from the excavators. The shout of triumph sounded strange among the silent ruins.

"O Khawaja, descend; we have got the head of Sitt Zeinab!" shouted the chief of the party, as he ran to the foot of the ladder, and in his excitement began to ascend the rounds with a large stone in his hands. The shouting brought a crowd of idlers around us, and in a few minutes about one hundred persons were holding an inquest on the head of Zenobia.

The head had been broken off a statue, and was somewhat disfigured. It was, however, the head of a Palmyra lady, with carefully folded turban. There was a broad jewelled band across the forehead horizontally, and other bands extending diagonally from the middle of the forehead downwards toward the ears, with jewels in each as large as beans.

The head was not so grand as we expected, and it was considerably battered, but after enduring the weather

and the buffetings of fortune for 1593 years, it was in a wonderful state of preservation. I was reconciling myself to it with the reflection, that perhaps, like heroes generally, the heads of female statues are less impressive on close inspection, when another yell of triumph, reinforced by a hundred voices, made the ruins of old Palmyra resound again. Nothing like it had been heard since the day that the Tadmor cavalry, with Zenobia in glittering armour at their head, drove Sapor the great across the Euphrates. Had Odainathus or Zenobia been about, they would have heard an echo of other days.

My excavators, seeing that I was pleased with their find, as I was tenderly removing the sand of ages from the folds of the turban, and doubtless thinking that I ought to be encouraged, had delved deeper and brought to the surface the female head of another statue.

There are circumstances under which one may have too much of a good thing. The second discovery rendered the identification of the first with Zenobia doubtful. The new head was purely Grecian in style and decoration. The hair came down low on the forehead, and there were holes in the eyes for jewels.

Turning from the interesting though mutilated heads, found by the column on which the statue of Zenobia once stood, and which may or may not have been intended for the great queen, I think it is almost certain that Bath-Zabbai was a native of Tadmor, and that, like most of the other Palmyrans, she was of Arabian descent, at least on her father's side. It is probable that on her mother's side she may have been Egyptian, and may, very probably, have received her education among her mother's people. It is certain that she was a Palmyra beauty, belonging to the military and governing aristocracy of the republic. Odainathus, a widower, *vir clarissimus consularis*, the favourite of Rome, of Palmyra, and of the desert, chose Zenobia, the fairest flower of the East, to share his fame and fortune and dangers.

The Roman historians have given us scant information as to the origin of this splendid woman, but they have given us pen and ink sketches of her personal appearance, and abundant details regarding her achievements.

Trebellius Pollio tells us: "She lived with royal pomp after the Persian manner, received adulation like the kings of Persia, and banqueted like the Roman emperors.

"She went in state to the assemblies of the people, in a helmet, with a purple band fringed with jewels. Her robe was clasped with a diamond buckle, and she often wore her arm bare.

"Her complexion was a dark brown, her eyes black and sparkling and of uncommon fire. Her countenance was divinely expressive, her person graceful in form and motion beyond imagination, her teeth were white as pearls, and her voice clear and strong. She displayed the severity of a tyrant, when severity was called for; and the clemency of a good prince, when justice required it.

"She was generous with prudence, but a husbandress of wealth more than is the custom with women. Sometimes she used a chariot, but more frequently rode on horseback. She would march immense distances on foot at the head of her infantry, and would drink with her officers, the Armenians and Persians, deeply, but with sobriety, using at her banquets golden goblets, set with jewels, such as Cleopatra was wont to use. In her service she employed eunuchs advanced in years, and very few damsels.

"She ordered her sons to be instructed in the Latin language, as befitting the imperial purple, in which she had arrayed them. She was herself acquainted with the Greek tongue, and was not ignorant of Latin, though from diffidence she spoke it seldom. She spoke Egyptian perfectly, and was so versed in the history of Alexandria and the East, that she made an abridgment of Oriental history."[1]

Cornelius Capitolinus, another Roman historian, declared Zenobia to be the handsomest of all Oriental women.

This supremely beautiful and accomplished lady must have been very young at the time of her marriage, and during the stirring years when she exercised so large an influence on the destinies of the world. Her youth and beauty had a magic charm, not only with the gallant

[1] Trebellius Pollio, Hist. August. p. 199.

spearmen of her race, but for all the Orientals that followed her standard and espoused her cause.

But she had still more solid claims to their allegiance and support. Her knowledge of languages alone showed that she must have been given to studious habits, and from the Latin and Greek literature within her reach, she had probably a wider acquaintance with the world than any of her generals, or than even Odainathus himself. Her perfect command of Egyptian as a living tongue implied an early education in the schools of Alexandria, and gave colour to the claim of kinship with the renowned Cleopatra; and while acquiring a knowledge of the Greek and Roman languages, Zenobia must have learned much of the character and influence of the Greek and Roman peoples. This marvellous woman did not, however, finish her education when she quitted the schools. She continued her study of Greek and Roman writers under the guidance of Longinus, who was as pre-eminent among the philosophers and scholars of his time as Zenobia herself was among the women of her day.

Cassius Longinus was probably born at Emesa in Syria, where he became heir to his uncle Phronto. His parents, being in easy circumstances, took him to travel, and he had an opportunity of visiting the chief places in the then civilized world. He had also the advantage of an education directed by the greatest teachers of his time. He studied at Athens under his uncle Phronto, at Rome under Plotinus and Amelius, and at Alexandria under Ammonius Saccas and Origenes.

Having learned in the best schools, he became a teacher. The famous Porphyry was one of his pupils, and he became the centre of the last brilliant galaxy of pagan scholars.

Longinus united in himself the subtlety of Greek form with Roman fervour. His "Treatise on the Sublime" bears in its luminous beauty that stamp of sense and form which, notwithstanding doubts as to the authorship, proves it to be the work of Longinus, who, on account of his great learning, was called "a living library."

No doubt Zenobia must have heard of the great Longinus during her school days, and it is probable she may have met him at Alexandria; but it is certain he became her instructor and secretary, and practically her prime minister and guide, and that he perished on the overthrow of Palmyra.

We find the following summary of his life in a preface to his writings by Suidas: "Longinus Cassius, philosopher, preceptor of Porphyry the philosopher, a learned scholar and critic, lived in the time of the Emperor Aurelian, and was cut off by him as having conspired with Zenobia, the wife of Odainathus."

Longinus, the chief counsellor of the widowed queen, favoured the policy of independence by throwing off the Roman yoke; and it was his policy, as we shall see, that led to the destruction of Tadmor, the captivity of the queen, and the forfeit of his own life.

Cassius Longinus, as events proved, was not a safe counsellor for the young and proud Zenobia. We do not know how he came to have the name "Cassius." Possibly he inherited it, but more probably he assumed it, through sympathy with the deeds of such men as Caius Cassius and Cassius Chærea. In any case, the associations of the name were distinctly anti-imperial and even regicidal. Besides being a Syrian, he would be ready to throw off the Roman yoke as soon as occasion offered.

On the death of Odainathus, Zenobia had to reconsider her position. I have examined the two inscriptions in Palmyra dedicated to Odainathus. According to the one erected in April 258 A.D., Odainathus was of consular dignity, and on that of August 271 A.D., he was declared king of kings. In the inscription which accompanied the statue of Zenobia of August 271 A.D., she is styled Queen. This title had doubtless been accorded to her by her husband, who was king of kings, and acquiesced in at Rome; but Zenobia, fearing that the rank and titles which she and her children enjoyed, in virtue of her husband's personal services, might be set aside at Rome, resolved to act as queen-regent during the minority of her son.

The state of the Roman Empire was favourable to the ambition of Zenobia, and the schemes of Longinus. Gallienus was a base, bad emperor. He takes rank in vice with Heliogabalus and Nero. His neglect of his duty to his captive father and distracted country had reduced the Empire to confusion and degradation. The Roman legions, when he was emperor, were driven back in all the remote provinces. The Roman seas were full of pirates.

An opportunity was soon given to Zenobia, if we are to accept the statement of Trebellius Pollio, to assert her queenship. On hearing of the murder of Odainathus, Gallienus despatched an army against the Persians under Heraclianus. Zenobia, resenting the encroachment, espoused the Persian cause, and at the head of a Palmyra army marched to meet the Romans. A battle was fought on the confines of Persia, which ended in the rout and destruction of the Roman army. Soon afterwards, Gallienus was murdered at Milan, leaving Syria and Mesopotamia in the hands of Zenobia.

Claudius came to the throne, and as he was fully occupied with enemies in Europe, he recognized the authority of Zenobia, and devoted himself to strengthening the Empire by reforms at home.

At that time, Probatus, a pretender, appeared in Egypt. Zenobia despatched Zabdas, the commander-in-chief, against him, with an army of seventy thousand Palmyrans, Syrians, and Bedawîn. He encountered Probatus at the head of an army of fifty thousand Egyptians, and gained a complete victory.

Zenobia had undertaken the Egyptian campaign in the cause of Rome, and had fought and conquered in the name of Rome, but she held the country in her own name, and as a part of the kingdom of Palmyra.

Aurelian, on coming to the throne, recognized the Palmyra conquest of Egypt. The statements of Roman historians regarding this period are contradictory and perplexing, but I have a coin, struck in Alexandria, with the figure of Zenobia's eldest son and the title *Imperator* on one side, and the figure of Aurelian and the title of *Augustus* on the other.

Aurelian was a soldier of fortune, who had risen from the lowest rank. He was called to be Emperor by the army, and during the two first years of his reign he subdued the Goths, Germans, and Vandals. At the same time, Zenobia was adding the province of Asia Minor to her dominions.

In 271 A.D., Aurelian had so reduced matters to a satisfactory condition in Europe, that he was able to turn his attention to Zenobia. A Palmyra garrison had been left in Egypt. Probus, who had been waging war against the Mediterranean pirates, was ordered to drive the Orientals out of Egypt. He was victorious, but Zabdas, being guided by Timagenes, attacked the Romans who had attempted to cut off his retreat, and defeated them.

The time had now arrived for a decisive struggle between the East and the West, between Aurelian and his veteran legions and Zenobia and her chivalrous Orientals. The contrast between the foes and their followers was very great. Aurelian had risen to power by courage, strength, and attention to discipline. He lacked culture, refinement, and education; but he had built up a Roman army which had become an irresistible engine of war. With this engine he hoped to crush Zenobia.

At the approach of the danger, the refined and cultured Zenobia paused in her literary and artistic pursuits, and called together the sons of the desert, who had planted her standard on the banks of the Nile and established her authority on the plains of the Seleucidæ. Swift dromedaries sped forth from Palmyra, in all directions, to warn the Bedawîn of the approaching foe. The Roman name had no terror for the freemen of the desert. In several encounters they had annihilated the famous legions; and even the Parthians had destroyed a Roman army, and held in slavery a Roman emperor. Zenobia's summons warned them of a common danger, and roused them to repel the common foe.

The prosperity of Palmyra meant the prosperity of the Bedawîn. The city in the desert was at that time the meeting-place between Europe and Asia, the market-place where the East and West exchanged their wares, and the tribes were the common carriers both east and west. What the Phœnicians were by sea, that were the Bedawîn by land; and during the ascendency of Zenobia, the Bedawîn were not only the carriers of the commonwealth, but the body-guard of the dynasty.

Zenobia's call to arms was splendidly responded to, and in a few days the sandy plains of Tadmor swarmed with warriors, ready not only to protect their beautiful and heroic queen, but also to guard intact the lines of their commerce. They came together with light hearts, eager to be led against the western barbarian.

COIN OF ZENOBIA.
(*Enlarged.*)

CHAPTER XIII.

THERE was one, at least, in Palmyra who was fully alive to the gravity of the impending danger. Zenobia did not despise her enemy, but with a prudence equal to her courage she began at once to reduce to order the innumerable swarms of motley warriors that covered the plains of Tadmor.

Three vast military camps were formed. Traditions live very long among the Bedawîn, who hand down to their sons, and their sons' sons, precise details of the deeds in which they had a share. A young sheikh pointed out to me the exact spot on which each camp was formed, and his information agreed with what I had gleaned elsewhere.

One camp, composed of the levies from south-eastern tribes, was formed, due south of the warm fountain, on the plain beyond the acropolis. Another, drawn from the Bedawîn of the south-west, between Palmyra and Damascus, was formed on the plain, opposite the Abu el-Fawaris springs. The third camp, which was intended for the northern and north-western tribes, was formed on the direct road to Emesa, beyond the Palmyra quarries, at a place called Marbat 'Antar, where, in a cleft in the mountain, there is a fine spring of water. The word *marbat*, the "tying-place," that is, the place where camels were tied, or the "camping-ground," may have taken its name from Zenobia's camp. Tradition links it with the name of 'Antar, whose horse was said to have cleared the chasm, two thousand cubits wide.

In this crisis Zenobia was more than a general. She visited each of the camps daily, surrounded by a brilliant staff of officers, and with helmet on head, and arms bare, drilled and reviewed and harangued her troops. Zenobia shared fully in the privations and fatigues of her men; and while the charms of her sympathy and beauty bound them to her by undying loyalty, her martial bearing and knowledge of war kindled their military ardour and enthusiastic confidence.

During the period that Aurelian was completing the conquest of the Goths, Zenobia continued the drilling of her soldiers; and as each division attained proficiency, she sent it forward to the Orontes valley, where forage was more plentiful.

Having subjugated the Goths, Aurelian crossed the Bosphorus at Byzantium. His progress through Asia Minor was much more rapid than Zenobia had anticipated. Her friends in Asia Minor who did not join the Roman army fell back before it. Ancyra opened its gates to

Aurelian, but at Tyana, on the river Sarus, a stubborn resistance was offered to his advance. The city, however, was opened to the enemy by a traitor named Heraclamium.

The Palmyra army marched to meet the Romans by three routes. The camels and cavalry proceeded by the Aleppo route as far as Hamam, and then turned in a more westerly direction and marched on Antioch. Another division, composed chiefly of mounted warriors, marched in a still more westerly direction straight to Hamah, past the wells of Marbat, Jaral, Barri, and Salimîyeh. The third and great division, composed chiefly of archers and sword and clubmen, marched by the Damascus route as far as Karyetein, and then turned off and marched to Emesa.

The Aleppo route was the more dreary, but there was sufficient water at long intervals for camels and horses. The route to Hamah, through groves of terebinth, was somewhat better supplied with water; and the route by Karyetein was the best supplied of all.

A short distance from Palmyra the third division passed the night at the abundant waters of Abu el-Fawaris. An early start and nine hours' brisk marching brought them to a reservoir at Kasr el-Hiyar, full of water drawn from the 'Ain el-Wu'ul fountain, which was secluded in the mountains about six miles to the south-east. Here the division spent the night, and, by an early start and ten or eleven hours' march, reached the great fountain of Karyetein. After leaving Karyetein, the division passed the fountains of Hawarîn, Muhîn, and Sudud.

I have examined these fountains, which are now neglected, but which, under the prudent care of Zenobia, rendered the passage of her armies a comparatively easy matter. Three years previously, as we have seen, Zenobia had despatched Zabdas to Egypt at the head of an army numbering, according to Zosimus, seventy thousand soldiers.[1] That campaign was undertaken nominally to punish a pretender against Roman authority; it was a mere matter of invasion. In the war on which Zenobia and her people were now embarked, kingdom and crown, honour and fame, life and liberty, were at stake.

It may, I think, be safely assumed, that in the great crisis of the kingdom, Zenobia had four or five times as large an army as that which sufficed for the Egyptian campaign. Tradition fixes the number at one million of all arms, but I think we should not be far wrong in supposing that from a quarter to half a million of subjects followed the standard of the beauteous and heroic queen.

From all parts this countless host of wild warriors concentrated on Antioch. As Aurelian and his legions climbed the Beilan pass, Zenobia, accompanied by her prime minister, Cassius Longinus, and her commander-in-chief, Zabdas, led her forces out from the neighbourhood of Antioch. So certain was she of being able to cope with the Romans, on a fair field, with no favour, that she did not attempt to block their way in the steep and narrow mountain defiles. Shortly after Aurelian emerged

[1] Zosimus, lib. i. p. 58.

THE GRAND COLONNADE.

on the plain, the struggle for mastery between the East and West began.

According to Eusebius, the great battle was fought in 273 A.D., but it is almost certain that it took place in the early days of 272. Zenobia, no longer acting as queen-regent, but as Queen and Empress of the East, rode forth equipped as a warrior to beat back the great army of the Roman Empire. The plain was filled with her serried ranks. Her heavy cavalry, clothed in complete armour of steel, led the van, the light archers followed, and the infantry of all arms brought up the rear.

Innumerable spearmen on fleet dromedaries were massed on the flanks of the Palmyra host, or tried to get on the flanks of the Roman army, with intent to cut their communications and turn their position.

The battle was joined at a spot which Ptolemy calls "Immae," where he says Zenobia in person directed her troops to battle.[1]

Zenobia, armed like Diana, but beautiful as Venus, mounted on a splendid charger, rode down the front rank of her mighty army and gave the order to charge. The cavalry advanced with irresistible fury, and bore down everything before them. But Aurelian had placed his infantry out of reach of the cavalry, and held them in reserve, till the Orientals had exhausted themselves by

[1] Mr. Skene, late British Consul at Aleppo, identifies the scene of the battle. He says: "One of the small plains surrounded by rocks was that of Immae, where Zenobia took her stand against Aurelian, and was defeated. It is now called Haeka, or the Ring." — *Rambles in the Deserts of Syria*, p. 138. London, 1864.

chasing a light and flying foe. Zosimus, the Roman historian, gives the following account of Aurelian's strategy : —

"Finding Zenobia with a great army ready prepared for battle, he met and engaged her. But seeing that the Palmyra cavalry confided very much in their armour, which was heavy, strong, and secure, being also very much better horsemen than his soldiers, he placed his infantry somewhere beyond the river Orontes in a place by themselves, and commanded the cavalry not immediately to engage the victorious Palmyra cavalry, but to allow themselves to be attacked, and pretend to fly, and continue to do so, till the Palmyrans and their horses should be thoroughly tired, through the excessive heat and weight of their armour." Aurelian's ruse succeeded.

The heavy Palmyra cavalry under the eye of their queen, chased the light Roman horse all over the plain, and, believing that the Romans were beaten and fleeing, as was their wont in the time of Gallienus, they followed them with exhausting energy, until they got separated from the main body of the army.

At this juncture Aurelian brought his infantry across the Orontes, and marched them into the space between the Palmyran cavalry and infantry.

"As soon as the Roman cavalry saw that their enemies were tired by their great exertions, and that their horses were scarcely able to stand under them, they stopped in their feigned flight, turned on their pursuers, and trampled them under their feet. By which means the slaughter of the Palmyra cavalry was promiscuous, some being killed by the sword, and others crushed to death by the Roman horses."

Though Zenobia issued her commands through her general Zabdas, she was seen by all her troops, galloping over the plain, with a glittering helmet on her head, and with arms bare, encouraging the hesitating, cheering on the wavering, and calling the broken and dispirited to make a stand against the advancing Romans. But the day was irretrievably lost, by the impetuous valour of the heavy cavalry. It was the Balaclava charge on a large scale, with no red line to fall back upon. Seeing that resistance was no longer possible, Zenobia collected the remnants of her shattered army, and retreated on Antioch.

At Antioch the Palmyrans had recourse to a curious device. According to Zosimus, "Zabdas, Zenobia's general, with the defeated Palmyrans, retreated into Antioch; but fearing a revolt of the people if news of the defeat should get abroad, he picked out a person somewhat hoary, much like the emperor, and clothing him in a garb such as Aurelian wore, led him through the whole city as if he had taken Aurelian captive. With this contrivance he deceived the people of Antioch, and stealing out of the city by night, marched with Zenobia and the remainder of the army towards Emesa."

A stand, however, was made by the Palmyrans at a strategic position near Daphne. Aurelian entered Antioch unopposed, and after reducing the city to order, followed the fugitives. He found them well posted on a hill. "He commanded his soldiers to march up to the enemy with their bucklers so near to one another, and in such close order, as to keep off darts and stones. As soon as the Romans had ascended the hill, they found themselves on equal terms with their foes, whom they put to flight. Some were dashed to pieces over precipices, and others were slain in their retreat. The Romans were again victorious, and marched forward, delighted with the emperor's success.

"Apamea, Larissa, and Arethusa opened their gates to him."

At Emesa, Zenobia had time to re-form the fragments of her broken forces while Aurelian was establishing law and order in the cities through which he passed. Both armies found abundant provisions along the fertile banks of the Orontes. Fresh new levies joined Zenobia, and preparations were made for a stubborn resistance at the native city of Cassius Longinus, whose anti-imperial feeling may have had much to do in bringing on the terrible war.

The plain to the north of Hums was splendidly adapted for a great Oriental battle-field. I once passed over it with Subhi Pasha, and an escort composed of several thousand irregular cavalry, village sheikhs, and princelings. All day long the horsemen galloped over the plain, engaging in feats of horsemanship and sham battles, their bright colours and picturesque garments lending special interest to the scene. With the field, that had once resounded with the yells of Romans and Palmyrans, before me, swarming with Orientals engaged in mimic warfare, I was able to form a vivid conception of the great struggle between Zenobia and Aurelian.

The emperor marched out of Restân, the ancient Arethusa, and the queen with her army moved out of Hums to meet him.

They met on the right bank of the Orontes, five or six miles north of Hums. The Palmyrans had the advantage of sun, and slope of plain, but otherwise there was no key of the position to be contended for, or that could give either side an advantage over the other.

According to her custom, Zenobia in armour marched at the head of her army.

Zosimus describes the battle that ensued: —

"Aurelian, seeing the Palmyra army drawn up before Emesa in a body, opposed them with the Dalmatian cavalry, the Mysians and Paonians, besides those of Noricum and Rhœtium, which are Celtic legions. Nay more, there were the best of all the imperial regiments picked out and chosen man by man, the Morisco horse, and the Tyanians, the Mesopotamians, the Syrians, the Phœnicians, and the Palestinians, out of Asia. All were men of courage, and the Palestinians, besides their other arms, had clubs and quarter-staves."

The battle was fierce, long, and desperate. The Palmyra cavalry had to avenge the overthrow of their companions at Antioch, and they almost annihilated the Roman cavalry. The battle, however, was finally decided by the staying power of the Roman veterans, who had borne the eagles to victory in Britain and among the fierce Alemanni and ferocious Goths. The Palestinian infantry seem to have exercised a determining influence on the issue of the struggle.

To this day the people of Palestine carry a club, which they call *ed-dabbous*—the pin. It has a large bulbous head set with spikes, and in strong hands it is a most formidable weapon. Such a weapon would not fail to bring to the ground either man or horse.

Zosimus thus describes the result of the battle: "The Palmyra cavalry were much too strong for the Roman horse, most of whom were slain; but the work of the day lay chiefly with the infantry. The Palmyrans were amazed to see the Palestinians fight so strangely with their clubs, and were not a little disconcerted by it. After a fierce encounter, Zenobia's hosts were put to flight, and they trod one upon another, insomuch that the field was covered with dead men and horses."

Translation of Palmyrene Inscription—NASHOUM, SON OF MALKOU.

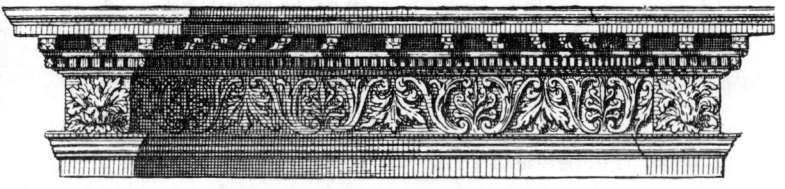

ENTABLATURE, TEMPLE OF THE SUN.

CHAPTER XIV.

ZENOBIA, with the fragments of her beaten army, retreated to her desert home. On their march, the Palmyrans destroyed all the wells, that they might not be available for the pursuing Romans.

Aurelian rested at Hums to prepare for the terrible ordeal of crossing the desert, and the siege of Palmyra. The delay gave the Palmyrans time to rally, and to prepare for defence, and when the emperor reached Palmyra, the city was in readiness for a protracted siege.

Aurelian quartered his soldiers on the three great camping grounds by the waters, where Zenobia had drilled her troops a short time before. The fierce and dogged West, the brilliant and chivalrous East, had reached their last ditch. How a great army within the walls of Palmyra, and a greater outside the city, were sustained in the midst of a howling wilderness, while they fought out their deadly feud to the bitter end, must ever remain a mystery.

I have, I think, solved the water question, as far as the host outside the city is concerned; and there are still the remains of water tanks attached to houses in the city, which may have rendered the besieged, for a time at least, independent of the outside fountains. Besides, I think it extremely probable that the tepid fountain Ephca may have been within the limits of defence. But the carrying of provisions across the desert for the Roman army alone was a task beyond the capacity of any commissariat of our time.

Aurelian's march across the desert with a great army, in the face of superior cavalry, was a notable achievement. Mommsen says: " The march was more difficult than the conflict. The distance from Emesa to Palmyra amounts in a direct line to seventy miles, and although at that epoch of highly developed civilization the region was not waste in the same degree as at present, the march of Aurelian still remains a considerable feat, especially as the light horsemen of the enemy swarmed round the Roman army on all sides."[1]

The march, however, of a strong, compact army, flushed with victory, and superior, as a whole, to anything the Palmyrans could bring against it, was a simple matter, compared to the work of keeping communications open, and the victualling of the besiegers by means of long trains of baggage animals through a dreary waste in the hands of the desert cavalry.

[1] The Provinces of the Roman Empire, Vol. II. 110.

It is more than probable that the country from which the Palmyrans had been beaten back had definitely taken side with the victorious Aurelian, whom they recognized as the legitimate Augustus.

Among the nationalities who fought under the eagles at Hums, there were divisions from Mesopotamia, Syria, Phœnicia, and Palestine. These were doubtless Palmyra legions who had joined the emperor on his victorious march through Asia Minor. The defection of these troops, and the march of events, would have a determining influence on the different districts.

Besides, Aurelian, recognizing that the different towns and peoples had submitted to Palmyran authority with the sanction of Rome, treated them with generous gentleness, and his final triumph was as much due to wise statesmanship as to skilful generalship. It is, I think, therefore, almost certain that the Roman communications, as well as their base of supplies, were to a large extent under friendly control. And even with the Bedawîn, Roman gold exercised a moderating influence.

We have no reason to doubt the statement of the historian: "Aurelian besieged the city quite round, and engaged the neighbouring nations to supply his army with provisions."

Poor Zenobia was now shut up in her beleaguered desert home, with her own beloved Palmyrans.

After the battle of Hums, the emperor, pointing to her losses in the Orontes battle, called on her to submit; but she replied that only her Roman troops were slain, and that she had still her own Orientals, who did not acknowledge defeat, to fall back upon.

She had fled to Palmyra in such haste, that she was unable to carry away from Hums her vast treasures of gold, gems, and silk, and these fell into the hands of her enemy.

The provinces which formed her kingdom had been wrested from her. In the year 270 A.D., her troops, after a desperate struggle, had been driven out of Egypt. Aurelian, in his victorious campaign, had wrested from her Asia Minor and Syria. The Parthians, whose assistance she expected on the Orontes, had failed her. The aged Sapor, doubtless recognizing that a Roman emperor of the genuine kind had arisen, and that the period of Gallienus had passed, prudently left his old foe Zenobia to her fate.

What, however, rendered the cause of Zenobia hopeless, was the fact that the Romans who had not abandoned her cause were slain. The triumphs of Zenobia, and of her husband Odainathus, were triumphs of the Roman arms. Her conquests were made in the name of Rome, and the steady Roman legions carried her to victory. But the power of Rome had revived, and the Oriental was a feeble reed in the face of the imperial storm.

In these circumstances, perhaps better understood by Zenobia than by any of her generals, the defence of Palmyra was undertaken.

Her archers manned the battlements, her engines hurled

great stones on the attacking Romans, her guards were massed at convenient places so as to be ready to move quickly to threatened positions. Zenobia rode from point to point, surrounded by her generals, and by her restless activity, as well as by her addresses to the soldiers, encouraged the defenders.

A very large area had to be protected. As we stand on the summit of the castle, we can easily trace the ancient wall, which I have already described as beginning outside the Ephca fountain, and running westward along the highest ridge of the hill, to the Damascus road, where there were strong forts; then turning in a northerly direction, and passing along the highest ridge of the mountain west of the city, and including the present castle, which probably stands on the foundation of an older structure, and having cleared the city by a circuit of a dozen miles, it turned in an easterly direction and passed around, completing the enclosure.

From the castle hill Zenobia could look down on the entire wall, and on every position of friend and foe, with the exception of the Roman camp at the Abu el-Fawaris water.

The siege was pressed with all the force at Aurelian's command, and resisted with chivalrous courage by the Palmyrans. Without her gold, and without her allies, Zenobia was hard pressed.

The sands of Palmyra are full of little copper coins. After strong winds the people of Palmyra gather them in handfuls. I bought hundreds of them for a few piasters.

They are generally adorned with radiated heads, gazelles, fishes, zodiacal signs, and such like emblems. They are probably specimens of the currency with which Zenobia resisted the siege.

The siege was fruitful of stirring incidents. Zosimus tells of the emperor approaching the walls, and being jeered at by the defenders, and of a Persian shooting with an arrow a Palmyran who had mocked the emperor to his face for not taking the city.

A letter from Aurelian to the senate shows the light in which he regarded Zenobia's defence:—

"The Romans tell me that I am waging war against a woman, as if Zenobia was contending against me with her own strength alone, and not with that of a host of enemies. I cannot tell you how many arrows and engines of war there are, how many weapons, how many stones: there is no part of the wall which is not furnished with two or three balistas; tormenting fire is poured from them. What more? Do you say she fears? She fights as if she feared punishment. But I trust that the gods, who have never been wanting to our exertions, will defend the Roman state." [1]

Aurelian had hoped to have taken Palmyra by storm on reaching it, but owing to the defences, and gallant resistance, the spring of 272 A.D. was passing away, and the city still held out. Again he summoned Zenobia to surrender. The emperor's letter and the queen's reply are both preserved. And remembering the acute

[1] Hist. August. p. 218.

crisis in which they were composed, I give them *in extenso:* —

"Aurelian, Emperor of the Roman world, Receptor Orientis, to Zenobia and the others united together in hostile alliance.

"You ought to do that of your own accord which is commanded by my letters. I charge you to surrender on your lives being spared. And you, O Zenobia, may pass your life in some spot where I shall place you in pursuance of the distinguished sentence of the Senate; your gems, your silver, gold, silk, horses, camels, being given up to the Roman treasury.

"The laws and institutions of the Palmyrans shall be respected."

Zenobia replied as follows: —

" Zenobia, Queen of the East, to Aurelian Augustus.

"No one, as yet, except thee, has dared to ask what thou demandest. Whatever is to be achieved by war must be sought by valour. Thou askest me to surrender, as if thou wert ignorant that Queen Cleopatra chose rather to perish than to survive her dignity. The Persian auxiliaries whom we await cannot be far off; the Saracens are on our side, as well as the Armenians. The Syrian robbers, O Aurelian, have conquered your army: what then if that band which we expect on all sides shall come?

" You will then lay aside the superciliousness with which you now demand my surrender, as if you were victor on every side."

These precious documents have been preserved by Flavius Vopiscus.[1]

Nicomachus declared that Zenobia dictated her letter in the Syrian tongue, and that he translated it into Greek, but Zenobia herself is said to have confessed to Aurelian that Longinus had dictated the letter.

On receipt of Zenobia's letter the efforts of the besiegers were redoubled. From the castle mountain the queen watched the eastern horizon with straining eyes, to catch a glimpse of the Persian succour which she expected. Towards the west she saw, among the billowy hills that stretched away to snow-clad Lebanon, only long strings of camels bearing supplies to her foes. Aurelian had intercepted the Persians, and bought over the Armenians and Saracens.

[1] Hist. August. p. 218.

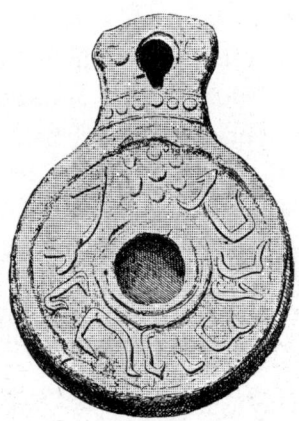

ROMAN LAMP, WITH SEVEN BALLS REPRESENTING THE SEVEN PLANETS.
Translation of Palmyrene Inscription—AGLIBOL AND MALAKBEL.

FRIEZE IN TEMPLE OF THE SUN.

CHAPTER XV.

IN these straits Zenobia resolved that she would go to Persia, and return with a relieving army. She visited the entire defences of the city, and charged the defenders to hold out to the last. Then she held a council of war with her ministers and generals, and sallying forth on a dark night, with a few companions, the heroic young Queen passed the Roman lines, and made a desperate rush for freedom.

She was mounted on a she-camel known for its wonderful swiftness. The point of the Euphrates at which she wished to cross was distant five days' journey. Fear, as well as the eager desire to bring succour to the beloved Palmyra, lent wings to the fugitives. With a few short snatches of sleep on the bare sand, she pressed forward night and day.

At last the green streak of the Euphrates appeared in the distance. The dromedary increased its speed to reach the water. Already Zenobia felt safe; but during the last half hour of the journey a little cloud of dust had been following her track, and seemed to be gaining upon her. After a time it became apparent that the cloud of dust was raised by a band of pursuing Romans. Many a time the desert has resounded to the yells of the pursuer and pursued, but never since or before in a crisis when so much depended on the result of the race. Swiftly and silently Zenobia's camel approached the great river. Zenobia slipped from her camel to the ground, and ran panting like a gazelle to a boat which was preparing to take her to the other side. She sprang into the boat. She is safe, and there is still hope for Palmyra! But a slight delay occurred in the starting of the boat, whether by entanglement, or treachery, will never now be known. The delay was sufficient to turn the balance in favour of the West and to alter the destiny of the East. With foaming horses the Romans came thundering to the bank of the river, and seized the heroic Queen just as the boat was putting off.[1]

The weary and baffled Zenobia was hurried back to Palmyra by her captors, and ushered into the presence of her conqueror. It was a bitter moment for the proud, fallen Queen. Addressing his captive, Aurelian sternly demanded, "How, O Zenobia, hast thou dared to insult Roman emperors?"

She replied, "Thee I acknowledge to be emperor, since

[1] Deyr, on the Euphrates, is believed to be the crossing at which Zenobia was captured.

thou hast conquered. I have not considered as chiefs [*'principes'*] Gallienus, Aureolus, and the rest."[1]

Palmyra fell with the queen under whom it had reached its highest renown. As soon as it was known in the city that she was a captive in the Roman camp, the Palmyrans sought the clemency of the conqueror. They thronged out of the city with presents and sacrifices, and the emperor, according to his enlightened policy, treated the people with generous kindness.

Very different treatment was reserved for Zenobia and her advisers. Leaving a small Roman garrison at Palmyra, the emperor returned to Emesa, leading with him the functionaries and officers whom he had marked for punishment. Vopiscus has left it on record that the soldiers clamoured for the queen's death, but Aurelian reserved her for his Roman triumph.

It is said that, owing to harsh treatment and intimidation, Zenobia, crushed by the magnitude of her misfortunes, admitted in a moment of weakness that Longinus had dictated the defiant letter which had so enraged the emperor.

Mommsen sums up the testimony of the Roman historian thus: —

"Zenobia, after she had for years borne rule with masculine energy, did not now disdain to invoke a woman's privileges and to throw the responsibility on her advisers, of whom, not a few, including the celebrated scholar,

[1] Trebellius Pollio in Hist. August.

Cassius Longinus, perished under the axe of the executioner."[1]

I have a strong conviction that this verdict of the historian is too sweeping. The brilliant Longinus was put to death at Emesa, his own city; but Aurelian, in such matters, did not found his decisions on the confessions of a crushed and helpless woman. The emperor, in his acts, was guided by state reasons. The name "Cassius," as we have already pointed out, was associated with anti-imperial and even regicidal ideas, and I think these were reasons of sufficient weight with Aurelian for ridding the Roman world of "Cassius" Longinus, without placing the blame at the door of Zenobia.

Longinus took a leading part in the war against the imperial authority, and the cause which he espoused having failed, he paid the penalty with his life. It was sad that the author of the great work on "The Sublime" should have perished so miserably, but Roman law had no exception in favour of philosophers who dabbled in treason.

Aurelian hurried home with Zenobia, and the spoils of war, to enjoy his triumph; but he had scarcely reached Europe, when a message from Palmyra caused him to retrace his steps. Possibly, in revenge for the slaughter of Palmyran chiefs, the people had revolted against Roman authority, and slaughtered the garrison.

Aurelian, in an incredibly short space of time, reached Palmyra. He entered the city without opposition, and

[1] The Provinces of the Roman Empire, Vol. II. 110.

fell upon the citizens without mercy. The palaces and temples were sacked and despoiled, and the place became, as the word Tadmor signifies, a ruin.

Nothing can so well describe the general havoc as a letter from Aurelian himself to Ceionius Bassus: —

"You must now sheathe the sword. The Palmyrans have been sufficiently slaughtered and cut to pieces. We have not spared women; we have slain children. We have strangled old men; we have destroyed the husbandmen. To whom, then, shall we leave the land? To whom shall we leave the city? We must spare those that remain, for we think that the few who are now existing will take warning from the punishment of the many who have been destroyed.

"The Temple of the Sun at Palmyra, which the eagle-bearer of the third legion, with the standard and ensign bearers, and the trumpeters, and clarion-blowers, have despoiled, I wish restored to its former state. You have three hundred pounds of gold from the casket of Zenobia. You have eighteen hundred pounds of silver of the effects of the Palmyrans. You have the royal gems. From all these make a creditable temple, and you will do a very agreeable thing to me and to the immortal gods. I will write to the senate requesting them to send a high priest to consecrate the temple."[1]

Aurelian once more turned his back on Palmyra, and set out in haste for Rome. The Syrian cities had experienced his clemency, but they learned from the fate of

[1] Flavius Vopiscus in Hist. August. p. 218.

Tadmor that he could be ruthless, and the Orientals did not need a second lesson. Palmyra having been destroyed, the Empire in the East was at peace.

Aurelian led in his train a number of Palmyra notables to grace his triumph; but in crossing the strait between Byzantium and Chalcedon all the captives were drowned, except Zenobia and her two sons.

The triumph of the conqueror on his return to Rome was the grandest ever enjoyed by a Roman emperor. Flavius Vopiscus has left us full details of the barbaric pageant.

Aurelian rode in a magnificent chariot, which he had taken from the king of the Goths; and the chariot was drawn by four stags, which the emperor, on his arrival at the capitol, sacrificed to Jupiter Capitolinus. Twenty elephants, two hundred wild animals, including tigers and elks, and eight hundred gladiators, marched before him, accompanied by the treasures of Zenobia and the spoils of Palmyra. There were also captives from the different peoples whom he had conquered, and ten Gothic women in complete armour. The carriage of Odainathus, overlaid with gold and silver and studded with precious gems, was there, and a splendid carriage, the gift of the king of Persia. But the object which gave to the procession its crowning interest was the captive Queen Zenobia. Every window, balcony, and roof was crowded by the maids and matrons of Rome, to catch a glimpse of the Oriental woman who had contended with Rome for supremacy.

Zenobia, in the days of her pride and power, had caused

COLONNADE OF THE TEMPLE OF THE SUN.

a splendid chariot to be built, and it was said that she had declared she would enter Rome, a conqueror, in that chariot. The Roman crowd saw the graceful and beauteous lady tottering through the streets on foot, in front of her own chariot, not in it, her hands bound with golden chains and a golden chain round her neck. Golden rings were round her ankles, and slaves supported her, as, laden with jewelry, she staggered wearily forward in front of her conqueror. Behind him the senate and the victorious army completed the show.

On that day Rome enjoyed her grandest triumphal procession and reached her deepest degradation. In all the annals of perverted patriotism and abused power there is no more brutal spectacle than the triumph of great and imperial Rome over that humbled and helpless Queen.

It is pleasant to reflect that Aurelian's swaggering triumph did not pass without protest, and that the conqueror's justification of himself is an abiding testimony to the greatness of the illustrious woman whom he had crushed, and sought to degrade.

In a letter to the senate he writes:—

"I hear, O conscript fathers, that it has been urged against me that I have not accomplished a manly[1] task, in triumphing over Zenobia.

"My accusers would not know how to praise me enough, if they knew that woman,—if they knew her

[1] "Quod non virile munus impleverim Zenobiam triumphando."— Trebellius Pollio, Hist. August. pp. 198, 199.

prudence in council, her firmness in purpose, the dignity she preserves towards her army, her munificence when necessity requires it, her severity when to be severe is just. I may say that the victory of Odainathus over the Persians, and his putting Sapor to flight and reaching Ctesiphon, were due to her. I can assert that such was the dread entertained of this woman, among the natives of the East and of Egypt, that she kept in check the Arabians, the Saracens, and the Armenians."

We have no certain knowledge of Zenobia's career after the triumphal procession. There are two traditions regarding her. One, which is the more generally accepted, represents her as married to a Roman noble, and living on an estate given her by the emperor, at Conche on the Tiber, where, as the mother of a numerous progeny, she lived and died a much-respected Roman matron. This tradition seems to rest on the fact that some of her descendants, a century afterwards, were men of senatorial rank and of high standing at Rome. But it must be remembered that Zenobia's two sons accompanied her to Rome, and the descendants referred to may have been their offspring.

The other, and I believe more probable, account, is given by the Roman historian Zosimus, who declares that, mourning over the utter destruction of Palmyra and her ruined fortunes, Zenobia refused all food, languished, and died.

As we have already seen, many circumstances, personal, political, and local, contributed to the sudden rise and brief glory of Palmyra, but the desert city had in itself no certain element of abiding stability. To the Roman connection it owed its wealth and splendour. The hand that made it for its uses extinguished it in a blaze of glory that lighted up a dark period, when it had ceased to be useful.

Other highways to the East, through Aleppo on the north and Bosra on the south, became safe for commerce under Roman sway, and the meteor-like glory of Tadmor became a thing of the past. The Roman hand, however, was not all at once withdrawn from the fallen city, and in accordance with the letter of Aurelian which we have quoted, the temple was patched up, but it fell far short of its former magnificence. Under the reign of Diocletian, the walls of the city were rebuilt round a smaller area; but Palmyra's queen was degraded, its princes slain, its culture and public spirit strangled, and natural laws were at work which carried the golden tide of commerce past its gates.

A Roman governor and garrison occupied the restored city, but they could not save it from decay, when its merchants were slain and its industry blighted, and it sank by degrees, so that when Justinian repaired it about the year 400, it had been for some time almost quite deserted. The Justinian walls are more circumscribed still than those of Diocletian, and it is by the area enclosed by the Justinian walls that modern travellers estimate its greatness.

At a later period it seems to have been a border town of

some importance, as it became the seat of a bishop, in the province of which Damascus was the metropolis.

After passing through many vicissitudes, Tadmor fell under the withering blight of Islam, and then its fate was sealed.

The finest structures were pulled down to erect Saracenic fortifications, and amid the ruined splendours of the Temple of the Sun the entire population now herd in clay huts.

SCROLL AND CAPITAL OF PILASTER, TEMPLE OF THE SUN.

FRIEZE, GREAT DOOR OF TEMPLE COURT.

CHAPTER XVI.

ON the forenoon of our last day at Palmyra, we were sitting on the brackets of the columns in the portico of the little temple, husbanding our strength for the return journey, and watching the wonderful play of light and shadow, of roseate hues, and golden tints, which overspread the ruins, and gave them their greatest charm,[1] when suddenly we heard the shrill war-song of the Bedawîn. In a few minutes we saw a straggling band of spearmen gallop through the pass, and down to the warm fountain. They disappeared from our view, and their war-song ceased; but as we had learnt coming along that the Bedawîn were in a particularly Ishmaelitish mood, we called on our servants to hand us up our breech-loaders and cartridges. We knew that the only law in

[1] Tourists generally speak of "the marble ruins of Palmyra white as snow." There is no marble in Palmyra, and the ruins are not white. The stone used is a close-grained limestone (except four granite monoliths) of a yellowish colour, streaked and flushed with pink. The ruins and whole landscape have a yellow, golden hue which is very striking.

force, or acknowledged, in the desert, was that of the strongest, and we resolved, in case of absolute necessity, to fall in with the law. I was just then busily engaged in fixing the position of the tomb-towers, and as I had an intelligent sheikh telling me their names, I took little notice of the Bedawîn, who were coming up slily at a canter, as if they meant to pass us; but just when they came within charging distance, the leader turned his horse and spear towards us, and went right at us.

My companion's coolness was inimitable. With his back against the column, and his legs dangling from the pedestal on which he sat, he smoked his cigar, and manipulated his cartridges as methodically as he plied his instruments when stuffing a bird, and with certainly more composure than he used to exhibit when under fire in the House of Commons.

He afterwards told me the secret of his composure. He felt safe from our own wild party, who could not shoot him from behind, through the column, and he was confident that we could empty the saddles as fast as they came up. We determined that we would not let the ruffians, who stripped women and stole donkeys, strip and plunder us with impunity.

For a moment, it seemed that we were in for a brush with real Bedawîn. Most of our guard were absent, and Brandy Bob, instead of calling his men to arms, got hold of a soldier's rifle, quietly lay down behind a prostrate column, and covered his man. Our soldier of the blind horse, with more prudence than his captain, got into the

GRANITE MONOLITHS.

temple, and putting his rifle through a hole laid his cheek to the stock and his finger to the trigger.

We marked out a wall about twenty yards distant, and resolved to fire as soon as the Bedawîn passed it. As they approached they quickened their pace, and the leader came on a little in front, with his spear pointed against one of our breasts, his teeth set, and his eyes flashing fire. The Arab war-song ceased, and there was no sound except the clatter of galloping horses, and my general order, oft-repeated, "Don't fire, till they are close upon us."

The fatal wall was approached, but just then Gazâway, who could contain himself no longer, rushed out from behind us with a double-barrelled gun, and hurled such a volley of Egyptian oaths at the Bedawîn, that he fairly staggered them. The whole party hesitated, wheeled to the right, and made a graceful and masterly retreat. Gazâway by his horrible howling saved us, but much wrath fell on him for his imprudence, so popular is a fight everywhere.

The Bedawîn then charged right up to the village; but the Palmyrans, who had been watching our tactics from the walls of the temple, met them in the gate with matchlocks and lighted fusees, and the robbers, again foiled, fell back and halted in the triumphal arch. In a moment they picketed their horses and threw themselves on the sand to rest.

I had often wished to see a foraging party of Arabs, for the tribes send out their best horses and arms, and only their picked men. I resolved to visit the party;

but Brandy Bob, who amused himself with aiming at the Bedawîn with a loaded rifle, declared that he would not consider himself responsible for my safety if I moved beyond our camp. I thought it well to relieve him from the weight of responsibility, and the opportunity was not to be lost, so I started alone for the Bedawîn, who were distant about a quarter of a mile. On the way I met some of our soldiers coming back to our camp, but crouching along hollow places, and behind ruins, so as not to be seen by the spearmen. The villagers also, who were in the gardens and fields, were stealing home and entering the temple through holes in the wall.

I walked very slowly, with the Bedawîn in view all the way, and in order that I might appear as composed as possible I examined all the ruins in my path, though I had seen them fifty times before. When I came within a few perches of the triumphal arch, one of the Bedawîn sprang to his feet, seized a club and a spear, and rushed at me like an infuriate bull. Never did I see a man, even in a mad-house, so utterly beside himself as that man appeared to be. He was livid with rage, and his passion seemed to be choking him, and as he hurled imprecations at me the foam flew from his mouth.

I met his exhibition of wrath with a laugh, and, pushing the point of his spear aside, I walked past him, as if I was accustomed to that sort of thing, and thought nothing of it. I went straight, and at my leisure, to the rest of the Arabs, and he followed me, roaring like a wild beast. The others received me with scowling looks, and none of them returned my salutation. I sat down upon a stone, fully believing myself in a trap, and tried to look composed, though I did not feel so.

"Who do you think I am?" thundered the wrathful Bedawi.

"I think," said I, "you would be a magnificent-looking fellow, if you did not spoil a handsome face by bad temper."

"Know, then," said he, "that I am the great Kufeiley, at whose name pashas tremble."

I said, no one denied that he was the great Kufeiley, but that I had seen as pleasant-looking a man somewhere previously; and then, seeing the necessity for a diversion, I added, pointing to a horrible-looking cut-throat, who stood *glowering* at me, —

"Look at the sweet and pleasant countenance of your friend there, on the approach of a guest."

The wit was of the feeblest quality, but it did its work, and a broad grin overspread every countenance, even that of the infuriate Kufeiley. A joke that leaves you to assume that you are superior to some one else is always appreciated.

In less than five minutes from the birth of the first smile we were deep in the politics of the desert and the city. Kufeiley had a grievance against the Turks — as who has not, that has any dealings with them? They had ceased to pay a stipulated tribute for the right of peaceful passage, and he would reduce them to terms, as he had often done before. He had come expressly to plunder us, by way of punishing the Turks, and as Allah was great, he would scatter us like dust on our return journey.

Then they examined everything I had, like big children, and asked me the price of each thing — my boots, my watch, my revolver, my hat; in fact, I believe they were making an inventory of my personal effects, to facilitate future division, after they should have relieved me of them.

I broached the question of the education of their children, but they answered, scornfully, "Do you want to make them clerks?" On further discussion, they promised to entertain the question, or submit to any other humiliation, if I would procure the release of some of their tribe, who were, they said, wrongfully imprisoned in Damascus.

I had now an opportunity to become thoroughly acquainted with the robbers. I found that Kufeiley was the leader of that branch of the Amour Arabs who frequent the desert between Palmyra and Hums. He did not exaggerate the terror his name inspired,[1] as he was one of the most active and bloody of all the Bedawîn. He was a short, thick man, with a short, black, shaggy head and bull neck, and with innumerable wrinkles concentrated round his crafty eyes and hard, relentless mouth. His flesh looked black and hard as dried Brazilian beef.

[1] Kufeiley was shot dead through the breast the following spring, near Hums, by a peasant whom he was plundering.

PALMYRA AND ZENOBIA.

Second in command, and in fame for bloody deeds, was Azzab, the father-in-law of Kufeiley, a tall, spare man. They all had the deep, suspicious eyes of their race. They were armed with lances, tufted with ostrich feathers, and most of them had clubs, and flint pistols, and crooked daggers; and there was one double-barrelled fowling-piece, which they seemed to regard with special affection. They exhibited it in triumph; but it was only a Belgian gun, which had got the name "London" engraved on it in Damascus.

They all appeared as if they had dressed at an "old-clo'" shop, as there was nothing like uniformity in their apparel, and they were doubtless arrayed in the garments of their victims. One man had hung about him the black clothes of a European, much too large for him, and sadly in want of buttons in certain places: the ventilation was perfect. Their horses were weedy.

While I lingered with the Bedawîn, the Turkish governor of Palmyra joined us, accompanied by a scribe. He and Kufeiley fell on each other's necks, and it soon became apparent why we and the Palmyrans had to defend ourselves, in presence of a Turkish garrison. The governor got a fair share of all plunder taken by Kufeiley, and he in return abstained from interfering with that chief's enterprises.

On our arrival at Palmyra, this Turkish official paid several visits to our camp, and always, on leaving us, sent his servant to ask us for a bottle of brandy. Our supply was limited to one bottle for medicinal purposes, but we yielded to his importunities in a moment of weakness. We could not, however, give him the whole bottle, and we were ashamed to send it half full; so we did as the brewers do who want to recoup themselves for the lately imposed tax,—we filled it up with water. Apparently the brandy was not up to the governor's standard of perfection, or he had got from us all that his heart desired, for he appeared at our tent no more, and his friendship was turned into hostility.

My interview with the Bedawîn was cut short by a mounted soldier, who came galloping up from Brandy Bob, delivered his message from a distance of twenty yards, and galloped away before the Arabs, who sprang to their feet, had even time to fire at him.

He wished me to return at once, and told the Bedawîn that if they did not retire from the triumphal arch in twenty minutes, they would be fired on. I thought he might be foolish enough to keep his word, and so I returned to prevent mischief. I left the Bedawîn without having effected a treaty of peace for our party.

On my return to the camp, our cavalcade were getting ready to start on their homeward journey. As we moved from the ruins, some of the Bedawîn went before us, and some of them followed us, but they always kept at a respectful distance. They did not attack us, for they prefer plundering to fighting; but they kept in a position from which they could have cut off stragglers, or caught a runaway horse or mule, had there been any such.

Passing into the long plain which stretches from Palmyra to near Karyetein, we kept to the right, about a mile from the mountain range on the north. The Bedawîn marched parallel with us along the foot of the mountain. In an hour and a half we reached the open mouths of a subterranean water-course. The openings were about eighty feet apart, and the water was eighteen feet from the surface of the ground. The stones round the sides of the openings were much polished and grooved by the friction of ropes drawing up water. This was the water of the Abu el-Fawâris fountain, which was the chief supply of Tadmor.

We pitched our camp by the water, at a point due west from the Castle of Palmyra. The place seemed to have been much used as a camping-ground. The plain around us was green with the *el-kali*, and another shrub, like a dwarf tamarisk; flocks of pigeons and vultures swarmed about us to get at the water; and the Bedawîn encamped at the foot of the mountain right opposite, and watched for an opportunity to attack us.

Danger in Syria soon loses the romance of novelty and the thrill of excitement. I remember with what feelings of horror I heard from our first landlord in Damascus, that two of his brothers had been murdered in the room which we had made our chief sitting-room. He had come in one gusty night to see how we liked our new quarters, and to keep us from feeling lonely, and with twitching mouth, he said, pointing to where we sat:

"There is where my two brothers were killed, and my father was murdered over there, and then they threw them all into that fountain outside."

The wind made horrid noises about the house that night, and for many a day I fancied I could see the purple stains through the white straw matting. But we soon became familiar with such horrors.

Three skeletons of murdered Christians were fished out of the well from which we had our first water in Damascus. Our colporteur was brought in to us with his head laid open; and a little boy who had been in our school, and our service, was murdered by Druzes, and eaten up by dogs. Our mission-field lay along the border of the desert, and in ten years we had come to look calmly at the deeds of city and desert Ishmaelites.

It was not, however, without a sense of danger that we lay down for the night in full view of a band of well-armed, hardy spearmen, who had vowed to murder us, and who had a will to carry out their vow. Our guard was sufficiently strong and well armed to keep the enemy at a distance, but they were only Turks, and the Bedawîn, on their nimble mares, might dash into our camp during the night, and overwhelm us in the confusion and darkness; and it was not pleasant to fancy a spear penetrating one's tent. I went round our sentinels several times, and they continued to swear, and brag, and keep guard, as long as we watched them; but no sooner had we lain down to sleep than they stacked their arms, rolled themselves up in their greatcoats, and lay down to sleep likewise.

A little after midnight my servant awaked me, and told me that our soldiers were "all snoring at the stars."

I walked through among them, and over them, and found them loudly asleep. I thought of the sleeping hosts of King Saul that had gone out to seize David, and I wondered if we could repeat David's trick on Saul.[1]

In a few minutes my servant had the soldiers' rifles carried to beside my bed, and not a soldier had stirred. He then mounted guard himself, but, as sleep under the circumstances was impossible, we roused our camp before dawn for the return journey. Then woke up the most indescribable babel.

The soldiers rushed about in search of their arms, frantic with rage, shame, fear. The cowardly Bedawîn had stolen their rifles while they slept, and would now fall upon them unarmed.

The officers screamed at the men, and the men roared at the officers, and the choicest epithets in Arabic, Turkish, Kurdish, and Armenian were hurled about with much waste of nervous energy.

When the noise had reached the climax, I called over Brandy Bob, and quietly asked him what was all the shouting about.

"Oh, sir," he replied, "I took my eyes off my men for an instant, and they have lost their rifles."

"Nonsense!" I said. "You bragged how you would guard us, and then you all went and fell asleep. There are your weapons. My servant brought them here to prevent the Bedawîn from getting them, and then mounted guard for you."

[1] 1 Sam. xxvi. 12.

The soldiers took their guns in silence, but, with the versatility of Falstaff, they all soon began to swear that they had seen me taking their rifles, and only wanted to humour me.

We struck our tents in silence and in haste, while it was yet dark, and marched to 'Ain el-Wu'ul, and on the following day continued our homeward journey as far as Karyetein.

But what of the Bedawîn who had encamped over against us? We had given them the slip, and got among the hills at the other side of the plain, before they were aware of our departure, and as they never suspected that we had discovered the 'Ain el-Wu'ul water, they pursued us, as they supposed, down the beaten track of ordinary tourists. All day long they spurred their animals in pursuit, and strained their eyes to catch a glimpse of us on the horizon before them. At last the gazelle-traps and gardens of Karyetein rose before them, and they felt that their prey had escaped.

A council of war was held, at which it was the unanimous opinion that we had hidden in some dip of the desert, or among the mountains, as it was clearly impossible that our baggage animals could have reached Karyetein in so short a time.

It was then resolved[1] that they should lie across our track until we came up.

All night long they watched in vain, but at eleven

[1] These details I had from one of the Bedawîn, who called on me afterwards in Damascus, and gave me all particulars.

o'clock the next morning, as they were about to give us up, a caravan suddenly appeared issuing from the mountains on the north. " Allahu Akbar!" (God is great) shouted the delighted Bedawîn, and tightening the girths on their hungry horses, and the girdles on their own empty stomachs, they rushed with a desert hurrah on their prey.

The caravan was conducted by the hardy villagers of Jebel Kalamoun, who were bringing provisions for their families from the Euphrates, and they had, besides, Persian carpets, and tobacco and other valuable merchandise for Damascus. They had just passed the most dangerous part of their journey, and had relaxed their ordinary vigilance, and were somewhat scattered, so that with the first onset, the Bedawîn cut off and captured a number of stragglers. These were withdrawn to a distance, and secured. The remainder of the caravan was then drawn up in a circle, and the camels were tightly bound together in a living rampart, from behind which the villagers fired on their assailants.

"The Arab force," according to the *Levant Herald*, "consisted of about twenty horsemen, accompanied by forty dromedaries, each carrying two armed riders. They were the Giath Bedawîn, a branch of the Seba'a tribe, accompanied by the 'Amour, under Sheikh Dabbous." They and their horses took a hurried meal of the food they had captured at the first onset, and then, flushed with victory and with the prospect of large booty, they dashed bodily against the living rampart. A desperate struggle ensued. The circular line swayed and staggered; but in a hand-to-hand encounter the Bedawîn had no chance with the able-bodied[1] villagers, and several of them were dragged from their horses and stricken down with clubs.

The Bedawîn then became more wary, and galloped round and round the circle, making a feint here and an attack there, till the villagers were weary of rushing round their rampart, and their ammunition was exhausted. Thus they continued hour after hour, till near sunset, when a wounded camel staggered and fell, and broke the line. The circle opened out and became a crescent. Quick as lightning, the Bedawîn rushed in at the breach, the camels started off in all directions, and the active horsemen, with their flashing spears, decided the victory in a few minutes.

The *Levant Herald* summed up the result of the raid thus: "The Bedawîn took possession of, and carried off, all that the caravan contained, — 120 loads of butter (*semmen*), and an enormous number of donkeys, mules, camels, horses, arms, valued at £4000. In addition to this they stripped all the travellers, and left them naked in the blazing desert. They even stripped the dead. The friends of the murdered men remained to watch the bodies, till animals were brought to convey

---

[1] The Bedawîn are much smaller-bodied men than the Fallahîn of the villages. Colonel Gawler, the late keeper of the crown jewels, informed me that the suits of armour preserved in the Tower were found to be too small for ordinary men.

them to the village. They succeeded in protecting themselves from the heat by day, and the cold by night, with rags from the furniture of camels that were shot in the *mêlée*.

"The unfortunate men were industrious people, inhabitants of Nebk, Deir-Atîyeh, Rahibeh, and one of them was from Damascus. They were mostly heads of hungry families, and paid taxes to the Sultan for his protection. There is no honest reason why this state of things should be permitted to exist. A few years before, Subhi Pasha kept the desert in almost perfect order. The Bedawi marauders are within easy reach of the government.

"When the case was laid before Halet Pasha, governor of Damascus, he merely said that Karyetein was outside the bounds of Syria. Those who were present corrected his Excellency's geography, and he caused a sharp telegram to be sent to his subordinates, and with that the matter rested."

This report, published at the time, in the chief newspaper at Constantinople, was, I know, correct in every detail. I knew several of the murdered men, and one of them, Shibley Kassis, of Nebk, was brother-in-law to our chief Protestant in that district, and a very amiable man.

What would the Bedawîn do with one hundred and twenty loads of butter?

They brought it, or rather, had it brought, into Damascus, and sold publicly.

What would they do with the splendid carpets and shawls from the looms of Persia and Cashmere?

They distributed them among their powerful friends in Damascus, in return for their efficient protection, and some of the best found their way into the gorgeous saloons of those whose duty it was to administer justice.

One of our Protestants found three of his camels in the hands of the robbers, in Damascus, and, though he got an official order for the restoration of his property, he was never able to get it carried out, and the robbers were permitted to keep his camels.

We rested a day at Karyetein, and had the pleasure of finding that our school had taken root among Moslems and Christians; and we saw Moslems and Christians sitting side by side in that land of violence and blood, and spelling out together the story of Christ's love to men. In the evening we heard that a battle was being fought near by, and I believe the report of the guns was distinctly heard; but the sheikh said the Turks were there to protect the district, and the Turks smoked their nargilles, and ejaculated "Allah is great," and did nothing.

PALMYRA TERRA-COTTA HEAD IN PROFILE, WITH SUN, MOON, AND STARS.
Translation—BEL PROTECTS THE SONS OF BARSA'A.

CORNICE SOFFIT OF TOMB TOWER.

CHAPTER XVII.

WE finished the day by visiting and receiving the visits of our friends, and on the following morning continued our homeward journey, before receiving the details of the battle. We passed several ruined khans, resting-places for caravans and travellers in more propitious times; had several spurts after gazelles with our Persian greyhound, caught a fox alive and a curious land rat; and after a weary ride, encamped at 'Atny, a few miles west of a salt lake that glowed and sparkled in the evening sun.

Here, too, we were met by "rumours of oppression and deceit." The Ishmaelites had been to the village three hours before us, and had carried off several flocks of sheep, and all the donkeys and camels and portable things they could find.

Any one who makes a tour through Northern Syria will be able to appreciate for the remainder of his life the advantages of a civilized government. He will there see as fine a peasantry as is to be found anywhere, — handsome, and courteous, but picturesque in rags; thrifty and frugal, but penniless; comparatively truthful and enterprising, but without credit or resources. They have broad acres which only require to be scratched and they bring forth sixty-fold; but they only cultivate little patches, surrounded by mud walls, and within the range of their matchlocks.

During the greater part of the year they dare not walk over their own uncultivated fields, for fear of being stripped of their tattered garments.[1]

And yet these poor people are the most heavily taxed peasantry in the world. They pay "blackmail," called *khowieh* (brotherhood), to the Bedawîn, who plunder them notwithstanding. And they pay taxes to the Turks, who give them no protection in return. The Bedawîn's claim is from time immemorial, and they enforce their claim by cutting off the ears of peasants from the defaulting villages, and by carrying off a number of the village children into the desert. The latter plan always brings the villages to terms. The Turks enforce their claims by imprisoning the village sheikhs in foul, pestiferous sties, without food, till they have paid "the uttermost farthing."

[1] The *Levant Herald* of 12th August 1874, referring to this subject, pointed out that "three villages, not the most important, had lost during the year 7680 sheep and goats, 55 camels, 32 donkeys, and an enormous amount of other property, besides shepherds and drivers killed and wounded. The other villages had suffered equal losses, and the people were in a state of despair."

BED

These spoilers follow on each other's heels, and that which the Turkish caterpillar leaves the Bedawi locust devours. With anything like protection or fair government, the peasantry of Northern Syria would be among the happiest in the world; but for the ten years that I knew them, they saw the fruit of their labour swept away by organized robbers, and they lived in a state of starvation and despair. All who can get away leave for Egypt and for the large cities, and the region is becoming depopulated year by year. Hundreds succeed in breaking the Turkish cordon, and in effecting their escape to America.

It was pleasant to see how lightly sorrow sat on the simple people of 'Atny. When we arrived they were plucking at their beards, and rending their garments, and calling for vengeance from heaven on their spoilers and on the Turks. Toward sunset, however, the ceremony of marrying the Sheikh's daughter, a mature maiden of twelve, was commenced, and the people danced, and sang, and shouted, and clapped their hands, and the women sent up shrill notes of joy, and the old Sheikh scattered sweetmeats among the revellers, and all seemed merry and light-hearted, as if they had sat all their lives under their own vines and fig-trees, with none to molest or make them afraid.

The bawling and screaming came to an end about midnight, but soon broke out again. Somebody's house had been plundered, and the people were all proclaiming it from the house-tops. The women's voices were still in tune, and they howled as if they had been robbed of their most precious treasures. I had been giving battle to a number of persevering mosquitoes, up till the time that this new disturbance arose. Finding, however, that sleep was impossible, and that my presence was no longer required by my companions, I started alone, in the dark, for Damascus.

I passed through Jerùd, Muaddamiyeh, and El-Kutifeh while the people were still sleeping. The dogs lay thick in the streets, and my horse had difficulty in threading his way among them. They were too lazy and sleepy even to bark at me.

The night was long, but at last the tops of the mountains were touched with gold, and as the plain of Damascus burst upon me through the Eth-thunîyeh Pass, the rising sun was pouring its first rays into a surging sea of verdure and beauty, and lighting up the minarets of hamlet and city with tongues of fire.

No wonder Orientals rave over the beauties of Damascus. At all seasons of the year, and from every point of view, Damascus is beautiful; but its beauty is enhanced tenfold by the fact that you can only approach it through a howling wilderness. Your eye has been resting on the heavens as brass and the earth as iron. Every green thing is a prickly shrub. Desolation and dreariness and sterility reign on every side. Suddenly you turn a corner, and your eye rests on Paradise.

A gallop down the hill, and I was among luxurious harvests. Then I passed through miles of orchards golden with ripe apricots, the paths overspread by fragrant walnuts. Crystal waters tumbled in cascades over the walls, and ran babbling by the side of the road. At last I reached Bab Es-Shurki, the eastern gate of Damascus, in which the Roman arch is still visible; and as I passed through where Khaled and his fiery Saracens first entered the city, my heart sank as I saw a Turkish soldier levying "blackmail" on a miserable Jewish pedlar. A minute more, and I was at home even in Damascus.

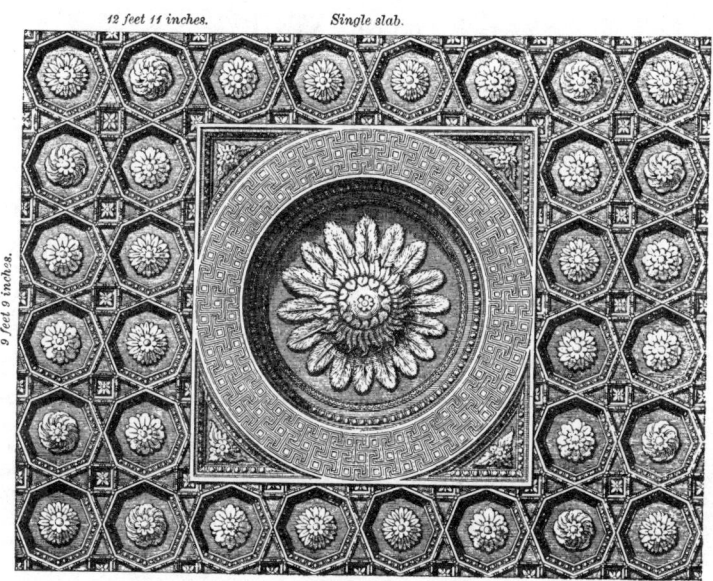

CEILING OF HOLY OF HOLIES, TEMPLE OF THE SUN.

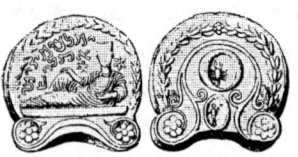 

Translation—JAMLIKOU, SON OF MOKEIMOU AKLEISH.
This is the man who, in the year 83 A.D., built the most beautiful tomb tower in Palmyra.

Translation—SOKAYI, SON OF WAHBALLATH.
Sokayi was one of four sons who in 112 A.D. built a tomb tower.

CHAPTER XVIII.

DURING my first visit to Palmyra, in 1872, I spent four days from dawn to dusk in incessant exploration. One of my companions, a wealthy banker, began with great zeal to collect curios. By the end of the first day his money had set the whole population in motion, to sift the sands, and rifle the tombs. He returned to the tent at night laden with a miscellaneous assortment of old Tadmor odds and ends.

He had handfuls of the beautiful little coins that are found in the sand, boxes of *terra-cotta* tablets with Palmyra inscriptions and figures, Roman lamps, inscribed gems, and a heap of skulls and limbs of mummies. The lower extremities of one of the mummies he inserted into a pair of his own under-drawers, the better to preserve them.

There is perhaps no pursuit that so quickly grows to a passion as the search for antiquities. The searcher is always finding something unique, and in Palmyra every glass bead is associated with the Sitt Zenobia. My friend had secured several objects of great interest, among which were real coins of Wahballath, one of Zenobia's sons.

The collector's passion soon culminates in fever. I had gone over the heaps of coins, gems, lamps, and tesseræ with my friend before going to bed, pointing out the archæological value of some of his discoveries. He spent a sleepless and restless night, tossing to and fro, and longing for the dawn. He woke me up in the night to tell him the name of Zenobia's son whose name was on the coins.

As soon as the day began to break he slipped from the tent, and gathering around him the entire population of Tadmor resumed his researches among the ruins.

I had ridden out early to the quarries from which the great stones and columns of Palmyra had been taken. We again met at nine o'clock, at breakfast, and I found his cup of satisfaction was full to overflowing. It is not easy to carry the full cup with dignity. He had no eyes for my bag of partridges, or ears for my story of the wondrous quarries.

When breakfast was over, he drew from his pocket a red silk handkerchief, and, calling us around, began very mysteriously and deliberately to unfold it!

"There," said he, disclosing a little ivory figure, "look at that. It is pure Grecian, of the best period. See the expression, the feeling, the spirituality of that idol. I have little doubt that it once belonged to Zenobia, and one cannot wonder that the lovely woman worshipped so lovely an object."

Our ladies thronged round the fortunate finder, to examine the beautiful idol. I was waiting for my turn to get a sight of the wonderful work of art, when my niece exclaimed:

"Why, you goose, it's the head of your own umbrella."

He turned on her with a look of scorn, and I thought he would have struck her to the ground. Then a most unsympathetic laugh burst from the whole party. He became ashy pale, as if he were about to faint. Before the laughter ceased, he had scattered all his collection on the sand, kicking the things about. Then he rushed out of the tent without speaking a word, and disappeared among the ruins.

The demand for antiquities had stimulated the supply. The Palmyrans, aided, I believe, by my friend's dragoman, had stolen the handle of his umbrella, and sold it to him for ten times its weight in gold. That transaction completely cured him of the archæological fever. He bought no more *antiques*, and declined to look at those purchased by us, or offered for sale by the natives, and he took no further interest in our explorations. His one and only desire seemed to be to get away from Palmyra.

For three days he urged me incessantly to leave the "God-forsaken place." Morning, noon, and night, at all our meals, and whenever we met in the ruins, he urged his one plea, that we should retrace our steps to Damascus. I reminded him that all our plans were laid to spend a week at Palmyra, that our contracts were made on that basis, that we were never likely to visit the place again, and that it would be a calamity to leave the place half explored.

As the week advanced, his complainings became harder to bear. They began to take the form of taunts and challenges. "If I had any one who could ride to accompany me," he would say, "I would return straight to Damascus, without spending four days dawdling by the way." He did not wish to ride back with a parcel of girls; though, as a matter of fact, the girls were the liveliest riders of the party.

On Thursday night I told him I would ride back to Damascus with him as quickly as he pleased. I had had a very hard day climbing the ladders to inscriptions and investigating subterranean chambers. We threw ourselves down for a brief sleep, and started a little before midnight.

I hoped to accompany our party well clear of Palmyra, and to leave them to follow the beaten track with their escort, while I pushed forward with my friend.

Noiselessly we stole out of the ruins, which are more impressive at night than by day. We swept silently down the plain, lighted on our way by the stars. The air was fresh and balmy, and quite exhilarating after the broiling heat of the day.

I was riding well ahead, when I saw our way blocked by an encampment about a mile in front of us. I stopped and called up our guard, and tried to get them well together so as to be ready for all emergencies.

As soon as my Bashi-bazooks saw the encampment, they

dashed forward with a wild yell, and charged down the plain. I was better mounted than they, and I got before them, and with my whip tried to restrain their impetuosity; but a wild spirit had taken possession of the whole party.

My cook rode past me on a baggage mule, brandishing an old pistol that would have endangered somebody's life if it had gone off; but so great was the general madness that seized our party, that a young and cool-headed friend, a distinguished metaphysician and gold medallist, who had been riding behind with the ladies, left his charge, and galloped furiously past me, holding his revolver in front of him, at arm's length, and shouting the one good Arabic phrase which he had at command, "Clear the way."

Our gallant charge was akin to panic, and would, I knew, in case of a real enemy, be equally disastrous.

It was for me one of the most anxious moments of my life. If we were in for a battle, I knew that my breech-loader and revolver, as they were both of the best, would be of service; but our ladies were behind in the darkness. I therefore rode to the rear, when I was needed in front, and my arrival was most opportune.

The ladies, one of whom was sister to the metaphysican with the revolver, had also charged when they heard of an enemy on the path; but one of the saddles had turned round in the confusion, and the rider's foot having caught in the stirrup, she was being dragged along the ground. In less than a minute she was again in the saddle, and we were all galloping towards the enemy. We heard a few sputtering shots and cries, and prepared for the worst; but when we arrived, we found the camp was only a caravan of Damascus merchants, and that the cries and shots were only let off for joy on the meeting of old friends.

My reception, as I brought up the rear, was far from flattering. I heard one of our escort saying, "The Khowajah was the best mounted and best armed of the whole party, but when the supreme moment came, he rode to the rear, and took his place among the women."

The Arab is a game-cock, and a fight is as popular in the desert as anywhere else; but I have an impression that when my escort gallantly bore down on the caravan of peaceful merchants, they knew that they were likely to be rewarded with brandy and tobacco.

Leaving our party on the march, my friend and I set out for our long ride to Damascus. The night had become piercingly cold, and we seemed to be always riding against a ridge about ten yards ahead; but we pressed forward for a couple of hours, without drawing rein. We were both well mounted. My companion rode a large-boned, serviceable chestnut of the *Kadîsheh*, or plebeian, order. I rode a blood-mare (*Asîleh*) of the Siklâweh-Jidrân breed. She was a beautiful bay, with deep chest, large soft eyes, cup-like feet and long pasterns, and springy step, and an unwritten pedigree stretching in point of time as far back as the bluest blood in England.

I was once able to render an important service to a

family of Arabs, who were being ruined by Russian Jews under English protection, at Damascus. I fell in love with one of their mares. They saw me fondling her, and giving her bits of sugar and biscuit, and, believing that I would be kind to her, they sold her to me, in defiance of their custom. She brought me safely out of many a scrape in the desert, and we became fast friends. She would stand stone still, if she saw me putting up my gun to fire, so that from the saddle I could shoot birds on the wing; and when I wanted to mount her she would come at my call, and stand rubbing her head against me, till I got into the saddle. She was larger than the ordinary desert blood-mare, and carried easily a weight of thirteen and a half stones.

When we had got opposite the 'Ain el-Wu'ul fountain, we found our way blocked by an Arab encampment. The twinkling lights seemed to fill the whole plain. All appeared to be fast asleep, but we knew that if one of the Bedawîn saw us, we should soon have the whole hornets' nest after us.

As the wind was coming from the fountain-side, we resolved to try to get round the other side of the encampment. We alighted, and, slinging the nose-bags on our horses, carefully led them as we moved round the Arab flank in the darkness.

It was an anxious time; for, had our horses whinnied, or a desert dog discovered us, we should certainly at least have been deprived of our horses.

By making a circuit of a mile or more, we got past

the northern flank of the sleeping host. A strong wind was blowing from the camp, laden with the odour of camels and camp-fires. Our mares, we knew, would not neigh like horses, and betray us; but lest they might be tempted to act contrary to their natures, we let them feed from their nose-bags as they walked silently and docilely by our sides.

As soon as we thought we had got past the Arabs, we worked our way back to the direct path, and started for Karyetein at a pace of twelve miles an hour. The track was hard, and the noise of our cantering horses roused the camp, which was nearer to us than we had supposed, judging from the glimmer of the camp-fires, which seemed in the darkness farther away than they really were. An alarm shot was fired, and then there arose a babel of sounds, in which the braying of asses, and barking of dogs, and shouting of men were mingled.

We kept steadily on our way, but we did not seem to be getting much further from the noises. When we had ridden for about an hour, we suddenly became aware that we were being pursued. The night had become very dark, and we could see nothing but the camp-fires in the distance, but we could distinctly hear the clatter of horses' feet, and even the hard breathing of horses which were being driven furiously.

Three courses were open to us. Either to stand and fight, or to race for our lives, or to give our pursuers the slip. There was little time for coming to an agreement, but my companion said, as we galloped side by side, "Take any course you wish. I am responsible for our difficulties, and I will do whatever you do."

To have fought would have been simple madness, for, from the noise our pursuers made, there seemed to be hundreds of them. It was doubtful if we could have escaped by hard riding, for our steeds were jaded, while theirs were fresh. I might have escaped on my *Asîleh*, at the best, but my companion's *Kadîsheh* would certainly have been overtaken. The darkness favoured the third plan.

We were then passing over rough ground, and having reached a *seil*, or the dry bed of a river, we turned up it at right angles to the path. In a few seconds we were quite out of sight, among the hills. We again hung the nose-bags on our horses' heads, and set them to feed, and I left both with my friend, and crawled back to a little hill by the side of the path.

I had scarcely got to the top of the hill, and peeped over, lying flat on the ground, when the troop swept past. There seemed to be about a dozen horses, and as many dromedaries, and as each dromedary carried two men, there may have been thirty or forty all told. There may not have been a score, for, with the greatest desire to be accurate, the conditions were such as to lead to exaggeration.

We now knew that we had no reasonable cause for fear. We both had breech-loaders and revolvers of the newest patterns, and we should have been able, if the worst came, to fire forty shots between us in a minute.

Our double-barrelled guns were charged with shot cartridges, and, barring accidents, we felt that we could run away from spears, and clubs, and empty saddles at our leisure. My companion, an old Wimbledon crack shot, was anxious to begin at once; but I was determined to avoid bloodshed if possible, and he took his orders from me.

We immediately mounted, and followed the Bedawîn, who thought they were following us. There was less than half a mile between us. We could hear them distinctly; but if they heard us, they must have thought we were some of their own party. When we had followed them for an hour or so, and they seemed to be getting further and further ahead of us, it became necessary to shake them off in some way or other, as we knew that the dawn would very soon reveal us.

My companion carried a little flask of brandy suspended by straps, as an ornament. I induced him to give it to me. We then rode into the desert to the left, and I took the muslin which was fixed on my helmet as a protection against the sun, saturated it with the brandy, and set fire to it on a heap of brushwood.

The flame rose suddenly, and the brushwood caught fire, and continued the blaze. I fired two or three shots, sending the bullets whistling after our pursuers. At the same time we walked our horses between them and the fire, and danced round it, so that we might seem more numerous than we were. Then we galloped back in the darkness to the road, and crossed out into the desert on the other side.

The ruse succeeded splendidly. The fire burnt itself out quickly, but the Bedawîn hurried back to the spot where they had seen it. We heard them leaving the road, and passing back, with much noise, through the brushwood. Knowing that our path was free, we returned to it, and sped as fast as we could on our way to Karyetein.

We were both profoundly thankful that we had escaped a real danger, and that we had not been obliged to shed the blood of even desert cut-throats.

It was a strange but intensely enjoyable adventure. I do not think we were afraid, but there were times, especially when I was lying on the hill as our pursuers rode past, when I could distinctly hear the beating of my heart so loud that I feared others might hear the throbs.

Our horses seemed to understand the position, and played their part well.

TESSERÆ FROM PALMYRA.

CEILING OF TOMB TOWER.

CHAPTER XIX.

WE continued our journey unmolested, at a slow gallop, and did not pause till it was broad day. Then we dismounted, and walked by our mares for a mile or so.

The Bedawi encampment was at least twenty miles to the rear. The Arabs were in motion, swarming up the high ground towards the fountain of the Ibexes ('Ain el-Wu'ul). We saw them rolling up the hill like a cloud-shadow, and disappearing into the mountain gorge, and we knew that the way would be safe for our friends and their escort, coming behind.

That was a very charming desert morning. First the eastern horizon became saffron, then it passed through all shades of orange, and the mountain tops glowed with a roseate hue, and the light poured in great streams into the plain, and objects were seen detaching themselves from the darkness, till every mountain base, and every deep ravine, and every dark crevasse was filled with living light, and colours, from lightest pink to deepest indigo, tinged and tinted the mountains, that stood like high walls on either side of the plain down which we sped as if fleeing for our lives before the avenger.

Shortly after the day was established, four horsemen coming from the hills appeared, bearing down on us on our right. They had long spears, and clubs hung to their saddles, and little arsenals of flint pistols and daggers in their belts. They were really small fry in our eyes after what we had passed through, and we looked carefully to see if there was a larger force behind them. We continued to gallop, and they doubtless thought we were afraid of them, and trying to escape, and they made a tremendous effort to cut our path, and intercept us.

It was a pretty sight to see the four sons of the desert bearing down upon us. At first their pace was the ordinary ambling or desert jog-trot, for which I know no English name. We have nothing that corresponds to it. It seems slow and sly, but it gets over the ground fast. Greater speed, however, was necessary to catch us though we did not press our weary horses. When we first saw them they were ten or twelve miles distant; but they struck straight for our path, and as they came nearer to it, they galloped as fast as they could to get before us. The horses were at full stretch, and the riders, with their short stirrups and high saddles, seemed to sit on the tops of their horses as if on seats, ready to spring.

They reached the road about four hundred yards in front of us, reined up their horses, and planted themselves right in our way. We brought our horses to a walking pace, and prepared for the worst. They shook their spears, and leaned forward on their saddles, as if about to charge; but they saw our shining weapons, and paused.

We approached till we were within eighty yards of the enemy, and halted. I said, —

"Who are you, and what do you want?"

One of them replied with a sharp bark. "You are trespassers on our land, and by Allah we will make you repent, you sons of dogs."

I said, repeating one of their own proverbs, "Violent language never yet tore a shirt. I can shoot the four of you through the heads in four seconds, and if you move one step towards us, I will shoot your four horses to begin with."

They did not like the prospect, and after exchanging words among themselves, one of them said: "No man has ever presumed to pass through our territory without leave; but if you surrender the horse you are riding, we will let you pass."

I replied: "Let there be no fooling. Since the day that Abraham your father, of blessed memory, passed down this same road, till this day, the way has been open. We are here to injure no man, not even the road; but if you attempt to stop us, your blood be upon your own heads."

My companion said, "Let me empty two of their saddles."

He had once tied with Sir Henry Halford for the Queen's cup.

I said, "No; if they attack us, we will shoot their horses first."

One of them said, "We belong to the great Anazi tribe, which makes pashas tremble, and we cannot let you pass."

I replied: "Your sheikh and I are friends, and I know his brother who spends much time in Damascus. I have just established a school at Karyetein, and I am only anxious to befriend the Bedawîn; but either you must give way, or we must give way. My friend wants to shoot two of you to begin with. We are the stronger, but I am loath to harm you. I now give you five minutes to make up your minds, and if you do not move off in that time, may Allah be merciful to you."

I said to my friend: "Be ready, but keep cool; they may make a dash at us. You had better alight, as your horse is restive."

He slipped from the saddle, and stood with his fowling-piece ready. I sat in the saddle, with my watch in my hand. "Four minutes are now gone," I said, "and the fifth is half sped." A few seconds later, I put my watch into my pocket, and as I lifted my gun to my shoulder they turned and fled before us, hurling a volley of imprecations at us as they went.

They galloped along the path before us, and we galloped after as if in pursuit. There were about four hundred yards between us. Several times they turned, and waited as if to stop us; but we galloped straight at them, putting up our guns to our shoulders, and when we neared them they broke and hurried away. We thought they might be playing at delay, till a larger force should arrive, but we could hardly take our eyes off them, to look back to see if others were coming.

My companion at last lost patience. "This thing," he said, " must come to an end, one way or another."

I called on them to halt, and then I told them that my friend had not so much consideration for them as I had, and that they must leave us altogether, or I could not restrain him from shooting them.

They then galloped off in a wide circle, riding round us at a respectful distance, for some time, and finally took up their position at a little hill on the left near our path. As we came near, they rode round the hill, out of sight; but one of them appeared suddenly from behind the hill, and discharging his blunderbuss at me, fled at full gallop with his companions, and disappeared among the hills.

We hurried as quickly as our horses could take us to the spot from which the shot had come; but the four horsemen were already a quarter of a mile away, and going at a tremendous pace. My companion dismounted and sent half a dozen bullets after them, but the distance was too great for effective shooting. He was very vexed that we had let them off, especially when he knew that I had been hit.

I had had a marvellous escape. A perfect storm of

slugs and pellets seemed to have swept me and my mare. The gun fired was a short, wide-mouth blunderbuss, such as several of our four escort carried. Such guns are charged with a quarter of a pound of powder and a pound and a half of pellets, slugs, nails, bits of iron, and split bullets. It is a most deadly weapon in a crowd.

The report of the shot was very loud, and the discharge tore up the ground round us, and it seemed to sweep my mare almost off her feet. She had received only a few scratches. I was not quite so fortunate. I had a slight wound in the left hand, and two in the breast. One of the pellets that struck my breast had passed through a thick part of my Norfolk jacket, and, being spent, only penetrated beneath the skin, and I was able to remove it with my penknife. The other buried itself out of sight in my left breast. It did not bleed much externally. It was painful at times, but I did not take any measures to have it extracted, and after a lapse of thirteen years it grew out and was removed without pain. It proved to be a little drop of lead, about the size of No. 1 shot.

This adventure was all over in less time than it takes to read the account of it, and we continued our journey in the increasing heat, and alighted at the new school in Karyetein at eleven o'clock, having ridden the whole distance from Palmyra in a little over twelve hours, including interruptions.

My first care on reaching Karyetein was to have my mare sponged down with soap and tepid water, and her back well washed with native wine. Then she was rubbed with a flannel cloth till she was perfectly dry, and her hoofs were anointed with olive oil. All this time she was feeding from her nose-bag, and gently moving about. By one o'clock we were ready to continue our journey; but it soon became apparent that I must continue it alone, for my friend and his steed were both thoroughly exhausted. I suggested that it would be a kind act for him to wait and escort the ladies past danger, during the remainder of the journey, and my friend acquiesced; and so, after the formidable formalities of leave-taking, the sheikhs and local functionaries, mounted on horses with gay trappings, accompanied me as I cantered out of Karyetein, at four minutes past one on Friday.

For the first hour I met several parties of mounted travellers, but in the baking heat we scarcely exchanged words. On the hill-sides there were flocks of goats, with tinkling bells, and here and there foul vultures were engaged in gorging themselves on the carrion of animals that had fallen by the way. A few pin-tailed grouse flew out of our way, and here and there I saw Persian larks; but the way became fearfully dreary, and as monotonous as the Pacific Ocean. Sometimes I felt as if I were derelict in the middle of a vast sea. There was no trace of human beings, or indeed of any beings, and no help could have come to me from man, had I needed help.

At four o'clock I met a wild-looking caravan of about fifty camels. Far down the plain before me I had seen them resting during the fierce heat, but they met me in motion about a mile and a half from their resting-place.

They had with them some women and children, but they were a most filthy, cut-throat-looking party. I saluted them, but they scowled at me and did not return my salutation. We passed, however, without damage given or received.

When I approached the resting-place of the caravan, I saw a striking illustration of the eagles gathering to their prey. The surly-looking party had left behind them a dying or dead camel. It was a bright Syrian day, and there was not a speck on the sky from horizon to horizon. But soon a vulture appeared, so high up in the blue vault that it did not seem bigger than a lark. Whether guided by scent or by sight, it came without delay, and with unerring precision steered its course to the dead camel. A veritable bolt from the blue, it dropped on its victim.

But the feast was not to be a solitary affair. Soon the air became filled with vultures, screaming and hastening to their prey, and, foul in talon and red in beak, they greedily settled on their victim. I allowed my mare to walk while watching the guests assembling, and when I passed the meeting-place the great birds were feeding as eagerly as if they had been at the Lord Mayor's banquet or a Corporation dinner.

It was pleasant to reflect during the remainder of the journey, when I saw vultures watching me from the cliffs, that a fatal accident to either myself or mare would not pass unappreciated. In fact, the vultures of the desert are as eager to take advantage of a passing misfortune or calamity, as are the vultures and sharks in civilized society.

And have they not their uses, in helping kindly nature to bury dead things out of sight?

In another hour I passed the foundation of a ruin, near which we had an interesting adventure, a few days before, on our way to Palmyra. Our ladies were riding about a mile ahead. We were all fresh, and ready for any adventures that might turn up.

Suddenly we saw our ladies leave the beaten track, and gallop off to the left into the desert at a splendid pace, with a tally-ho! We all put spurs to our horses and galloped furiously after them. The ladies stopped shyly at a little hollow, beside something that seemed to be moving. When we arrived we saw a sad object, not, however, wanting in a comic element.

Our ladies had actually discovered a naked man. He was a soldier, and had been carrying a government message from Jerûd to Karyetein; but some Bedawîn had taken his arms, mule, and clothes, and left him like Adam in innocence, before he bethought him of the fig-leaves.

What were we to do with this derelict waif of humanity? It was suggested that the ladies who had found him should cast lots for him; but it was a matter for something beyond jesting. Our native escort was disposed to leave him where he was, to feed the vultures, a score of which were soaring around.

Fortunately I had taken a waterproof coat with me, which I was not likely to require, and it served him for a complete suit. I happened also to have taken a half loaf in my pocket, at luncheon time, to feed my mare with when walking beside her, as was my wont.

The poor fellow was weak with hunger, and unable to walk; but, clothed in my waterproof, with my mare's luncheon in his hand, he was hoisted on to one of the baggage mules, and carried into Karyetein. His gratitude knew no bounds, but our sense of satisfaction at acting the Good Samaritan was an exceeding great reward. We received no official thanks for rescuing the soldier.

SOFFIT OF SIDE DOOR OF THE TEMPLE.

SQUARE ENTABLATURE IN GREAT TEMPLE.

CHAPTER XX.

CANTERING down the dreary plain, towards Jerûd, I came in sight of two horsemen who were riding before me. As I was going much faster and steadier than they, I gained rapidly on them, and at last overtook them. They were splendid-looking fellows, well mounted and well armed. They carried, in addition to their spears, and daggers, and horse-pistols, the *dabbous*, which was the weapon I feared most in Syria. The *dabbous* of Arabia corresponds to the genuine shillelah of Ireland. Its growth is watched over for years. Branches are removed, leaving the single stem, and when the root has become large and bulbous, the sapling is taken up, seasoned, and dressed. Then steel spikes are driven into it, and the heads, which stand out, are filed to rough, angular points.

The *dabbous* is a much more powerful and deadly weapon than the shillelah. I cannot say that I ever feared the firearms of the Arabs. They always seemed to be more formidable to friend than to foe. And the spear, notwithstanding all that has been said in its praise, is an unwieldy and ineffective arm. But the *dabbous* is a lethal weapon, and one blow of it is sufficient for either man or horse.

Travellers have plenty of room to pass each other in the desert, without inconvenience, and so I attempted to give a wide berth to the horsemen on their right; but they circled round to the right, and drawing up their horses in front of me, so as to bar my way, one of them shouted to me, with a voice of command, "*Shallih, ya Franji!*" ("Strip, O Frank!")

In the desert, as I have already said, no law is recognized but that of the strong arm and keen blade, and opportunity is often the occasion of violence. The Arabs will not enter into a contest lightly, unless the chances are greatly in their favour; but being two to one, and fortified with all the orthodox weapons of their calling, they thought they saw a fine opportunity for transferring to themselves my mare, my clothes, and my arms, with pocketfuls of money besides.

I knew well what "*Shallih*" meant. A party of Arabs had, on one occasion, surprised my colleague, Dr. Crawford, of Damascus, at a well in the desert. They screamed "*Shallih*" at him and his companions. The companions who showed signs of resistance were knocked over with spears, and then they peeled off every stitch and shred of garment that they wore, and humbly handed all to the robbers. Dr. Crawford would not strip; but his naked companions, seeing that the Arabs were going to kill him, removed all his garments, as he stood passive and motionless — even his boots and socks — and handed all over to the lords of the desert. He pleaded for his hat, as the heat was fierce, and it was of no use to them; but they ran their spears into it, and tore it into small fragments.

"*Shallih!*" shouted again one of my would-be despoilers, the words hissing from between his white teeth as we sat on our steeds staring at each other.

Keeping my finger on the trigger, and my eye on the robbers, I said, very slowly and calmly: "You are both absolutely in my power. I can fire twenty shots with this gun, and six with this revolver, before you have time to lift a hand. Ask pardon from God, and plant your spears instantly in the ground, and I will spare you."

There was a space of ten or fifteen yards between us. I lifted my gun, and my mare, thinking I was going to fire, stood steady as a rock. Instantly both men stuck their spears into the ground, and, leaping off their horses, ran towards me as if to kiss my hand or stirrups.

"Stand back," I shouted; "leave your rusty old daggers and pistols with your spears, picket your horses, and come and eat with me."

On several critical occasions in Syria, both when alone, and in company with others, I succeeded in averting bloodshed by an assumption of authority. The two would-be robbers did as they were told, and then followed me to a hillock, two hundred yards or so from their horses. I spread out my biscuits, dates, and cheese, and we all three sat down to the frugal fare. They added dried olives and salted pistachios to the feast. They handed me some of the salted pistachios, and as soon as I had put one into my mouth, they said we were brothers, and then they proceeded to kiss my hand. I then felt perfectly safe with them, and proceeded to show them the mystery of my arms, telling them how glad I was that I had not been obliged to slay them.

One of them said, "Are you a Franji?" "No," I replied, "I am an Inglizi."

"Ah," said he, "you are ruled by a woman, live on calico, and drink brandy."

I responded: "My people never '*Shallih*' at the bidding of another, or show their backs to a foe, or take what is not their own. They make calico, and build ships, and cultivate the ground, and live in peace without fear. Some of them, I added, are not Christians, and they get drunk and make others drunk, and try to '*Shallih*' the weak, and either flee to other countries, or get shut up in prisons."

"Are you," he asked, "one of the Nazarites, who worship images and saints?"

"No," I said; "I am a Christian. We worship God only, and if you come to my church in Damascus you will see no pictures and hear no mention of saints."

"Do you believe in Muhammed?" he asked.

"Yes," I said; "I believe in Muhammed as a famous

Arab. He slaughtered the idolatrous Nazarites who had departed from the pure and holy religion of Jesus Christ; but he was a gross, cruel, and licentious Bedawi."

"Our law," said the robbers, "permits us to take by force from a hostile tribe, from the people of a village, from a desert caravan, and from a traveller like yourself. It is lawful spoil, not theft, is it not?"

I said: "Your law is cowardly, and cruel, and cannot have the approval of God, whatever Muhammed may have thought. It permits you to rob the weak. Christ's law is, 'Thou shalt love thy neighbour as thyself,' and he enjoins on all his followers to do to others what they would wish others to do to them."

"W'Allah, is that so?" ejaculated both at the same time. "We have heard that two great princes contend in your country for the mastery. Prince Kladstone wants to make all the Turks Nazarites, and the Jew prince wants to make all the Nazarites Turks. Is it so?"

I tried to explain that Christians were never made by the sword, as Muhammedans had been, but by love, faith, and voluntary surrender; and then, giving to one the Gospel of St. John in Arabic, and to the other the Gospel of St. Matthew, and exacting from both a promise that they would read the portions, I remounted my mare and galloped off.

Long afterwards, one of the two recognized me in Hamah when I was travelling with Subhi Pasha. He attached himself to me with the most dog-like fidelity, and it was he who procured for me the gypsum by which

I was able to take casts of the Hittite inscriptions. He assured me that he and his companion had agreed on the distribution of my arms, money, and clothes, and on the disposal of my mare. When we met in Hamah he had read the Gospel of St. John with delight, and still carried the portion on his person.

The benedictions fell as thick at our parting as the maledictions had fallen at our meeting. Firmness with kindness works miracles even in the desert.

My mare galloped for hours along the homeward track. The scenery was bleak, barren, and desolate, with no living thing except the *jerboas*, or ground rats, that sat at the mouths of their holes, and whisked in when one came near. The sun was sinking behind the western mountains, and after it disappeared the brief but glowing twilight faded into darkness; a cold wind swept across our path; but my mare went forward with the steadiness and untiring energy of a steam-engine. Such is blood.

I became very sleepy, and slept for hours in the saddle, but occasionally I was suddenly brought to consciousness by my mare stumbling into the holes of the *jerboas*.

That was the longest night I ever remember, but the dawn came at last, and the sweet and beautiful plain of Damascus was in view, and in it all the trees of the forest and the garden blended their many shades of colour, and extended for many a mile, and held the desert at bay. And the great pearly domes and graceful minarets rose from out the ocean of emerald green that surged around and over the city, and Hermon, grand in its snowy shroud,

PALMYRA AND ZENOBIA.

gleamed beyond. And along the dusty tracks, beneath spreading walnuts, and past tumbling cascades, we held on our way, and entered the city as the sun touched the snowy crest of Hermon, and the criers from the minarets summoned the faithful to prayers.

SOLITARY COLUMN.

BAB ES-SHURKI, DAMASCUS.

ADVENTURES AMONG THE RUINS OF BASHAN.

CHAPTER XXI.

I HAD made complete preparation for a thorough inspection of the ruins of Bashan, and for becoming acquainted with their inhabitants. I had undertaken several preliminary visits, and had gained the confidence and friendship of most of the sheikhs and spiritual chiefs of the Druzes. With my colleague, the late Rev. J. O. Scott, I had formed projects for occupying the whole of that interesting district with a network of schools, which should receive our constant surveillance. Circumstances prevented this plan being carried out.

I resolved, however, to go and offer the Scriptures to every individual in all that region. The Rev. Prof. Andrew Harper, then an Australian student, who had completed his studies in Scotland for the ministry, and who was giving a few months to the study of Oriental languages in Damascus, previous to his return to his own land, eagerly entered into my project, and zealously assisted me throughout. The British and Foreign Bible Society placed a colporteur at our disposal, leaving me to choose the man. I chose Khalîl Dawoud, a member of our church in Rasheiya, whom we had formerly employed as colporteur at the expense of the same society.

When we were about to start we made the acquaintance of a pleasant party of Englishmen, who were travelling for the purpose of growing beards, and for other similarly cogent reasons. We all agreed to start on the following morning, and cross the "field of forays" together, to Burâk; but their master the dragoman determined otherwise, fearing the length and danger of the way. The next morning we waited for our new companions till an hour past the appointed time, and then started alone. As soon as the dragoman perceived that we were gone, he brought his party to my house to assure them of the fact also, and then taking them a few hours out of the city, encamped them for the night by a miasma swamp.

We left 21 Straight Street on the 4th of April, about half-past ten o'clock A.M. As we passed along the street eastward, we encountered a string of camels entering the city, laden with olive-wood for fuel. The husbandman during the fruit season marks the trees that are unfruitful, gives them special attention and cultivation, and if they still continue to "cumber the ground," they are cut down, and carried into the city on the backs of animals, and sold by weight as fire-wood.

It is not pleasant meeting a row of camels with these

SKETCH ROUTE OF BASHAN.

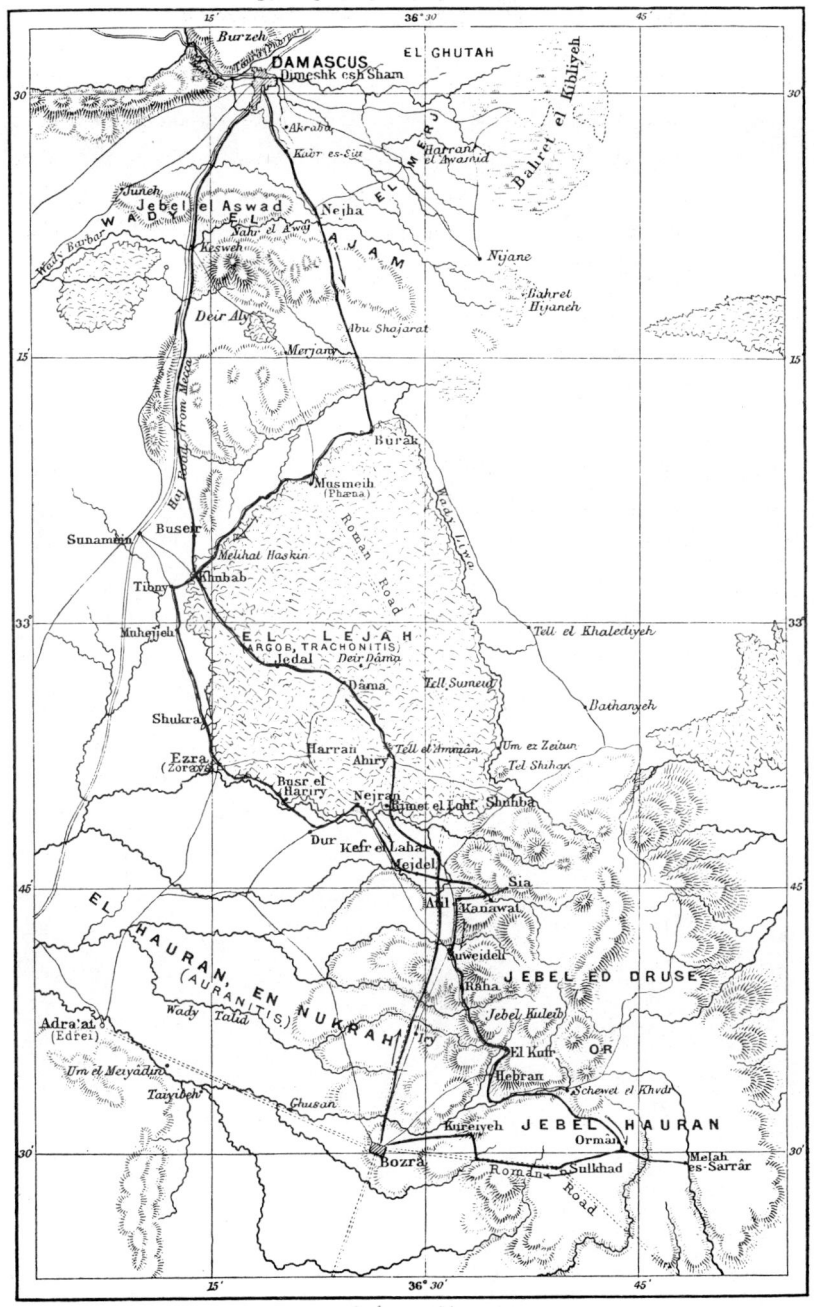

crushing loads. Their cushioned feet make no noise on the pavement, and they swing so in the narrow streets that there is always some dexterity required to evade them. They are conducted along, often without halter or bridle, and as they are exceedingly timorous, they dart and jerk about in the most unexpected manner, like huge uncouth birds.

Camels are very subject to panic. In the desert, a whole caravan of them will sometimes scamper off over the plain, in the wildest manner, like a flock of startled birds, and are only overtaken twenty or thirty miles off. A camel panic is a fearful event in the city. They rush along the narrow streets wildly, and nothing in their path need hope to live. The cry "The camels are coming!" precedes them, and the people rush into their shops and houses. The torrent of camels sweeps along till one slips and falls. The next in succession falls upon it, and so on till the last, when the street is one throbbing mass of living camel.

Here and there on the right we see sides of columns peeping out of the mud walls. These are the remains of the north side of the double colonnade that stretched for a mile down the two sides of the Roman *via recta*, and made "the street called Straight," in the days of Paul, a splendid thoroughfare, unsurpassed in the magnificent capitals of modern Europe. We passed out of the city by Bab es-Shurki (eastern gate), through one of the Roman side arches. The great central arch is broken down, and filled up with bits of columns and blocks of Roman masonry. The other side arch is entire and filled up. Through this gate Khaled, "the sword of the Lord," entered by treachery in A.D. 634, and filled the adjoining streets with Christian blood; and near this, in 1148, the Crusaders, under Baldwin III., made their last feeble and vain attempt to capture the city.

The Crusaders carved the *fleur-de-lis* on a stone outside the eastern gate, and they scattered coins in the ditch, where they are sometimes picked up, but they left no other memorial at Damascus.

As we looked down the walls, in which we recognized pieces of the Roman period, we saw houses on the ramparts, and windows overhanging the ditch. From such a place was Paul let down on the night of his memorable escape from Damascus.

Our road lay through the native Christian cemetery. It is a horrible field of death. Many of the vaults are wide open, tainting the air for miles around, and attracting the dogs and other wild animals from afar.[1]

Among these vaults is an oblong building arched over with a slight curve at the top, and with a little air-hole in the end. Into this were gathered the fragments of some seven thousand Christians murdered in 1860.

[1] The people believe that the rapid decomposition of the body indicates a happy state of the soul, and it is a cause of great grief and scandal to the friends of any one should his body be found after the lapse of a year not sufficiently decomposed. Probably it is to prevent such a calamity that the cemetery is left unwatched, and the bodies uncoffined, a prey to wild beasts.

RUNAWAY CAMELS IN THE DESERT.

When the order was given to stop the massacre, all the pieces of the mutilated Christians that the dogs had left were deposited in this mausoleum. There is an Arabic inscription on the soft limestone in the wall, now much defaced; but on my first visit to the place, eight years before, I copied it. It is in rhyme, and runs thus, literally translated: —

> "This is what the people of Shem (Damascus) have done unto us. O Lord, let not justice be lost unto us!"

In this we recognize the old Miltonic spirit expressed in the lines: —

> "Avenge, O Lord, thy slaughtered saints!"

On the other side of the way the ground is strewed with long, wedge-like stones, covered with Hebrew inscriptions dating back several centuries. This was the burying-ground of the Karaïte Jews, who have long since disappeared from Damascus.

In the corner of this large Jewish cemetery stands the neat little Protestant burying-ground. In the matter of burying the dead the Protestants have given an example of a more excellent way. The Protestant cemetery is surrounded by a high wall, overhung by fragrant walnuts. The ground is marked off for graves by rows of shady 'Pride of India,' and bordered by damask roses. All further attempts at ornamentation have been frustrated. Yew-trees, those "constant mourners of the dead," were planted, but they were soon carried off. The well that was sunk for the irrigation of shrubs and flowers was destroyed. The ornamental gravestones were broken, and the non-ornamental were stolen and sold.

In the midst of the chaos of neglected open graveyards a closed substantial door is a mark for fanatics, and so the cemetery door is thickly peppered with shot and slugs, and blue bullet marks appear on the stones at each side, showing fanaticism in excess of skill; and sometimes the gate used to be smashed in several times in one year.

To that little cemetery the mission and consular families have made large contributions, giving sad proof of the unhealthy climate of Damascus. In one row, side by side, lie eight of the missionaries' children. Near them is the grave of the Rev. J. Orr Scott's beautiful young bride; but he, though due to Damascus, lies far from her he loved so well, in the bare, red sand of Suez. The Rev. J. Frazer and wife in death are not divided. And there is here the grave of William Hamnets, an English mechanic and man of God, who was brought to Damascus by an Arab company to set up machinery, and lodged in a feverish sty, till he died.

And here lies Buckle, who, with much pretentious scholarship, erected a literary pyramid with its base upwards, and received the last kind offices from the people whom he had laboured hard to misrepresent, by means of his wondrous stores of second-hand learning, and by all the arts of a fascinating style.

By the side of this man of letters, spoiled chiefly by the adulation of women, lies the unfortunate Countess Teleky, in accordance with a wish she had often expressed, even before her visit to Damascus.

At a short distance from these rests one of a different type, — William Broomfield, F.R.S., the kindly Christian gentleman and profound scientific scholar, whose memory is green in the love and esteem of all who knew him.

And here also lies the beautiful and cultured Lady Ellenborough, known at Damascus as "The Honourable Mrs. Digby el-Miserab," who lost her way in London in the seething slough of fashionable society, and after a wild, passionate, and reckless career, closed her days in peace, as the wife of a Bedawi sheikh, and died in the Christian faith, "in sure and certain hope of a blessed resurrection."

We were now fairly on our way — colporteur, cook, and two muleteers — when the colporteur, seated between his two boxes on his little horse, dashed past us like a bolt, disappearing in a cloud of dust, which streamed behind him like the smoke of a railway train. "Bravo!" shouted the muleteers; but it was not a case for bravo, as the race was entirely involuntary on the part of the rider. He soon appeared again, shooting off at a tangent in another direction, and presently, with a general crash, the horse disengaged himself from rider and boxes, and then turned round in the most gallant manner to learn the result.

We rode up, fearing the worst; but as Dawoud had only fallen on his head, there was no harm done. A leathern water-bottle, however, had got crushed in the fall, and its precious contents, Scripture type of the evanescence of life, was spilled upon the ground, and could not be gathered.

The gardens and orchards through which we now passed were very beautiful. The light-green apricots, and dark-green walnuts, and silvery, evergreen olives, interspersed here and there with red-brown pomegranates and white-stemmed poplars, quivered in the bright spring morning, each leaf catching from its neighbour sunbeams, and each flinging back to each burnished diamonds; and beneath the trees was the broad, level carpet of green, fresh corn; and Hermon, in his glittering shroud, ever and anon shone like burnished silver through the vistas formed by the arching branches. In front, at a distance of seven or eight miles, the sombre wall of the black mountain seemed to cross our path, each ravine flooded with wondrous tints, from roseate and pale violet to deepest indigo.

In about an hour we passed the Moslem village Babîla, with its dome and minaret and saint's tomb. By the saint's tomb there was a tree with thousands of rags fastened to its branches. Every one who fastens a rag to a branch of this tree does a meritorious act, and some of these festoons are sometimes taken away to serve as charms.

Passing the village, we were in the open, level plain. Away to the left, in front, the mirage was playing fantastic tricks with the little conical tells of the Safa, elevating them into considerable mountains, mantled with groves, and crowned with villages and fortresses, and girt around with seas, which reflected the shadows of the trees and towns, and gave to the whole a wonderful appearance of reality. I never passed that way without seeing the mirage in one form or another, but always wonderful.

Leaving the cultivated ground, we entered on a part of the plain where the grass grew deep and thick as in an Irish meadow. Large flocks of cattle and camels were browsing about, and innumerable swarms of sheep and goats covered the face of the whole district. After this the ground was thickly covered with scented southernwood, the little shrubs being about a foot and a half high, through which our horses had to pick their steps. Here numerous storks, called by the Arabs "the father of luck," stepped out of our way in a stately, dignified manner, and eyed us with curiosity from a distance of twenty yards, as we passed.

We struck the basaltic formation at one o'clock, and in half an hour more, having passed through a ruin on the eastern spur of Jebel el-Aswad, we alighted for lunch in a little grove of poplars at Nejha. Nejha was the last village in the Damascus plain on our road. It was built on a rising ground, and contained about eight houses and forty souls, all Moslems. A duct, led off from the 'Awaj, supplied it with a little dirty water. The men had an evil look, and two of them, with long guns and heavy bludgeons, were very anxious to take us in charge; but we disliked their looks, and declined their escort—of course with great civility, explaining to them the nature of our guns, which blazed away at the rate of thirty shots a minute, rendering guard or escort unnecessary.

The women had a gipsy appearance. One blue calico shirt, closely fitting at the neck, and extending to their toes, was their only garment. A sooty-looking cloth was wrapped round their heads, leaving the crowns, that never felt a comb, bare, and permitting the hair to hang down their backs in coarse plaits. They wore an ornament stuck in their noses, and all had bracelets of glass or brass. Their tawny faces were horribly tattooed, from the lips down, and they had sharp, quick, restless eyes, such as are seen in confirmed pickpockets; but they had the most lovely teeth, perfect in form, and white as the purest ivory. Unlike village women generally, they were as fanatical as their sisters in Damascus, and we could not get from them a pleasant look or word.

The village contains no ancient ruins, but it has two Latin inscriptions on an inverted column in the little mosque. They contain the names of Diocletianus and Maximianus, Constantinus, Constantius, and Constans. The column may have been brought from a distance.

A few minutes after leaving Nejha we reached a broken bridge over the almost dry bed of the 'Awaj. This river has its origin in the springs of Hermon, passes Kefr Howar and Sasa, and flows into the Hejâny marsh. It is very tortuous in its windings, and hence is called 'Awaj, namely, "the crooked." For several years this river has been called by travellers the Pharpar, and has found its way into modern maps under that name, without, as far as I can ascertain, a single claim, logical or archæological, to be so honoured.

"Are not Abana and Pharpar, rivers of Damascus, better than all the waters of Israel?" The language of Naaman, the Syrian captain, was, no doubt, a jealous burst of patriotic indignation; but the great general would not have made himself ridiculous in the eyes of his followers by ranking the brook 'Awaj higher than the river Jordan, or by declaring that it was a river in which he could bathe at all. Nor would he have called it a river of Damascus, seeing that it is distant from the city a ride of three hours, and interposes between itself and the plain of Damascus the whole range of the Jebel el-Aswad. On the other hand, the meanest follower in the Syrian's train would have endorsed his leader's boast, as would every Damascene in the city to-day, that the Abana and Pharpar were better than all the waters of Israel.

In riding through that heated land I was never able to resist the temptation of a cold bath, when one offered; but after two attempts to bathe in the 'Awaj, I can safely say that its waters have now no attraction for me. On my first attempt I lay down on the pebbly bed of the river, held to the bottom by my nails, and let the water and sand run over me. I came out of the turgid stream as if I had been whitewashed. On my second attempt I plunged into what seemed to me a considerable pool, and found myself up to the knees in mud, surrounded by tortoises and frogs and leeches. If Naaman meant the 'Awaj when he declared the Syrian waters superior to those of Palestine, he was certainly open to experience.

236 PALMYRA AND ZENOBIA.

The rivers of Damascus are its one great and abiding charm, and every Damascene loves them passionately. The Barada is split up into different channels, several miles above the city, and these all flow through Damascus, bearing different names as rivers, and are supposed to have different degrees of excellence. The river whose

VILLA ON THE BARADA, DAMASCUS.

water is most prized is called the Abanias (doubtless the Abana), and passes through what was once a fashionable suburb, the "Southern West End" of Damascus, overhanging the green *merj*. Another river of Damascus passes through what was the northern West End suburb of the city, until Tamerlane destroyed it. It is now called

THE BARADA AND MERJ.

the river Taura, which name we find in an old Arabic version of the Bible instead of Pharpar; and Benjamin of Tudela identified the Taura with the Pharpar.

The "Wady Barbar," said to be at the source of the 'Awaj, and which was supposed to contain in its name the word Pharpar, is now known to have no existence; and as there are at Damascus a number of rivers,[1] known by distinct and different names, there need be no question that the same rivers with various names flowed through the city in the days of Naaman and Elisha.

And there is no reason to doubt that the great Damascene mentioned in his haughty boast the two rivers he had most enjoyed. And if the various rivers of the Syrian capital now sparkle in fifty-eight public baths during the decadence of the city, who will doubt that the same sparkling waters were as extensively used for purposes of luxury in the palmy days of the Ben Hadad dynasty? Nor is it for a moment to be supposed that the great Syrian leader, who knew the refreshing charms of the Damascus rivers, would mention as on a parity with one of them the brawling little 'Awaj.

[1] Nahr (river) Taura, Nahr Abanias, Nahr Kanawât, Nahr Yazid, Nahr Barada, Nahr Deirany, Nahr Akrabany. Each is called a river.

COIN OF ARETAS.

CHAPTER XXII.

AS we crossed the river 'Awaj into a rich loamy plain beyond, we came up with a caravan of mules and donkeys laden with jars, on their way to the Hauran. The men rushed towards us as we approached and made an attempt to kiss our feet and stirrups; and then followed a little torrent of jerked-out ejaculations, along with which the hands were held up to heaven, thanking God for sending us to be their protectors.

One of our servants shouted out, "God is great," the usual solace for all difficulties, and we were in the act of riding on past them, when they appealed to us so piteously that we had not the heart to leave them. They pointed to their little donkeys, and their fragile burdens, and told us how many mishaps they had had on that same road, on their way to Burâk. They assured us that the Arabs would without doubt sweep down upon them from behind some hill, if we left them, "And, oh! my lord, we have only you and Allah to trust in." Their appeal was successful, and we lingered with them, much against our will.

They had been waiting for us all the morning, as our muleteers, who were their friends, had informed them of the strong escort that our travelling companions would have, so they had ventured to come the nearer but more dangerous way in hopes of being protected.

Our route lay over a high stony table-land, with hills to right and left. As we proceeded we met an almost naked shepherd, walking towards Damascus, followed by his sheep, from which our potters first inferred that the country was safe, as a shepherd and sheep could move through it unmolested; and secondly that there was great danger, as the shepherd was only coming from some tribe in the vicinity.

A deputation of potters now approached us, headed by their most eloquent spokesman, who by the most fierce and extravagant tales, in which they or their ancestors had put to flight or slaughtered hosts of Bedawîn, endeavoured to arouse our valour, or at least to prevent it from "oozing out at our finger ends." When I hinted to them that my mare was very timorous, and very fleet, and would, no doubt, bolt at the first sight of the Arabs, but expressed the hope that from their hereditary proficiency in the art of disposing of their enemies, they would never miss me, they suddenly changed their tone, and told how they and their ancestors had been "killed" by the Arabs without any power of retaliation.[1]

[1] An Arab always speaks of a beating as a killing. "I ate a killing" is a very common phrase.

Of course every second word was punctuated with an oath. The spirit of "brag" had now seized our party, and they boasted and swaggered, and hurled great stones feebly at the heads of imaginary Bedawîn, and kept up a regular fusillade from their one gun; but they would have collapsed, like their earthen pots, before any serious blow. When we remonstrated with them that their tumultuating and firing were calculated to attract the enemy, they assured us that the Arabs would know from their firing that they were armed, and should they see us with them, they would take us for their armed escort. Thus what seemed to us folly was only strategy in their eyes.

Following some partridges on a ridge to the left, I found that there were artificial hollows in the ground, a few hundred yards from our path, in which a large number of Arabs might lie concealed, and pounce almost instantaneously on passers-by. Such a discovery suggested watchfulness and preparedness, especially as we were on one of the paths most frequented by the Arabs. My faith, however, in Bedawî attacks had been growing weaker and weaker for eight years, till I had almost become a confirmed sceptic. I knew that they seldom make a serious attack unless the odds are tremendously in their favour.

The most conspicuous object in view for a long time was a solitary tree, high up on the side of a hill to the right in front. The hill was called *Abu Shajarat*, "the father of one tree." This part of the desert was exceedingly stony and barren, but yet it showed signs of former occupation, by foundations of houses, by traces of fields, and by stone walls stretching miles in a straight line over hill and plain. We passed also a place where water could be had, and where there were numerous sheepfolds surrounded by circular single stone walls breast-high.

We now reached the spot celebrated for Bedawî gazzos (razzias). To the left there was a high conical hill, called Abu Muraj, behind which the Arabs lie in wait and form. A trustworthy man with good sight lies on the top of the hill, so as to be unseen from the road, and, when the proper moment arrives, he starts to his feet, and gives the signal, whereupon the Arabs sweep round the base of the hill with a fiendish noise, and with quivering lances make their sudden flank attack on the passing caravan. Clearing the hill, they find a piece of ground admirably suited for their peculiar hostile operations.

If the caravan is properly equipped and commanded, it forms instantly into a circular rampart, the animals being firmly braced the one to the other. The men who have guns fire away in succession as fast as they can over the backs of the mules and from under the bellies of the camels, and those who have no firelocks stand by their animals with clubs and stones, waiting for the onset at close quarters. Should the Bedawîn have the caravan at their mercy, and no blood-feud exists to embitter their feelings, they are seldom wantonly cruel. They approach with such shouts as, " Surrender, and we will spare your lives, and be content with the half of your loads"; "Give up your guns, and we will leave you your mules."

If an easy victory is not certain, the Bedawîn, chary of their own blood, but especially of that of their mares, gallop round and round the caravan, endeavouring to cut off stragglers, and making feints here and there at full gallop to break the living rampart, but in the moment of feigned assault they wheel their horses round on their own length and gallop off. The affair generally ends with much curvetting, much dust, and a horrid din.

But we had evidence before us that these gazzos do not always end so bloodlessly, for the district around is a cemetery. Here and there are black mounds, where friend and foe rest heaped together, as in more civilized lands, "after a glorious victory"; and in other places there are little mounds and solitary head-stones which mark the scene of insignificant skirmishes and foul murders.

We now descended to the level plain. Here I had an exciting chase after a bustard, about the size of a large fowl, called by the Arabs *hibari*. My mare was so excited at being taken from the rest that I could not fire from the saddle, and so I sprang to the ground and pursued it on foot. It kept its distance, about one hundred and fifty yards from me, and when I stopped it stopped too. At last I made a final effort down the hill, and gained upon it till there was only about one hundred yards between us, when it took to its wings, and flew about five hundred yards further, and so I was obliged to leave it.

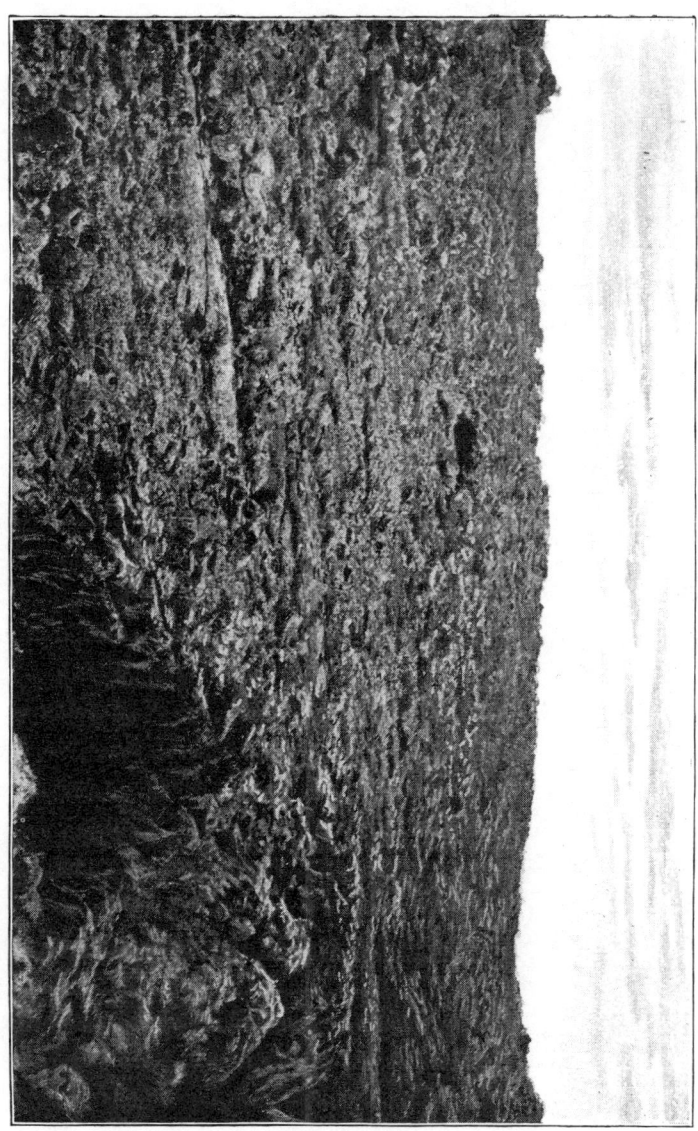

BASALT BED OF THE LEJAH.

The sun was sinking in the west when we reached the level plain. Before us a weird-looking, dark wall crossed our path like a low, gloomy sea-coast. A thin strip of green corn seemed to be sweeping like a sea around the headlands and up among the creeks. And the wondrous Lejah (Argob of the Hebrews, Deut. iii. 4, 14; Trachonitis of the Greeks) lay before us, having all the features of a sea — a troubled sea. From no place could we have had a more curious view of the Lejah. The setting sun touched the tops of the rocks and the bushes, and in contrast with the black shadows they shone like the crests of waves, and the dark shadows appeared like the deep furrows of the waves.

It was hard not to believe that the Lejah, as spread out before us, was a heavy sea, rolling great billows from west to east. The sun went down upon us as we neared the edge of the plain, and in the brief twilight we saw the heads of watchers looking out upon us from the rocks. We rode up a tortuous path unto the edge of the Lejah, and pitched our tent in the dark, among the ruins of Burâk.

We were surrounded by a motley crowd of muleteers and camel-drivers, who were waiting for the cover of the night to proceed to Damascus with their precious loads of wheat. Hearing that we had seen no Arabs on the way, the caravan filed off immediately. The people of Burâk also gathered sullenly round, but neither helped nor hindered us.

When I renewed my acquaintance with the sheikh, he

gave me to understand that their water was entirely exhausted; and though we were willing to pay for it at any price, we could only obtain about two pints, which had been treasured up all day in a dirty skin, having been carried seven or eight miles on the back of a donkey. The tea manufactured from this fluid was of a hue that would have delighted the eyes of a Persian, but its taste was strongly suggestive of leather broth, and as no amount of sugar would neutralize the flavour of raw hide, we swallowed down the bitter beverage like medicine.

Our attempts to sleep in Burâk proved even a greater failure than our attempts to make tea; for though the colonists of the place are not numerous, they have brought a very abundant and healthy supply of black and *white* fleas with them, which seem to live and thrive among the ruins of the town, rendering sleep all but impossible.

The first man I saw, in looking out from my tent, was a soldier whom I once found in the north of Syria robbing some peasant-women of truffles that they had spent the day in digging. The women appealed to me, and I forced the soldier in a somewhat high-handed manner to return the stolen property. I had therefore doubts as to the footing on which I should meet the bandit; but as soon as I issued from the tent, he came up and claimed me as an old friend.

We were at once reminded that we were in the Lejah — " the refuge " — the region to which Absalom fled after the murder of his brother, and the place where the ruffian soldier is safe, after having stabbed a shepherd to the heart for defending his sheep. That rock-girt land has been in all ages the home of the enemy of man, and there are few men in the whole district whose hands have not been defiled by some foul deed.

And never was land more suited to its inhabitants. Black discharges from the bowels of the earth "gloom the land," with a scene that might become the landscape of Dante's Inferno; and amid these scenes and landscapes lurk to-day assassins of every hue, and communities red from the perpetration of wholesale massacre. Nor is the right hand likely to forget its hideous cunning among these congenial scenes; for on my first visit to Burâk, the tall son of the sheikh, then a barefooted lad, boasted that a few days before he had killed four Arabs with his own hand, and the boast was confirmed by others with circumstances of time and place.

Leaving exact measurements and architectural details to the Palestine Exploration Fund, I could not help expressing disappointment with the actual ruins, especially after the exaggerated accounts of them which I had read.

The style of architecture is peculiar, but not wonderful. There is little wood, but much stone, in the region, and as security is the great end in view in building a house in the Lejah, the people find stone much more suitable than wood. It is curious, no doubt, to see stone roofs, and stone doors and windows, on a house, but it cannot be considered wonderful that the people made their houses of the material which was most abundant and most suitable to their wants.

The people of the Lejah built their houses as the feudal lords built their castles: they could fight outside the walls, retreat to their courts, and finally retire within the stone keep, and sleep soundly behind the stone doors and shutters. Thus the houses, though peculiar, are exactly suited to the circumstances of the country and the necessities of the people.

A few of the houses are in a sufficiently perfect state of preservation to enable one to get a good general idea of the habitations of Bashan. The walls of the houses are from three to five feet thick, and from eight to twelve feet high, built of squared basalt stones well fitted together. Stone plank-like slabs, three or four yards long and about half a yard broad, are laid across from wall to wall, and rest on a projecting cornice which runs around the room. In some of the houses there are very massive semicircular arches, on which the roof rests. The doors and windows, which are generally small, are of black stone. Some of the doors, however, even of private houses, are nearly six feet high.

The doors are generally folding, and they are hung by means of pivots, which project from the doors into holes in the lintels and thresholds. They are sometimes ornamented with panels and knobs and flowers, but those in Burâk are mostly plain, well-dressed solid slabs, from six to ten inches thick. A few of the houses had second stories, but owing to the accumulation of *débris* the lower stories of some of the houses are almost concealed.

As in all the villages of the Hauran, the houses seemed

to stand on a mound of black earth, while in reality they are built on the foundations of houses of a more remote antiquity. I descended in one place a depth of sixteen or eighteen feet, to see some pottery lately discovered, and I found the walls at that depth formed of enormous undressed and unsquared stones, unlike the stones of the superstructure, which are smaller in size, and have been better prepared for the walls.

Burâk must have been a town of considerable importance in comparatively peaceful times. It was built upon the rugged rampart that surrounds the Lejah with its "munition of rocks," and was thus easily defended. As far as we penetrated the dreadful lava bed at Burâk, we found few signs of cultivation, though there is pasturage for goats; but there are vast arable plains that sweep up like a sea to the rock-girt coast on which Burâk stands.

A few Druze families who now occupy Burâk cultivate a patch of the plain, within musket range of their houses, and are amply rewarded. They plough, and sow, and reap, with primed muskets slung from their shoulders; but if they were protected from the raids of the Arabs, thousands of men would here find a remunerative field for their labour. Even in comparatively peaceful times a good harvest may be gathered into the threshing-floors among the rocks, where the villagers can defend themselves.

The position of Burâk, on the edge of an immense fertile plain, must have rendered it an important town.

But it had other advantages. It was the nearest port to Damascus, on the coast of the Lejah, being the most northern town of that region. It also lay on the nearest route to Bathaniyeh, or the Druze mountain, and was thus an emporium of exports and imports. From these abiding causes of prosperity we should naturally suppose that Burâk, like Damascus, would be too tempting a prey to the destroyer to have many ancient buildings remaining; but as Burâk seems to have fallen early under the destroying blight of Islam, and never to have recovered, the ruins are of considerable antiquity.

There can be little doubt that most of the houses which are still standing were built in early Christian times, and when Christianity was triumphant; for we find on all the best houses crosses and other Christian emblems, which are evidently of the same date as the buildings themselves; and some of these crosses and Christian emblems are to be seen on lintels of doors, which have been so buried up that they are now lower than the surface of the streets. The Greek of the inscriptions appears to be that of the period between the second and fifth centuries of our era. The Kufic inscriptions were evidently scratched on the stones *in situ* in the walls, and do not, I believe, mark the date of any building in Burâk. All the coins and medals which I found in Burâk were those of Constantine and his immediate successors.

There is reason to conjecture that Burâk is the ancient Constantia, whose bishop, Solemus, was present at the Council of Chalcedon, in the fifth century (A.D. 451).

Hierocles places the episcopal city Constantia among the cities of Arabia, and by the side of Phæna, the modern Musmeih; and Mr. Waddington[1] remarks that inasmuch as the name Flavius is found on all the inscriptions of Burâk, it confirms the supposition that the town was founded or embellished by Constantine.

Whatever may have been the ancient name of the town, there is no doubt that the ruins which we now see are on the top of ruins older still, and in the walls of the most ancient-looking structures we see bits of lintels and fragments of ornaments rifled from more ancient structures.

Towards the outskirts of the town there are rude houses, sometimes built over caves, and against the stones of these houses no tool has ever been lifted up; but as these houses are composed of material in its primitive state, it would be equally bold to predicate either their great antiquity or otherwise. That the town is of great antiquity, however, does not admit of a doubt, since its structures date from the time of the Roman occupation of England. Nor will it be doubted that beneath that raised mound are buried the remains of one of the "threescore cities" that once existed in Bashan, and which still exist under changed circumstances, sometimes under different names.

The present name of Burâk signifies *tanks* or *reservoirs*, a name which did not suggest to us that our poor horses would have to pass the night without water, or that we

[1] *Inscriptions Grecques et Latines*, p. 576.

ourselves would have to put up with a few cupfuls of greasy fluid that no dog with any self-respect would drink. Names in this country are generally significates, and south-east of the town are extensive aqueducts leading to a large tank or reservoir in the suburb. The aqueducts are, of course, broken down and neglected, and the reservoir was filled up with stones by Ibrahim Pasha, the Egyptian (of whom more anon), as a war measure, when he sought in vain to bend the Druzes to his will.

This barbarous custom of destroying the water supplies of an enemy has been practised in this land since the days of Abraham (Gen. xxvi. 15). The Philistines of war stopped up the wells, and the innocent and the guilty suffer together. And this act of impotent wrath on the part of the great Egyptian has rendered this village uninhabitable, except after rainy years.

When Burckhardt and Porter visited this place, they found it entirely uninhabited. When I visited it last it contained six or seven families who had come from Aleppo, under the leadership of Abu Khattar, their sheikh. For the first few years after their arrival they were comparatively happy, as they had only the Arabs to contend against. If the Arabs came in small bands, they fought them, and a fight is always popular; but if they came in large numbers, they gave them *blackmail*, known in Arabic by the name "*brotherhood.*" The government has now found them out, and a good deal of their time is spent in concealing their property and their numbers from the official tax-gatherers, who are, as a rule, only legalized brigands. From force of habit, they attempted to conceal their numbers from us, but we shall not be far wrong in estimating the entire population at sixty souls.

Leaving the village, we wound down over the rope-like lip of the Lejah, into the margin of the plain. On the previous year, four days later in the year, when I visited Burâk, the whole plain was covered with a little lilac flower which made the air heavy with its rich perfume. Scarcely a blade of it was now to be seen as we passed along. The difference may be accounted for by the former spring coming after a wet winter, and the latter succeeding a dry winter. Swarms of Greek partridges were running over the rocks about us, and as we did not wish to abandon our servant, who was delayed in the village settling for the teapotful of dirty water that we got the night before, we occupied the time during our halt in knocking over a few partridges for dinner. We abstained, however, from killing more than we needed.

The process of bagging partridges in Syria is very different from the same operation in England. The partridge in Syria is a larger and stronger bird than the common partridge at home, and as game laws are unknown, the birds look sharply after partridge preservation themselves. An old cock, with a good eye and voice, is generally stationed on a prominent rock, and when danger approaches he gives a peculiar cry of warning, and then slips down off the stone, and runs from the danger, and all the partridges in the neighbourhood follow the sentinel's example. They run about as fast as a common dog, and the sportsman must go at the speed of a greyhound to overtake them.

The usual and most successful method is to walk slowly towards the partridge till it disappears behind the rocks, then rush with all your might to the spot where you last

LEJAH PARTRIDGES.

saw it, and continue running till the bird rises. This it does with a tremendous screech and whirr, and you must fire quickly, or it is gone like a rocket.

The natives conceal themselves about wells and springs, and slaughter the poor birds when they come to drink, and they sometimes employ a decoy partridge in a cage to call its free friends to their doom.

Those who, like us, travelled through the wilds of Syria without the luxurious *impedimenta* of a dragoman, find these partridges, which are equally distributed over the country, a great source of comfort and economy, especially as without them we should have had to buy a whole sheep, and slaughter it, every time we wished to indulge in the luxury of a meat dinner.

The cook sat on his mule and plucked the partridges as we went along, and on our arrival at a village at night they were placed in a pot with rice and water, and a stew was soon prepared, which was always very palatable after a ride of thirty or forty miles. We soon procured our supply of partridges for the day, and galloped back to the village, to extricate our servant out of financial difficulties.

The statement that Druzes received no return for their hospitality sounds patriarchal in books, but is not at all in accord with the facts of our experience. When they expect to receive a revolver, or a telescope, or a pocket-compass, they do not permit money to be paid, lest they should not also get the valuable instrument. And they are also very generous to travellers with consular recommendations, or with consular influence, but they are thereby building up a debt of obligations which they will take good care shall be cancelled by the consul. The Druzes, however, are the most generous and most hospitable and most gentlemanly of all the inhabitants of the land, and I hope I shall not be detracting from their virtues when I say that we were always able to pay in full for everything we received in the Hauran.

STONE WINDOW (HAURAN).

CHAPTER XXIII.

ON leaving Burâk we proceeded in a south-westerly direction, along El-Luhf with the raised edge of the great lava-bed on our left, and an immense ocean-like plain on our right. It was impossible to get rid of the impression that we were moving along the tide-mark between a great ocean and its rugged shore.

The Lejah (Argob), which is raised twenty or thirty feet above the plain, runs out into promontories, and is indented with bays and creeks, and all the headlands have their ruined towers, like lighthouses, and the bays have their little black ruins, like fishing-villages; and low grey tents here and there in angles of bays and creeks, propped up with sticks, reminded us of nets and fishing-tackle drying; and out on the ocean to the right, camels, steering in different directions, and greatly magnified by the miragy atmosphere, heaved and tossed about like boats; the thick, fat smoke of an occasional Arab's fire hung black in the air, like the smoke of a steamboat starting on a voyage; and the small, round stones on which our horses stumbled ever called to mind the "pebbly beach."

The real objects around us had all the marks of sea and shore; but, in addition, as usual, the mirage was playing all kinds of fantastic tricks, throwing up beautiful wooded beaches with castellated crests, and spreading out glassy seas which mirrored all the surrounding objects.

We coasted along, keeping clear of the headlands, crossing bay after bay in succession. In several of the bays were little Arab encampments of five or six tents each. The men were away with their flocks, and the women, who were hideously tattooed and frightfully dirty, were occupied in churning goat's-milk. The churn is a goat's skin which has been drawn off the goat like a stocking. All the openings of the skin are tied except the neck, and when the milk is put into the skin, the neck opening is tied too. A woman then gets down on her knees beside the skin and rolls it backwards and forwards with her hands on the ground, which is the churning process. She uses her fingers as a strainer to separate the butter from the milk, and she then places the butter separately in another skin.

I have sometimes partaken of such butter, but it smells of camel and tastes of leather, and no one could look at it without sympathizing with the Yankee, who guessed it would be better to serve the butter in one ball and the hairs in another, and then he could exercise his discretion.

The first time we passed this way we had a most

exciting chase. Our party consisted of several clergymen and a celebrated painter and his wife. I ascended a rising ground to get a view of the landscape, and just as I reached the top of the eminence I came face to face with an armed Bedawi. He was a scout sent on in advance by a party of Arabs who wished to pass that way, to see if the country was free of Druzes. As soon as he saw me, he galloped off in a most frightened manner, and I, not knowing what he might be, summoned our Druze escort, and we all started in pursuit, our lady companion among the foremost.

As long as the Bedawi kept his distance he made straight for his companions; but when he found we were gaining upon him, he doubled like a sly old partridge which wishes to decoy the enemy from its young. The day was bright and bracing. The ground inclined gently in the direction of the chase. The Arab, like the "man-slayer" fleeing before "the avenger of blood," bent to his horse's neck, parallel with his spear, and seemed to fly over the plain. The Druzes, like the avengers of blood, thundered along on his track. Our lady friend and her companions galloped along promiscuously in the rear, and thoroughly enjoyed the chase.

Those who have seen the excitement of huntsmen, after a miserable little hare or fox, can form some idea of the feelings in this wild chase, when the quarry was a son of Ishmael on his own ground, and our fellow-hunters were the chivalrous Druzes, his inveterate enemy. The Bedawi fled for dear life, but after a brief course he was brought

BEDAWIN OF THE HAURAN.

to the ground. He of course expected instant death at the hands of the Druzes, and he seemed to bear himself, when we came up, as if the bitterness of death were already past; but his manner instantly changed when he found that our presence secured his safety. We kept him as a hostage till near night, and then sent him away happy, with a good backshish.

Near the same place we came upon game of another kind — a large bustard and a flock of katha, or pin-tailed sand-grouse. This bustard was the first that my companion or I had ever seen at large, and so we stalked it carefully from different sides. We both got within long range of it, but did not succeed in bringing it down.

I have since seen the same magnificent birds in the wide plains bordering the Orontes. There the young chieftains of Hasya catch them with hawks, which seize the wing of the great bird and bring it to the ground. I succeeded, however, in getting several specimens of the katha, and I was the more anxious to have them, as I knew that Hasselquist and others had declared they were the quails by which the children of Israel were miraculously fed in the wilderness.

I once saw the katha migrating, and they seemed sufficiently numerous to feed all the hungry tribes of the desert. They swarm so thickly in the desert that the Arabs snare them, and knock them down with sticks, and sell them for one half-penny apiece. At Haushhoush, near Bora, Burckhardt declares, "The quantity of kathas is beyond description; the whole plain seemed sometimes to rise, and far off in the air they were seen like moving clouds." Russell says, "A donkey's load of them may sometimes be taken at one shutting of the clasp-net."

They lay their eggs on the desert, and so thickly are they strewed over the ground, that they are gathered every morning like manna. The Arabs go forth two and two, carrying a skin between them, with its mouth open like a sack. Other Arabs, men, women and children, scamper about, picking up the eggs, which are of a black-greenish colour, and as large as pigeons' eggs, and throw them into the bags. The eggs are, of course, all broken up, but the compound is strained through a hair sieve into other skins, and then served out like molasses for use.

The finest specimen I got was nine and a half ounces weight, and between the size of a partridge and a blue rock pigeon. Its colours and tints were very beautiful. A broad band of chestnut, edged with dark green, encircled the breast, and the upper surface of the body was streaked with alternate bars of yellow and green and silver grey, and on the centre of the feathers were yellow, heart-shaped spots. When flying, it shouts "Katha, katha!" from which sound it takes its Hebrew and Arabic name, and it takes its English name, "pin-tailed," from the fact that the two central feathers of the tail are elongated about seven inches, and stand out forked.

We found its flesh dark and tasteless, like that of an old pigeon, and much inferior to partridge. There are many circumstances in favour of these being the quails of Scripture, but I would suggest that the kathas are the kath of Scripture, birds strictly unclean to the Israelites. The Hebrew name for quails is almost the same as the Arabic, and they migrate through Syria in enormous numbers every spring.

After a ride of two hours a raised promontory stretched out before us, and on its isthmus rose massive, black,

TEMPLE AT MUSMEIH — PHÆNA.

jagged ruins. We worked our way with difficulty along what was once a Roman road, and entered the city Musmeih, the ancient Phæna. The most conspicuous ruin was a temple in a good state of preservation, and the most striking object in the temple was an enormous scallop shell in the semicircular recess in the back side, opposite the

INTERIOR OF THE TEMPLE.

door. The columns which supported the half-fallen roof were curiously wreathed with oak chaplets near the top. There were niches round the walls for statues, which would, no doubt, be found Dagon-like, on their faces, if the *débris* were removed; and one still saw traces of yellow and purple frescoes on the plastered walls.

The spirit that seeks immortality by scribbling on walls was abroad when the temple was erected. Hence, on the lintel of the door, and over the niches to right and left of the door, and on the stones of the architrave, are long and beautifully cut Greek inscriptions. Some of these inscriptions contain forty lines, and in some of the lines there are over seventy letters. What a paradise for the "Dryasdusts"!

The inscriptions, however, are of great importance. The longest is a letter from the legate to the citizens touching the lodgment of soldiers and strangers. It begins thus: "Julius Saturninus to the Phænians in the metropolis of Trachon greeting." We ascertain that Trachonitis, of the Tetrarchy of Philip [1] (Luke iii. 1),

---

[1] I have a coin of this tetrarch struck at Cæsarea-Philippi in the twelfth year of his reign, and eighth A.D.

and the modern Lejah, are one and the same, and that Phæna was the Roman capital of that region. From another inscription we got the date of the building, which was a little after the middle of the second century of the Christian era.

From the date of this building we may approximate the dates of the other buildings.

The palace, or residence of the legate, now tenanted by swarms of blue rock-pigeons, is three stories high. Around this are grouped the other official residences of the city. The style of architecture is the same in all the buildings: well-built walls of moderate sized stones, roughly dressed; roofs of long, hewn, finely dressed stone slabs, closely jointed, and resting on cornices round the walls, and on central arches; stone windows and doors, whose pivots project from above and below into lintels and thresholds. These buildings of Musmeih have a light, airy appearance seldom met with elsewhere in Bashan.

The native part of the town is of the usual low, gloomy character, and the Roman structures beside them strike one at first sight as being of yesterday in comparison; but then the native houses are generally built of the undressed old stones brought in from the lava beds, and the structures look as aged as the materials of which they are built. On the other hand, the Roman part of the city has a fresh and modern appearance, being built with stones dressed and chiselled, and fresh from the quarry.

The accumulation of rubbish, however, is as deep about

the Roman houses as about the native houses, and in most cases deeper, which would seem to prove that the native houses are of more recent construction. And this view is not unreasonable when we consider how much less solidly they are built than the Roman structures, and how much less fitted they are to endure the wear of ages. On the other hand, the native houses stand on much higher mounds of accumulated rubbish than the Roman houses, — a fact which points to many reconstructions of the native houses.

These facts, however, in no way go to disprove the remote antiquity of the city, but only the remote antiquity of its present buildings. It may be added that there are structures in the suburbs, half cave, half house, which might be of any age. There is, however, little accumulation of rubbish about them, and they show few signs of occupation.

Musmeih is not a comfortable place to linger in. Tall men, armed with long guns, which reached a good distance, whether they carried far or not, followed us stealthily, and watched all our movements from afar. Their teeth were glittering white, and their black eyes had a peculiar, uncertain light. Their only garment was a shirt, reaching from neck to heel, which, from colour and circumstance, seems to have been born at their birth, and to have grown with their growth. Through this garment peeped lithe and brawny limbs of a dark olive colour. A camel's-hair rope two or three times round the head, and a broad leathern girdle, with knives and charms pendant, completed their toilets. They were all barefooted, and as they were little encumbered with flesh or garments, they ran over the ruins like tigers.

When approaching a group of ruins, you heard the crowd following with such a tumultuous noise, and with such vigour of epithets, that you supposed they were coming to blows. You turned and faced them, and they shied back like fish in a pond, and there followed a great calm. As you entered the ruin you saw a form emerging from it at the other side, and when you paused in the centre to get an idea of the structure, you know that a score of pairs of eyes were converging upon you, as in a focus, from every part.

They peeped at you from every window, from over the wall, in at the open doors, and down from the portions of the roof still remaining. When you looked at one of these gazers, he returned your look with furtive, pickpocket glances, and soon disappeared. When you moved on to another position, they hurried after, noisily comparing notes, and again scrambled up the walls like monkeys, and took up their positions as mutes.

Everything you do is wonderful in the sight of these wild people. A compass is an instrument for pointing out the position of hid treasures. A cylinder that lets out and in a long measuring-line is looked upon as an inexplicable work of the Jân. But the greatest wonder of all is my Prince Pless breech-loader, which they endow with virtues that would make it the idol of the military powers of Europe.

Before these unsophisticated creatures, it is the custom with some travellers to swagger and to bully any of them that come in their way, and this conduct sometimes meets its reward in the bully getting thrashed; for these men, though shy and sheepish-looking, are not cowards when their blood is up, and as they live like wild beasts in dens they fear no law or government.

I have always found that a joke, or anything that makes them laugh, gains their confidence in a wonderful manner. They are astonished to hear you use their own language, and a question or a proverb which interests them throws them off their guard at once, and you can send them flying over the place, searching out inscriptions, and bringing you antiquities, in a manner that the Sultan himself could not command.

There were more people among the ruins than on my former visits, owing to the supply of water holding out, while it was exhausted in other villages. We led our horses to the water at the west of the town, and found swarms of women at the different tanks or cisterns, drawing water. The tanks were very numerous, and seemed to be half cave, half well. The women were partly gipsies, and partly from the Arabs in the neighbourhood. They were lightly clothed like the men, and horribly tattooed. They had the white teeth of the wild animal, and the piercing glance of the basilisk. Their speech resembled the sharp barking of a dog, and as they drew up their skins of water they screamed and swore at each other like fiends. They were a most unlovely-looking set, who had seldom during their lives heard or uttered a kindly word, and who had not, so far as we could make out, one attractive feature; and yet those black, buttered tresses, escaping down their shoulders from under sooty bands, were eagerly sought to adorn lovely brows in the saloons of civilization. There was in the town a ruffian who watched those hideous harpies till they fell, and then, vulture-like, rushed upon them and tore off their hair to supply raven locks for the European hair-market.

When we attempted to continue our journey south-west, we got inextricably lost among tortuous mazes of lava, and though we were in the midst of Arabs, no one would tell us where the path was without first receiving two *bashliks* — over two francs. At last a woman with a remnant of the instinct of her sex, pointed in the right direction; and after dragging our horses up and down black waves of rock, that rang metallic under their feet, we emerged on a path flagged with broad stones worn slippery as glass. We soon reached the coast-line, and for a mile or so I walked along the high edge of Argob, parallel with my party, in order to get a better idea of the strange and awful district.

The lava lay in great, petrified waves, and these huge waves were generally split along the centre of their ridge, and the two sides falling away, left a yawning chasm, wide at the top, but narrowing towards the bottom, and disclosing the heart of each wave. The scene had a weird, unearthly appearance. Here we crossed the party that had engaged to start from Damascus with us, but were being led about through the land, and past the most important ruins, at the will of their dragoman.

We coasted along the edge of the Lejah in a south-westerly direction, crossing broad bays which ended in narrow creeks, and skirting headlands with their lighthouses in ruins. We passed, likewise, four considerable towns, with high towers, on the coast of the Lejah, and a number of smaller ruins. The country on our right was entirely under cultivation, and towards night we joined in a long string of farm labourers returning from ploughing. The ploughman generally rode a little donkey, carrying his plough across the saddle before him, and leading his two oxen behind. The men were strong, healthy, and hearty.

They were going to Khubab, and so were we, and we swept along together. As we entered Khubab, we met all the youths of the place drawn out in a line to receive us, headed by the priest, the sheikhs, and the schoolmaster. As we passed, all bent to the ground to honour us, the holy father lowest of all. It soon appeared that some mistake had been made, and that honours had been given us that were not intended for us; for the sheikh, an old acquaintance, darted forward, and shook hands with me in the most familiar manner.

For the moment, Sheikh Diab was the most envied man in Khubab, for Lord Amadhon's dragoman had sent a report before that a prince was coming, and the simple people beheld with wonder and awe their own sheikh shaking hands with the prince.

It was curious to hear them telling one another that they felt assured from the beginning that I had nothing princely about my hat; but when the real scion of nobility did come, his appearance impressed them so little, that they let him pass without a nod, though they had been waiting all the evening to give him a princely reception.

He that would rule Easterns must not neglect appearances. When the Crown Prince of Prussia visited Damascus, he was looked upon as of little account, chiefly, I believe, because he did not wear a crown on his head through the streets, and nothing seemed so inexplicable in that wonderful Franco-German War as that so quiet-looking a man could be a soldier at all.

A Russian prince entered Damascus in princely trappings, and the effect was marvellous. An old Moslem who stood by my side exclaimed, " W'Allah, such a giant!" and then he went off into the following soliloquy: "Praise be to God who raises up men like themselves to destroy them." Of course he meant the English, whose mission in the world is to fight the Russians whenever the Sultan of Turkey calls upon them to do so.

COIN OF PHILIP THE TETRARCH,
Struck at Cæsarea-Philippi, A.D. 8.

CHAPTER XXIV.

KHUBAB is a large Christian village, built on the two marginal waves of the Lejah. An old inscription in the neighbouring village, Zobeireh, in which there is a reference to Britain, gives the ancient name of this village, which was Habiba. Khubab, or Habiba, an entirely Christian village, under a Christian sheikh, contrasts most favourably with the places we last visited.

The Druzes at Burâk are a parcel of outlaws, watching for the police, or their other natural enemies, the Arabs. The people of Musmeih are wild animals with some little clothes. They have a limited field for vicious practices — nobody worth the killing, and nothing to steal; but I have reason to believe that they have fair natural talents for dastardly deeds, which would improve with opportunity and practice, for my companion dropped his rug from the saddle, and it disappeared among the rocks like a flash.

Khubab is an agricultural village, wheeled round so

far west from the Arabs as to be comparatively safe from their attacks; but sometimes the Arabs sweep over their fields, and leave them clean enough; and sometimes, also, they gut and ruin the village. There are a few houses in the village of the best Hauranic style, with the ceiling slabs ornamented; and these are solid enough to defy the Arabs. The villagers also hide their wheat in pits (*nawawis*) in the earth, which they stop, and cover over with dung, rubbish, and stones, so that the Arabs do not always find their grain treasures; but they sometimes torture the sheikh to make him disclose these granaries, and they have refinements in cruelty worthy of the ancient inquisitors.

The men of Khubab labour in the fields during the seasons for labour, and, during the remainder of the year, cut and dress basaltic mill-stones, which are rolled to Akka, and there shipped for the Egyptian market. The women spin and weave and attend to household matters, and keep themselves comparatively clean. One of their occupations exclusively is kneading the cows' dung and sticking it on the walls to dry for fuel. When dry, the balls are gathered and stacked for winter use, as is done with peat in Ireland. There is not a shop in the town. Pedlars visit it with Manchester prints of the brightest colours, Egyptian sugar, bracelets, and other commodities, and get wheat, eggs, cheese, and such local products, in return for their merchandise.

I proclaimed that we had books to sell, and the whole village turned out and swarmed to our tent. The people had a sufficiency of curiosity, and curiosity sometimes leads to knowledge. We had a fair prospect of selling all our books at the first market; but the schoolmaster came with a stick, and drove away his pupils, and after him the priest arrived, with great bluster and noise, and forced his flock back into the village. He declared that they had done sixty years without our Bible, and they would not permit it to enter among them.

We were startled to hear an almost Scripture expression drop from his passionate lips, —

"These people have turned the world upside down in Beyrout and Damascus, and they are come here also."

It was in vain I told him he was rejecting God's book and Christ's gospel, and mentioned that already he had one of our Bibles on the altar of his church; for he was wrathful and inexorable, and he drove his flock away, but one of his *lambs* carried off a Bible without paying for it.

The sheikh and another man came to our tent by night, Nicodemus-like, and eagerly bought two Bibles; and a pretty little bride, Feride, — a *rara avis*, — who had learned German, and become a Protestant, with the Prussian Sisters at Beyrout, bought from us a Bogatzky's "Golden Treasury"; but her husband, still under the yoke of the priest, compelled her to return it on the morrow.

We spent Sunday at Khubab, and had a good deal of conversation with the people, for they kept coming and going in a perpetual stream all day. Their questions and modes of thought were very interesting.

During the day we strolled up to the top of the chief ridge, on which the village was built. We stopped beside a little graveyard in which women were swaying themselves backwards and forwards and wailing for their dead. Each grave is walled up with a single-stone wall about four feet high, which tapers in towards the top. The district is cut up into little gardens and fields, and walled around with high walls which have no entrance. But in these enclosures there is neither soil nor shrub — nothing but the bare grey stones. If they were ever gardens or vineyards, both soil and roots have entirely disappeared.

The country about the village is not so rocky and rugged as at Musmeih. The greatest waves of the lava stopped a mile east, leaving a ridge-like formation, on which stand two conspicuous towns that were finally destroyed by the Bedawîn about six years before our visit.

Looking towards the Druze mountain, the great basaltic lake or plateau does not appear so fearfully desolate as when seen from the north; patches of green with yellow flowers relieve the dreary scene.

Between us and Mount Hermon there stretched a vast level sea of green growing corn, dappled with red fields left fallow; and here and there black villages with white domes and tall minarets, rose like islands; and conical hills and low ranges of mountains prevented the green flat sea from running up sheer to the edge of the mountain.

Hermon itself, streaked and zebraed with snow, presented from our standpoint one of its finest side views.

However modern vulgarity may affect to despise Hermon, for not being the biggest mountain in the world, it is by far the finest object in the whole Syrian landscape; and we do not wonder, when we view it from all quarters of the land, that it impressed so deeply the minds of patriarchs and prophets.

About us, where we stood, the only signs of vegetation were a few patches of nettles and mallows, which grew among the blasted-looking, desolate graves; but there were patches of green down below in the hollows, and as we looked down on the village, it presented a cheerful appearance — girls trooped about in their bright Sunday dresses, and heads of families lay about in little grassy fields, with their children tumbled around them. The scene came as near a picture of home life in a country village as anything I had seen in the East.

From the point where we stood we were able to count fourteen round towers in the Lejah, and a great number of mortuary tombs resembling in a small way the Palmyra towers. Being once detained a day at Khubab, in consequence of my horse having lost a shoe, I visited the round tower due south of the village, and succeeded in getting a good photograph of it.

The tower stands near a fort at a well. It is built of basalt, and tapers from the base. The circumference one yard from the ground is sixty-eight feet. It has thirty-seven layers of stone in it, the one with the other of which would be nearly a foot high each. The walls are four feet thick; the height of the door is five feet five inches, and its width three feet three inches. A central column of cylindrical stones supports a stone loft at the height of fourteen feet, and a spiral staircase, the stones of which project from the wall, and are much worn by wear, ascends to this loft.

By the Hauran tower I place, for comparison, one of the Palmyra mortuary towers, which I found to be one

HAURAN WATCH TOWER.   PALMYRA MORTUARY TOWER.

hundred and eleven feet high, and to contain *loculi* for four hundred and eighty bodies.

On our way back from the tower we visited one of the ruins that are so numerous, and that no one thinks worthy of a visit. We chose Melihat Hezkîn, inasmuch as no European, as far as we knew, had ever visited it. We reached it on foot in less than an hour, and on our way we got both partridge and quail. We met three women who were out gathering a kind of wild rape, which they cook and eat. We found the village just like all other Hauran towns, in a small way. The doors and ceilings and windows were of stone. Each house, however, seemed to have more than the ordinary number of compartments.

At one corner of the village, near the village tank or cistern, was a square tower forty or fifty feet high, with a spiral staircase ascending to two stories. The upper floors were broken down, but enough remained to show the character of the building. The stones in the narrow streets were worn smooth, and the fireplaces showed signs of much use, but the place had been a long time utterly abandoned.

At the northern corner, a little modern square building domed over contained the grave of Sheikh Hezkîn, covered with a green cloth. Pilgrimages are made to the tomb, and each pilgrim leaves a staff stuck into the wall near the grave, so that the chamber is a magazine of staves. The only sign of life in the place was a solitary dove that flew out of the only tree in the village, which is that in the court of the mosque.

On the 7th of April we started for Ezrá, a town on the margin of the Lejah due south. The morning was raw and cold, and yet women and boys were hanging about our tent. As we worked our way once more to the coast-line, we only saw, of animate things, pensive donkeys, meditating among the black rocks — pictures of long-suffering misery. When we pushed out from the black shore, the ground became covered with flowers; among others I saw pink convolvulus, lilac mallows, yellow-hearted daisies, and scarlet pheasant's-eyes.

We first passed through fenced and cultivated fields, much resembling parts in Ireland, Scotland and Wales, and we soon emerged on the broad unfenced plain, where the neighbours' landmarks, large black stones, show the boundaries of the different cultivators. Tibny was in front, on an eminence, like most of the towns of this region. I galloped to the village, according to my custom, in advance of the cavalcade, shouting or singing something to bring the people out of their dens. I found that the most effective cry on such occasions was "fresh haddock" with a County Louth accent, and as we were in the character of pedlars, the cry was not very unbecoming. In Druze villages we tried a stave of the Druze war-song, and it not only brought the people around us, but put them in good humour, as they were no doubt charmed with our style of singing it.

Most of the villagers came out to meet us, and salutations over, I pointed to the colporteur, who was opening his boxes, and told them that he had books for sale, God's books, and explanations of them by good and learned men. I then took an armful of books, and leaving the crowd around the boxes with the colporteur, I literally took a walk over the town, jumping from roof to roof, and saluting the people down in their courts, till I had a sufficient crowd around me; and, then sitting down on an aged stone, I read them passages that seemed to turn up by accident. I thus had an opportunity of seeing the whole town, and of offering our books to every soul in it. Sometimes the crowd became menacing, and then I became aggressive, and questioned them in such a manner as to turn their attention from me to themselves.

When it became a case of "throwing pearls before swine," I commenced to purchase their old coins and medals, like other travellers.

Frankness and good temper and firmness carry one safely along, while a little swaggering, or assumption of mystery, would get us turned out of the village, and perhaps something more. I always returned to the colporteur with an enormous following of savages — climbing over walls and houses, and swarming out of lanes and dens, and all converging towards the books.

Here a widow, with impressive eagerness, bought a Bible for her son, who could read, and she not only paid for it, but poured blessings upon us for bringing it to her. "My son will read it to me, and I shall learn everything for myself," she exclaimed.

Tibny, like most of the other towns, consists of two parts. The Roman official part, temple and all, is in ruins. The native inhabited part is on a mound of ruins, and is of more recent construction.

Leaving Tibny, we passed a number of men ploughing up the fallow ground. They refused to buy our books, on the plea that they had no money; but when I offered them free they had no desire to possess them. Five other villages similar to Tibny lay along our path. At Muhejjeh there are long Greek inscriptions, and pieces of Greek sculpture; but the inhabitants were the most surly Moslems we had met. On the principle of offering our books to all, we urged them to buy, taking no notice of their churlishness.

The women of Muhejjeh have their legs tattooed in pretty patterns, so that they seem to have on blue open-work stockings, through which the white skin appears. They wear their petticoats short, and tucked up, in order to show their ornamented legs.

Shukra, in the midst of a red plain, turned out to be a Christian village, and we could see that Christianity, even in a very degraded form, has a thew and sinew that renders it superior to Islamism. The people seemed alive and eager to see and know. I found such people, as a rule, better than their priest. They *bought* books, but the old priest *stole* one.

I watched the priest with much interest stealing the book, but did not interfere with him, as I knew that he could put an end to our selling if he chose. In the accomplishment of his little purpose he bought a Psalm-book, and shuffled it and a Bible together, until he thought no one saw him, when he slipped the Bible to his wife, and she carried it off home under her apron. When he had the Bible secured, he pretended to discover mistakes in the Psalm-book, and got back his money.

Shukra has also its Corinthian capitals lying about, and several Greek inscriptions built into the walls with the wrong side down. It has all the Hauranic characteristics of the other towns, and from its modern walls peep the eloquent fragments of a higher civilization and more prosperous times.

Bearing to the left, we entered Ezrá over a horrible path, partly the Roman road, and partly the black basaltic rock worn smooth and slippery as polished steel. Ezrá is a large ruin, situated at the base of a rocky promontory, on the south-west corner of the Lejah. This ruin has recently been identified as the Edrei of Og, king of Bashan, but without sufficient reason, and contrary to overwhelming evidence.

Edrei of Og was well known to the Greeks and Romans under the name Adraa, and this rendering of the Hebrew name in Greek corresponds to the rendering of other Shemitic names by the same people, especially in the bilingual inscriptions of Palmyra.[1]

In Roman times Adraa (Edrei) was one of the chief towns of the Arabian province, and, like Bosra, had liberty to coin its own money, and I have in my cabinet several imperial Greek coins struck at Adraa.[2]

Now we are left in no hesitation as to the position of Adraa (Edrei.) The Bible declares it to have been on "the way to Bashan" for an army marching from Heshbon.[3] Eusebius places it on the road to Capitolias and Gadara, twenty-five miles from Bosra, and the Peutinger tables place it twenty-four miles from Bosra, in the same direction.

On one of my visits to Adra'at I approached it from Bosra along the route indicated by Eusebius and the Peutinger tables, and after a march of twenty-four or twenty-five miles we came upon the extensive ruins of

[1] De Vogüé, Inscr. Palmyr., p. 4.
[2] On the reverse of one is the uncouth figure of an enormous giant, a lingering tradition of Og.
[3] Deut. iii. 1.

Edrei at the place where our path was crossed by "the way to Bashan."

Accompanied by Dr. Thomson, the author of *The Land and the Book*, I started from Bosra on April 10th, and proceeded by a track parallel to the Roman Road, which runs straight as an arrow from Bosra to Adra'at.

The country through which we passed was exceedingly fertile and well cultivated. Vast spaces green with corn alternated with immense tracts red in fallow. Furrows a mile in length were turned by the plough in the basaltic ash, of which the soil is largely composed.

On our path, and to right and left, there were many agricultural villages which marked, by decaying ruins, the sites of important towns, and there were many rocky patches and basaltic outcrops here and there; but as we stood high in our stirrups and gazed around us, we seemed to be steering through a vast sea of waving corn, and villages and rocks appeared as black islets in the green ocean.

Adra'at we found beautifully situated on a rising ground, enfolded in a bend of the Wady Zeidy. At Jisr et-Taiyebeh, a river, flowing in the Wady Zeidy, crossed our path from right to left, ran by our side on the left, sometimes quite close to our path and sometimes at the distance of a mile; but at a quarter of a mile from Adra'at it recrossed our path from left to right and flowed in a beautiful curve round the north of the town.

During the whole journey I inquired from every person

we met the name of the town on the hill to which we were going.

"What is the name of that town?" I would ask, gently, pointing to the place. Invariably the Bedawîn would answer, "Adra'at."

As if I had not heard distinctly, I would ask the question again and again in a higher key, and they would bawl out again and again, aspirating every letter until the word might have torn their teeth out, "A-d-r-a'-at."

Almost as uniformly the Fellahîn called it Derá, but as the Bedawîn always preserve the oldest pronunciation, and their rendering agrees with that of Abu el-Fida, Edrisi, and the Arab geographers generally, I propose to follow it in this book.

We had a discussion regarding the right name of the place on the bridge below the town as hot as any that has been waged by Western scholars over the name. A great caravan bearing wheat to Akka was passing over the bridge as we approached it. The drivers in charge of the *kufl* were Bedawîn, but a number of the Fellahîn to whom the wheat belonged were in the party.

"What town is that?" I said to a Bedawi, as I handed him a few dates from my pocket.

"Adra'at!" shouted the Bedawi. "Derá!" shouted the Fellahîn. Then there arose Babel on the bridge, and we could occasionally catch fragments of sounds —such as "Ibn el-Kelb" (son of a dog), "Adra'at," "Majnoun" (idiot), "Derá," etc. In fact the sons of the desert were almost as rude and noisy as critics and controversialists at home, and they sought to settle the matter in dispute by strength of assertion like our own positivists.

While the controversy raged we forded the river with difficulty, and ascended the sloping sides of the green hill to Adra'at. We passed several Bedawi tents on the acclivity, with men and children squatting at their doors. The people of the town were at first sullen, especially the Moslems; but when they found we could talk their language they became more pleasant, and were ready to sell us anything they had.

Adra'at stands in the midst of green and beautiful rolling hills. It must always have been a great agricultural centre, and it is still the most populous town in Bashan. As it is situated on the edge of a most fertile district, it has been more constantly occupied than Ezrá in the Lejah, and hence it is smothered with great heaps of dung, which have grown up higher than the houses and over them. The land needed no manure, and all refuse remained where it was first flung.

Adra'at is a town of four tiers. The modern habitations are on the top, and next to them are the Roman foundations, and beneath on the chalk are the ruins of Og's city. But below all there is a subterranean city, with houses and streets excavated out of the solid rock. I explored some of the passages, but as the work was both dirty and dangerous, and as I had no change of garments with me, I thought it better to be content with Wetzstein's description till such times as the Palestine Exploration

Fund could take up a thorough investigation of the underground city.[1]

A small portion of the ancient Adra'at is now covered by the modern village. We explored the place, keeping along the tops of the great dung heaps and looking down into the squalid dwellings. There are still many ancient ruins which have not yet been engulfed by the ever-growing refuse. There is a curious square minaret of the truncated pyramid pattern. There is a large mosque which seems to be a transformed monastic building, and at the southern end of the rectangular enclosure one sees the apse of the church, the chord of which was thirty-eight yards. There are also the remains of ancient baths and many other ruins which testify to the civilization and luxury of the place at a remote period. All the structures appear to have been built from stones rifled from older buildings. We had our best view, however, from Tell Karak, which stands higher than Adra'at, and formed the citadel or north-eastern suburb of the city. We saw the aqueduct, bearing the name of Pharaoh, by which the water was brought from Dilly, and carried across Wady Zeidy by a bridge of five circular spans, now partially in ruins.

---

[1] Merrill, in his interesting book "East of the Jordan" — London, 1881, pp. 350-352 — has translated Dr. Wetzstein's description; and Mr. Schumacher, in his work "Across the Jordan" — published by the Palestine Exploration Fund, 1886, pp. 136-144 — has given a minute description with plans of an underground exploration carried out by him. He does not, however, seem to have come across the part explored by Wetzstein. Nor did I.

The bridge, though ancient, was also made from odds and ends taken from other edifices.

We spent some hours on Sunday reading on the top of Tell Karak. A large group of natives sat open-mouthed around us as we read in their own tongue the twenty-two passages of the Bible in which Og, the king of Bashan, is referred to. As we read and looked at the natural features of the landscape around us, the whole scene became vivid before us. "And they turned and went up by the way of Bashan: and Og, the king of Bashan, went out against them, he and all his people to the battle at Edrei." [1]

The Israelites, flushed with their victory over Sihon, king of the Amorites, poured down the sloping sides of the Zulmeh Hills from the south-west, and on "the way of Bashan," at Edrei, gained a decisive victory over King Og, who dwelt at Ashtaroth and Edrei, and reigned in Mount Hermon and Salcah, and in all Bashan. . . ." [2]

It is clear from the narrative that the great battle was not fought *in* Bashan, but *on the way to* Bashan. "Then we turned and went up the way to Bashan: and Og the king of Bashan came out against us, he and all his people, to battle at Edrei." [3]

As we read these and kindred passages on the summit of the old citadel of Adra'at, we had no room for even a doubt that we were in the very centre of the ancient battle-field, on which the kingdom of Bashan was won for the half tribe of Manasseh. Og's two capitals were Edrei and Ashtaroth, and he reigned in Salcah and Hermon and

---
[1] Numb. xxi. 33.   [2] Joshua xiii. 11, 12.   [3] Deut. iii. 1.

in all Bashan. The inspired writer might have stood where we stood when writing his narrative, so vivid is his description. To the south-east Salcah (Sulkhâd), its castle erected on the crater of an extinct volcano, dominated the district. Far to the north-west towered the lofty Hermon, snow-clad to its base. Between these two lofty landmarks stretched the kingdom of Bashan with the threescore cities of Jair.

Og's two capitals were Edrei and Ashtaroth. From Edrei he could see the lofty extremities of his kingdom. But where was Ashtaroth? Standing on the highest tops of Tell Karak, I asked the crowd of Arabs who surrounded me the names of the tells in view. Beginning on the eastern horizon and sweeping round the north to the west, they pointed out Tell 'Arar, Tell el-Faras, Tell Abu Nida, Tell el-Jumna, Tell el-Jabia, Tell el-Harrah, and a score of other tells which were either extinct volcanoes or artificial mounds.

One of the tells mentioned in the general summary was Tell Ashtarah. I did not affect any surprise when I heard the name, but I said quietly, "Where is Tell Ash'areh?"

Half a dozen voices shouted out at once, "There is Tell Ash'areh, but yonder away beyond is Tell Ashtarah." As I stood on the highest point of Edrei, I could distinctly see not only the remote boundaries of Bashan but also the Mound of Ashtaroth towering from eighty to one hundred feet above the surrounding plain.

Edrei was Og's great industrial and political capital, but Ashtaroth was his sacred and ecclesiastical capital, and the sites and ruins accord with this view. Edrei stood on the cross-road and meeting-place of industry and commerce, and the ruins tell of large resources and great prosperity. Ashtaroth stood on a sacred mound, apart from the highways of secular life, and the scattered ruins and foundations on Tell Ashtarah are such as might be expected in connection with the worship of the local deity.

In contrast with these obvious landmarks of the ancient Edrei, let us look at the three reasons given for identifying Ezrá of the Lejah as the City of Og.

First: *The situation.* It occupies an "impregnable site," whereas " Adra'at lies in the open country."

To this we reply, that the city Bosra was in the open country too, and in the open country became much more great and famous than Edrei. Besides, King Og was strong enough to live in a city in the plain. And when the Israelites "went up the way to Bashan" (Deut. iii. 1), Og did not retreat to some impregnable stronghold, but went out to meet them on their march, confident of victory.

Second: *The antiquity of the massive walls of the dwellings.* The chief advocate of this theory acknowledges that the buildings may be "as old at least as the Roman dominion"!

The reply to this is obvious. Roman ruins, however massive, cannot be taken in evidence in the identification of the city of Og, king of Bashan.

Third: *The correspondence of the Arabic name to the Hebrew name Edrei.* So far as this argument goes, it tells in favour of Adra'at, which is practically the same as the Hebrew name.

It was not, therefore, up among the rocky fastnesses of Bashan that the giant leader and his host were overcome by the hosts of the Lord, but on the plains, as the Israelites "went up the way to Bashan."

We must not, however, overlook the testimony of the ancient dwellers in these parts, for their vanity often led them to write the name of their city in conjunction with their own names. Thus "I, Smith," or "We, the Smiths of such and such a place, erect this monument at our own expense," etc. On this question the evidence of ancient Smith is conclusive. For he declares, with *cutting* emphasis and frequent repetition, that the name of the place in Greek and Roman times was not Edhra or Adraa, but Zorava. The name of the city Zorava stands as conspicuous as a signboard on two large stones near the minaret, and engraved on the walls of the two churches — St. Elias and St. George.

Og, king of Bashan, was one of our earliest and tallest friends. He and his wondrous bedstead had a large place in our imaginations ere we heard of "Jack the Giant-Killer" or "Giant Despair." We owed his giantship a small debt of gratitude, and we have now paid it, by restoring our tall and ancient friend to his own city and rightful inheritance.[1]

---

[1] In this question I agree with Burckhardt, Wetzstein, and Waddington. The invaluable work of the latter is conclusive on this subject, but it is unfortunately beyond the reach of the public.

COIN OF HEROD THE GREAT.

CHAPTER XXV.

EZRÁ is an extensive ruin three or four miles in circumference. Some of the buildings are very massive and look very old, as they are half-buried in accumulated rubbish; but when one sees in a massive wall a Greek inscription wrong side up, showing that it was taken from some other building, he rationally concludes that the structure is not older than the ruin from which its literary ornaments were rifled.

Probably the most interesting edifice in Ezrá is the church of St. George. It is one of the oldest Christian structures in the world. From an inscription we learn that the church was erected in 410 of the Bostrian era, corresponding to 515 A.D. It owed its construction to John Diomede. He built it on the site of a pagan temple, and dedicated it to St. George, who appeared to him, not in a dream or vision, but in reality. The tomb of St. George, containing his bones, is in the church, and is an object of veneration to Moslems as well as to Christians.

The form of the church is that of an octagon described within a square. Eight piers support the lofty dome, which has an external gallery running round it. This church of St. George was built after the pattern of the church at Antioch, which was the first octagonal church ever erected, and dates from the time of Constantine.

As we pitched our tent, we were joined by the Greek priest, who, probably, had the true succession from the Greek priest, his predecessor, who ran away with Burckhardt's money. He showed a disposition to take limited views of European society through the small openings of our tent. When admitted, he told a harrowing tale of Moslem persecution and murder, which broke down under examination. He was a very ignorant and unclean priest, and a very importunate beggar, and a very disagreeable man in every way.

The inhabitants of the place were about half Moslem and half Christian. The Moslems of the place were sullen and morose, but I visited them all, notwithstanding. The Christians were keen and active, and they all visited us. As a rule, the men of Ezrâ are tall and well made, and the women would be handsome but for the tattoo marks on their faces. The children are very beautiful, and the old women are simply hideous. Several villanous-looking characters, probably the same who made the murderous attack on Porter, were hanging about the camp, on pretence of looking at our books; and they became very much interested in the books when we watched them, but as they held the wrong side of the books up, it may be presumed that they were not profiting very much.

We were informed that we might expect to be robbed during the night, as the caves about the village were infested with robbers. Our muleteers, though unarmed, threatened loudly, and in the most emphatic language, that if any one appeared during the night, they would blow them into a thousand atoms. I showed my gun as a curiosity, and the rapidity of its fire, twenty shots a minute, was very impressive, and probably helped to secure us an undisturbed night.

We left Ezrá by a path at right angles to the one by which we entered, and crossed the promontory due east in the direction of Jebel Kuleib. The road was similar to that by which we entered, the black surface of the rock being worn smooth by traffic, till it had a metallic polish, and there were here and there, especially in the hollows, fragments of the Roman pavement, polished and slippery also by much wear.

In our descent we met several very fine-looking village women, who would have been counted handsome in any country but for the horrible blue tattoo ornaments worked on their faces and lips. Here also we got our supply of partridge for the day.

In twenty-five minutes we reached the bay on the eastern side of the promontory, and launched once more on the vast green sea, with the indented and ruin-crowned coast of the Lejah, or Argob, on our left. After a lovely sail of two hours, we turned in to the left, behind a headland, to visit Busr el-Hariry. We reached the ruin over an execrable road, and found it scattered over the two sides of a wady.

The ruins were extensive, ancient, and massive, and contained, as usual, many Greek inscriptions. We found the women at the cisterns, but the water was so exhausted that we could scarcely, even by paying for it, get enough for our horses.

Both men and women surrounded us here with the pale assassin faces we saw in Damascus, and gazed at us in the calm silence of suppressed fanaticism; and there was lightning in those pale, clouded brows, but lest it should dart forth on us, we drew their attention from ourselves by urging them to buy books. The only civil man in the place was the old green-turbaned keeper of the mosque, which was the most conspicuous object among the ruins. He held our horses, and permitted us to copy all the inscriptions, and we rewarded him.

Quitting Busr el-Hariry without regret, we embarked once more on a green sea of "poppy-growing corn." We passed Dûr, a large village, with a high square tower standing at a distance from the houses, and we saw a number of smaller places of the ordinary Hauranic type. We had here a typical Moslem for travelling companion. He was an intelligent ploughmaker, and we had conversation with him on many subjects. His theory about the Koran was that it has superseded all other revelations; and he added, of books in general, that they are an impertinence to both God and man, as the Koran contains all knowledge. He was the first Hauran Moslem we had met who did not seem preternaturally stolid.

I hope my readers will pardon the use of nautical phraseology thus far, for I could not divest myself of the feeling that I was sailing along near the tide line, with a black, rugged coast on my left, and a vast green sea on my right. Indeed, my companion, who was more of a geologist than myself, suggested that the molten flood may have been poured out from the bowels of the earth, ere the shallow sea had retreated, and hence the horribly contorted forms into which the seething mass finally settled down.

We had now coasted round more than half the well-defined border of the Lejah, and at midday we turned inland north-east to Nejrân. When I had last approached Nejrân a battle was going on within its walls. We heard the guns and the tumult of battle, and turned away, and on the morrow heard the result in killed and wounded. The wonderful unanimity of the Druzes, which is much applauded in books, is less the fruit of religious principle than the result of external pressure from their enemies.

We entered Nejrân through a savage wilderness of gloomy rocks. We found the town half in ruins, and the population half Druze and half Christian. The Druze sheikh, Fendy Abu Fakhr, gave us a hearty welcome. He led us to an open veranda covered with mats, and spread a felt rug on the ground. Then he ordered up *laban* in a lordly bowl, and we all three sat down on the rug and cemented friendship by eating together. The sheikh called up his little son to kiss our hands, but we refused to allow him to do so, on the ground that we were Christianity teachers; but in the meantime the native Christians came hurrying in to see us, and on entering the veranda, they all, even the old men, kissed the hand of the sheikh's son, though he was only a child of seven years old.

It was humiliating to see the manner in which the Christians cringed before the Druzes. They immediately, however, fell fiercely on us for calling ourselves Christians, and eating in Lent, which gave us a fine opportunity to give them a lecture by way of self-defence.

A tall lady, whom we took to be the sheikh's wife, acted as our hostess, and to her we gave our fee; but discovering that she was not the sheikh's wife, we paid backshish over again, for we found that we were always more welcome where we paid our way. The lady, however, was so different from all the other women that we had seen in the Hauran that she deserves a passing notice. She was dressed in a long blue skirt reaching down to her feet, and over it a blue calico robe, lined with red, which she folded back to let the red appear. She wore great coarse boots, reaching half way to her knees, and a black handkerchief on her head, over which she had a turban of red and green; and encircling her brow, and around her head, she had strings of gold coins. She was tall and slender, in contrast with the thick, stumpy Druze women. Her face was long and pale, her forehead high, her features well cut and very animated when she spoke.

Her eyes, dark as a gazelle's, shot from under artificially arched brows, and the arches were magnified by carefully applied pigments. She carried in her hand a cherry pipe with amber mouth-piece, and worked over with a filagree of gold thread. Every one seemed to treat her with the greatest deference, and her will was law at the sheikh's board.

When she saw me buying old coins, she asked me to go with her and she would sell me a few. Instead, however, of leading the way into the sheikh's house as I expected, or to some house in the village, she marched straight out of the town, and for the first time I found she was not the sheikh's wife. I followed her through labyrinths of congealed lava, not without some misgivings; but I had my revolver with me, and at worst I could make a good race back to the village. Nor would my Druze friends allow me to be drawn into an ambush.

About a quarter of a mile from the town we reached a solitary tent pitched on a little patch of green among the dismal rocks. She invited me into her "house of hair" with the vivacity of a Frenchwoman; and though my curiosity was roused to the highest pitch, a vision of strong-minded women from Jezebel to Lady Macbeth rose up before me, and I felt more comfortable standing outside and peeping into her tent after her. From what I saw I concluded that she lived in this tent entirely alone, but neither from herself nor from the villagers was I able to learn anything of this remarkable woman.

She soon emerged with a handful of old coins — Kufic

and Constantines, and Remus and Romulus tugging at the wolf; but among the common rubbish I found one which is a real treasure, and especially useful in the identification of Edrei. It is the imperial Greek coin, referred to above, struck at Adraa. There is a huge, ill-shapen giant on the reverse of this coin that was struck in the city of Og. He bears in his left hand a club like "a weaver's beam," and in his right hand a skull. One of his feet also seems to rest on a skull.

COIN OF EDREI.

The Romans permitted towns to place on the reverses of their coins their tutelary deities and traditional heroes, and so we see on coins of Sidon, Astarte; on coins of Dium, Dagon; and here, doubtless, on this coin of Adraa we have a remnant of the tradition of Og, the last of the "remnant of giants" (Deut. iii. 11), preserved by the people of his native town.

On my return to the village the sheikh took me away very mysteriously to the roof of his house, and when I expected to hear some state secret, which (à la Tancred) would shake a thousand thrones, he merely informed me that he wanted "to be in the purse of the English Consul."

Having no political mission, and not wanting to hamper myself by inconvenient promises, I answered, "You are a very big man, and the Consul's purse is only a few inches wide." He then explained that he wanted English protection, and to be a protégé of the Consul.

I replied, "O, Sheikh! your own proverb says, '*Too much tying loosens.*' Everybody knows the good-will the Druzes bear to the English, and the protection the English extend to the Druzes. Do not loosen the knot of friendship that exists between you by any attempt to tie it tighter."

A proverb may not always be logical, but if it be aptly applied it is always conclusive in Arabia. He came down from the roof apparently as well satisfied with my reply as if I had made the present debtor to the future by a score of extravagant promises which I could never have hoped to perform.

Our visit to Nejrân was one of the pleasantest we made in the Hauran. We had a good sale for our books, and a most pressing invitation to stay during the night; but we pushed on to Mejdel, the residence of my friend Sheikh Hazimeh, the most powerful of all the Druze sheikhs.

FOLDING STONE DOOR (HAURAN).

CHAPTER XXVI.

ON our arrival at Mejdel, Sheikh Hazimeh was absent, but his son, a handsome lad of fourteen, received us with hereditary courtesy and hospitality. In Mejdel we could once more move about without our revolvers, and without wishing we had eyes in the backs of our heads to guard against sudden surprises. However, as I wandered in the suburbs of the village, I became the object of a very ridiculous demonstration.

I had left my colporteur with the crowd, and while copying an inscription at the end of the village, a Bedawi woman came up and slipped her hand into the open pocket of my coat. The action was so quick and skilful that I did not perceive it. Finding that she had only secured a central fire cartridge, she returned it to me with a look of disgust. She then commenced a jerking Bedawi dance, shouting or singing with a shrill voice, " W'alla, w'alla, look at the smallness of his legs!" Her screams and laughter drew a crowd of Bedawi women, and they imme-

TELL SHEEHÂN.

diately fell into a ring round me, and all clapping their hands together, joined in the chorus, "W'alla, w'alla, look at the smallness of his legs, just like pipe shanks!" When they saw that I rather enjoyed the scene, the din became deafening; but a Druze came to my rescue, and they all slunk off to their lairs, withered hags as they were.

These women belonged to a sub-tribe of the Bedawîn, which is always stationary in the neighbourhood, and while the Druzes protect them, they act as "hewers of wood and drawers of water" to the Druzes. They have the same gipsy appearance wherever seen. They are small and lean, have sharp, pinched features, which are all covered with blue marks, and their clothes are a bundle of grimy rags. They all have the same deep-set, small, piercing eyes, and the same uncombed but buttered locks.

At Nejrân we first came

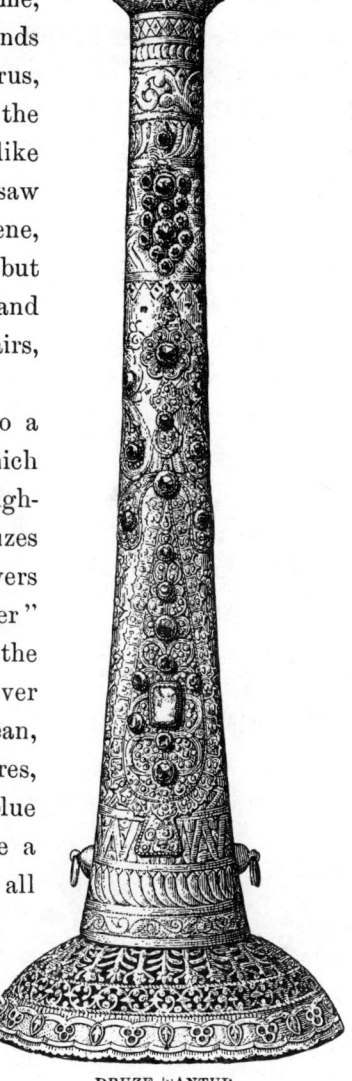

DRUZE TANTUR.

upon the Druze women wearing the *tantur*, or wonderful horn, which in many places they have since ceased to wear. The horn is a silver tube from twelve to twenty inches long, and three or four inches in diameter, tapering to the top. It is like a drinking-glass, greatly elongated, open at the bottom and closed at the top, and it is generally embossed with flowers and arabesque patterns. The horn is placed with its mouth on the tarboosh, or red felt cap, on the top of the head, slanting forward, and it is fastened by strings attached to hooks on the horn, and passing under the chin and behind the head. Over the horn a white veil is thrown, which falls down over the shoulders, and a hair rope passing round the head outside the veil keeps the horn in its place. The head-dress is then the shape of the "grenadiers' hats" which we used to make of rushes.

The remainder of the toilet of those horned females consists of wide calico trousers, and a kind of blue calico shirt falling over all to below the knees. The feet are generally bare. In this strangest of costumes, which gives a "Mother Hubbard" appearance, they engage in all works — some of them are said to sleep with their horns on at night; and as one sees them going to the wells, with jars on their shoulders, and horns on their heads, they form a very striking picture.

All the women wear massive ornaments, so that on the same arms you will see bracelets of glass, brass, gold, and silver, the one above the other. A well-dressed, fashionable woman in the Hauran will have on her person fifteen or seventeen pounds' weight of jewellery. The Christian

TEMPLE AT SULEIM.

women dress exactly like the Druze women, barring the horn. The children all wear little red caps with coins and charms suspended from the tassels.

On the 9th of April we cantered out of Mejdel on a clear bracing morning. Lebanon and Hermon appeared very distinct, and very high, and the snows on their summits glowed like amethyst as they were lighted up by the rising sun. To the north-east, Tell Sheehân stood gazing open-mouthed at the unlovely sable flood which it had vomited forth on the plain. The morning shadow lay dark on the mouth of the crater, showing very distinctly whence came the discharges which now drape the land. We believed we could trace the wavy outline of the fiery deluge that issued from its rugged throat; and the other smaller truncated cones around showed, by the deep gashes in their sides, that they were no idle spectators of the dismal work.

The stones were here gathered out of the fields, and the corn was growing luxuriantly around the cairns. In a few minutes we crossed the Roman road which runs from Phæna to Bosra through the centre of the Lejah. On my previous visit I got a small bustard at this place. It was larger than a partridge, but the partridge was preferred at dinner.

In a little over an hour we reached Suleim, and the Skeikh Abu Shahîn met us with the ever-ready Druze welcome. The sheikh was very proud of his new house, which he had built in the flimsy Damascus style. Into the walls he had built stones with inscriptions and bits of Greek ornaments, as he naively said, to save Englishmen from ranging through the town to look for them. On one stone there were the figures of two animals like lions, with wings and very long necks. They were much defaced, but they seemed to have had the countenances of men.

North-east of the village there is a fine temple in ruins, and hard by the large village cistern. The Druze women,

TEMPLE OF KANAWÂT.

as they stooped to fill their jars along the brink of this cistern, appeared from a distance like huge birds with their long beaks pointing down to the water.

DRUZE LADIES OF LEBANON.

From Suleim we struck up the hill to Kanawât. The country most pleasantly reminded us of home, — extensive cultivation and abundant vegetation, and the whole district wooded like an English park. On our left, on the curve of the hill, stood "*Kasr Mabroom*," a round tower, the most conspicuous artificial object in the whole landscape. We crossed a mountain stream opposite the Kasr Mabroom, and close to the ruined base of another round tower.

RUIN AT KANAWÂT.

We now ascended among the evergreen "oaks of Bashan," doubly pleasing in shade and colour, after the dismal and sterile districts which we had been traversing. Through the breaks in the trees on our left we saw a curious ruin, and, after vainly attempting to bring our horses up to it, we tied them in the thicket and approached it on foot. It was a huge round tower, with the side fallen out of it. The stones of which it was built were dressed, and did not seem very old; but there were hard by a number of foundations of other round towers that had·a very ancient look.

A considerable stream flowed close by these towers, and partridges roosted in the oaks that covered them. As we reached the edge of the wady on which the city stood, we came upon other foundations of round towers, one of which, with a little inscription lying beside it, was twelve yards in diameter.

The ruins of Kanawât are among the most important in Bashan, and they date from the early centuries of our era. One of the earliest inscriptions in the Hauran is a fragment (of course rifled from an older structure) now in the wall of one of the churches. In this fragment, Agrippa (presumably the elder) reproaches the people for having lived up to that time as if in the dens of wild beasts; and the remainder of the inscription, which is wanting, no doubt called upon them to build themselves houses and live like men. The testimony of Josephus and others corroborates Agrippa's tablets as to the habits of the people up to that period, and the ruins of private houses, as well as palatial residences, stand as proof that, at that time at least, they took to building houses.

From the time of Agrippa to the time of Justinian a gleam of sunshine fell upon Bashan, for to that palmy period of Roman rule belong all her wondrous monuments. Before and after that period, dark and troublous times were the portion of Bashan. But a wave of prosperity then passed over the land, leaving behind it monuments which, in the grace and grandeur of their massive ruins, have been attributed to the giants by travellers of the nineteenth century.

This ruin has been hastily identified as the Kanath of the Bible; but the theory is one that must be thrown down. There is little in the Bible about Kanath, but that little goes to prove that it could not have been at Kanawât.

When the Manassehites were settling into their possessions east of the Jordan, " Nobah went and took Kenath, and called it after his own name" (Num. xxxii. 42). Kanath is but once again mentioned in the Bible (1 Chron. ii. 23); but under its changed name, Nobah, we meet it again, in connection with other towns which approximately fix its location.

When Gideon pursued the flying Midianites across the Jordan, touching Succoth and Penuel in his pursuit, "he went up by the way of them that dwelt in tents on the east of Nobah and Jogbehah, and smote the host" (Judges viii. 11).

Now, Succoth, and Penuel, and Jogbehah belonged to Gilead (Josh. xiii. 27; Num. xxxii. 35), and Jerome places Succoth east of the Jordan, opposite Scythopolis,[1] at the place where Burckhardt found its ruins.[2]

We would thus expect to find Nobah on the east of Gilead, beyond the places mentioned in connection with

[1] Jerome *ad Gen.* 33. 17.
[2] Burckhardt's *Travels*, p. 345. Beisan is now finally identified by the P. E. F. party as Scythopolis.

it, certainly not on a remote mountain distant from them a march of three or four days. But when we read that " he went up by the way of them that dwelt in tents on the east of Nobah," we see from the slightest knowledge of the country that Nobah could not have been Kanawât, for the country east of Kanawât is mountain, and to have gone up by the people who dwelt in tents east of Kanawât, Gideon must have taken his noble three hundred round behind Jebel ed-Druze, into the distant and inhospitable desert, El-Kra.

We thus see the utter absurdity of identifying Kanath or Nobah of the Bible with the Kanawât of the Druze mountain. Kanath must be sought for much nearer Gilead; and it is of the utmost importance, in the interests of Biblical geography, that attention should be called

COIN OF KANAWÂT.

to fanciful identifications which have already taken up recognized positions on the maps.

I wish to trouble the reader with as few as possible of these crude identifications; but I should be inexcusable did I give the approval even of silence to so manifestly incorrect identifications as those of the Pharpar, Edrei, and Kanawât.¹

There is little doubt that Kanatha, or Kanawât, grew into importance as the summer residence of the Roman rulers of Bashan. It was the *sanitarium* of the district. Even Florentinus, whose great tomb is at Petra, is supposed to have had a summer residence at Kanawât, and his name remains over the door of a private house to this day. What Simla is to the English of India, and Bludân to the European resident at Damascus, that was Kanawât to the Romans, whose presence brought order and prosperity, for the first and last time, to the manifold districts of Bashan.

At Kanawât they had wooded hill and bracing air and ice-cold springs and murmuring streams, and the scene of their stewardship spread out before them like an open book; and so they builded temples to their gods, which were no gods, and when Christianity became patronized by the Constantines, they pulled their temples about and made them into Christian churches. And they had their baths, and their theatres, and their hippodrome, and their promenades. And when the city was plucked from the feeble grasp of the Byzantines, the blight of Islam, whose

[1] In Roman times there were two cities in Bashan, Kanatha and Kanata, and writers have not been sufficiently careful to distinguish between them. I have in my cabinet coins of both cities. Kanatha is Kanawât, and Kanata is supposed (Waddington, p. 549) to be Kerah, a ruin in the vicinity of Bosra. This Kanata has been pointed out with some probability as the Kanatha of the Bible; but though it answers better to the Scripture account of it than Kanawât, I believe it is also too far distant from the Jordan to be the Nobah, to the east of which Gideon went up with his improvised and famishing little troop.

genius is destruction, fell upon it, and from that period to the present day time and man have united to make this lovely town once more like a burrowing-place of wild

GATEWAY, KANAWÂT.

beasts. Their success has been considerable; but as we gaze on the airy columns that proudly rise above the oaks, and stumble over statue and column and capital, and listen to the partridge, and see the gazelles roaming tamely through the evergreen parks, and drink the crystal waters, and then turn to the wondrous landscape, stretching away to Jordan, and Hermon, and Lebanon, we can form still a conception of the paradise which Roman energy and taste created in this mountain dell.

I was glad the sheikh was not at home, for he was so warm a friend of mine that he would certainly have encumbered us with kindness. Unimpeded by friend or foe, we roamed over the whole ruins; but we were not a little surprised to find that all the men carried arms ready for use, and wherever we came upon any one suddenly his first instinct was to grasp his weapon.

I returned from my explorations, having sold every book I took with me.

The women are just like those we spoke of at Mejdel, and they wear an additional red robe under the blue one, doubtless necessitated by the greater altitude of the village. The horn is more common, and the size and weight of the numerous bracelets worn on the same arm are more striking. They all have a trick of drawing the veil that hangs from the horn coquettishly over the face, leaving only a little hole for the right eye to peep through, — a bright eye in a sooty setting.

The Druze women were all busy, and always busy, nursing babies, kneading bread for food or dung for fuel, or carrying water in jars, or grinding at the mill, or making rays and baskets of straw, or spinning with the distaff.

A short distance up the hill from Kanawât we came upon the interesting ruins of Sia. The temple was dedicated "to our Lord, King Herod the Great," and was adorned with groups of sculptured birds and animals, and festooned fruits and flowers. Herod's statue, of which one foot remains, was destroyed probably by the early Christians, who bore no good-will to the murderer of the infants.

This monument to Herod the Great is exceedingly interesting, when taken in connection with a statement by Josephus. Herod commenced the work of civilization in Bashan, and Josephus (Ant. Jud. xvi. 9, 2) tells us that "he placed three thousand Idumeans in Trachonitis, and thereby restrained the robbers that were there." On the stones about there are Idumean inscriptions, and it has been plausibly conjectured that Herod placed the three thousand in Kanawât, and that they erected the monument of Sia. And this conjecture seems almost certain, when we remember how badly the great king's efforts at civilizing these wild regions were appreciated; and, indeed, so unpopular was he with the people, that a monument could only have been erected in his honour in a place protected by his garrison.

Descending from Kanawât, we passed one of the loveliest ruins in the Hauran. On a knoll to the right, a number of beautiful Corinthian columns stand on a raised platform, towering over the wooded landscape. Time has made gaps among them, so that they stand charmingly irregular, like the trees of the field around them.

We passed down to Atîl through a lovely wooded country, in which every piece of open ground waved with luxuriant wheat. Streams murmured between grassy margins, and the air was heavy with the scent of haw-

PERIPTERAL TEMPLE AT KANAWÂT.

thorn and other blossoms, and on the grassy slope our horses crushed, with iron heel,

> "The little speedwell's darling blue;
> Deep tulips, dashed with fiery dew;
> Laburnums, dropping wells of fire."

When our minds wandered, led by the association of ideas, to the "days that are no more," we were generally abruptly called back to the reality of our position by the appearance of some ruffian among the trees, braced in the antique armour of his hereditary robber race.

In Atîl, the ancient Athila, there are two temples and many inscriptions, one of which was addressed to the Idumean god Theandrias, who was worshipped elsewhere in Bashan, especially in Bosra. Several broken statues, some of them equestrian, are lying about, and there is one fine bust built into a garden wall.

Here first we met the Druzes armed and excited, but as yet we did not know the cause. A young Druze, who was once in a Protestant school, recognized me, and we had a good sale of books.

The whole village pressed upon us more familiarly than was pleasant, and I found one man whose hand had strayed into my pocket. He seemed greatly amused when I asked him if that was an ordinary custom among them.

We discovered in Atîl a wonder such as no traveller has, I believe, seen in the Hauran since or before. It was nothing less than a Druze woman reading a book. She had the "notable horn between her eyes," like the other unicorns, and was sewing with her book propped up before her. The book was a manuscript, written, she said, by a Magraby, containing the traditions of the Pharaohs; but it was really a miserable work on magic. I could not get her interested in the Bible, but she bought a copy of "Henry and his Bearer" in Arabic.

Here, during a halt of an hour, we sold thirty-three different books; and when we left, an armed Druze followed us for a tract, and as he paid for one he snatched

RUINS AT KANAWÂT.

another by force from the colporteur, and ran away with it in triumph.

From Atîl to Suweideh our path lay for the most part along the Roman road. Nothing in that land gives one such an idea of the earnest, stern purpose and iron will of those old Roman teachers of order as that road, striking straight as an arrow over rock and hollow, through the whole length of this dismal land. We passed what seemed to have been roadside inns at regular intervals on the road.

CARVED HEAD, KANAWÂT.

DOORWAY AT KANAWÂT.

CHAPTER XXVII.

WE entered Suweideh in company with an enormous flock of little horses returning from their pastures. My old friend Waked el-Hamdân gave us a most fatherly welcome, and his sons looked on our visit as a pleasant incident. Bashire, our old guide on a former tour, but grown very fat and puffy since I last saw him, made a great fuss over us, and recounted all the fine things we then said and the wonderful things we did.

It was arranged that he should give our servants everything we wanted at a fair price; and he gave us to understand that from him we could get a list of all the Englishmen who had sponged on the sheikh for the last ten years, and of all who honestly paid their way.

Bashire is a refugee from the Lebanon, where, in consequence of his great activity in 1860, his head was eagerly inquired after. We found him a trusty guide, and, like Falstaff, he was the occasion of much wit in others, by the wondrous tales he told of himself.

We read in books of the unfailing loyalty of the Druzes to hereditary rank, and the statement sounds patriarchal. If it were correct, however, Waked el-Hamdân would have been chief of all the Druzes in the Hauran; but as in other states hereditary claims are set aside for political considerations and personal fitness, so in the Hauran the valiant and turbulent, though plebeian, Atrash family had eclipsed the gentle and humane, though princely, house of Hamdân; and at the time of our visit there was a radical movement among the Druzes to strip Waked of the last remnant of nominal power, and confer it on Ibrahîm el-Atrash of Kureiyeh.

Nor was this to be wondered at when we remember that the Druzes were engaged in a desperate struggle for national existence. On the one hand, they had to guard against the encroachments of the Turks, and on the other, against the encroachments of the Bedawîn; and occasionally they had a desperate war with the Christians. In such a state of society the fiercest valour is the highest virtue. Waked el-Hamdân was a tall, handsome man, of a most gentle and impressively sweet disposition, and his virtues were such as are recognized in more tranquil times.

All points of etiquette complied with, we declined the proffered banquet, on the ground that it would take up too much of our time, which we wished to spend in selling books and seeing the place. The sheikh the more readily consented to our leaving him for a time, as some question of deep interest was agitating the Druzes, and there were dusty couriers arriving and fresh couriers galloping off. There was also much whispering, and cleaning up of old armour. On our return to our tent we heard a loud voice " proclaiming from the house tops " the programme of the morrow. Part of the proclamation was in the secret language of the Druzes, and it ended in plain Arabic, forbidding, to our surprise, the departure of the caravan for Damascus.

We conjectured the cause of all this, but resolved to go on with our work, asking no questions, until events should reveal themselves.

We explored the ruins the next morning, and found them very extensive, but very much tossed about and crushed into heaps. The place must have been of considerable importance in the past as well as in the present; and the fact of its not being mentioned in history is easily accounted for, on the supposition that its name was changed in the early centuries of our era from Soada to Dionysias, and this conjecture receives confirmation from the fact that "Smith," in a Greek inscription, calls Dionysus the founder of the city.[1]

If it were Dionysias, it had considerable fame, ecclesiastically and otherwise;* but the identification is only a plausible theory, *and it ought to remain a theory until proved.* The necessity for this last observation will appear the more obvious when we remember how many

[1] Waddington's *Inscriptions Greques et Latines*, p. 531.

TEMPLE AT ES-SUWEIDEH.

Hauran theories have been already set aside. We were assured in books that two Greek inscriptions among the ruins of Suweideh had been erected by two companies, which were prototypes of our East India and other famous companies; but when the inscriptions were carefully examined, they turned out to have been no companies at all that erected them, but two historic Arab tribes. Nor is it easy to understand how this blunder was made, for the Greek word translated "company" is rendered by the word "tribus."

There was a large population among the ruins, and among them some Jews and Christians; but the door was effectually closed against missionary operations by late impracticable attempts to open it.

Waked el-Hamdân was not one of those who "welcome the coming and speed the parting guest," and so he would not hear of our departure; but we finally succeeded in taking leave of the kindly old patriarch and his amiable family, and galloped out of the town to show we could ride.

At first we passed among fields with high stone walls, and with many bases of round towers here and there, seven or eight being in sight at once. Druze women were in the fields gathering loads of yellow weeds out of the wheat. They all wore horns, and had unusually dirty veils thrown over them. They had a very ingenious way of getting the loads on their donkeys. They tied up one of the animal's legs and threw it down, and having rolled the sack of weeds on its back, they tugged at its tail till it got up. The poor animal in trying to rise generally stumbled and fell two or three times with the load upon it, so that this system of loading donkeys cannot be recommended on humane grounds.

Passing over a hill, we came in sight of Raha, and we saw on the rising ground to the left twenty-three yoke of oxen ploughing in one field. It was here a custom with the Druzes to meet together and plough each other's land in company. Our way now lay across stony meadows. On our left was Kuleib, *the pivot*, or *little heart*, a lofty cone at the southern end of the Druze mountain. It was once a volcano, and the crater is still lying open before us.

The trend of the lava from Kuleib was in a south-western direction, and we were anxious to know if the basalt stretched any further, and whence came the lava which is east of the mountain. Our curiosity was of short duration; for as we passed east of the extinct volcano Kuleib we still found the basaltic lava-bed continued, and there were many cones, large and small, with the peculiar gash in their south-western sides, and we could see clearly that the basalt south-east of Kuleib was traceable to these numerous exhausted volcanoes.

Following a little stream, we came to a fountain called 'Ain Mousa, with a Greek inscription over it, containing the name of "Isaac, the jeweller." By the fountain there was a shepherd boy playing on a reed pipe to a flock of goats and lambs. The music was of the simplest, there being only, as far as we could make out, two notes; but the boy was so "charmed with the sound himself had made" that he scarcely noticed us as we passed; and never did "high-born maiden in her palace bower" give more rapt attention to the strains of some distracted lover, borne on the midnight air, than did these appreciative sheep and goats to the serenade of the modern David. In fact, they shut their eyes, and nodded, and rocked from side to side, and seemed lulled into drowsiness.

A little beyond the fountain we entered El-Kufr, through high-walled fields, and rode round the town before going to the sheikh's house. When at length we reached the house, we found a number of Druzes armed and in conclave in a large, dark room. One of them, Abu Ali, whom I had once assisted in getting a friend out of prison, recounted what I had done, and so I became immediately a great hero. Abu Ali, however, was sorry he could not tell me what all the arming meant, but assured me that we were perfectly safe as long as we were among the Druzes.

Having used all the compliments we could think of, three or four times over, and a silence ensuing, we mounted amidst the most hearty hand-shaking and rode away. We then passed through lovely meadows, "o'er the smooth, enamelled green," to a wooded upland.

As I stopped on the knoll waiting for my party in the rear, I watched the efforts of a butcher-bird to secure a lizard. The lizard was one of the long, yellow kind, and several times it escaped from the bird's beak, and made for a heap of stones; but at last the butcher-bird carried it off in triumph and impaled it on a thorn. There were different kinds of butcher-birds about, and warblers that I could not see, which sent forth from the bushes a strange sweet song; and there were, in the open patches among the trees, storks, with stately steps, that had not forgotten their season.

We visited Hebrân to the right on the hill, and had a magnificent view of the landscape. We explored the churches, which were once idol temples, and read the Greek inscriptions which, even on this wild summit, "Smith" has left behind him. A cuckoo, a rare bird in the land, flew out of the ruined church as we entered it. The church had no other tenant except the lizards on the walls.

The Druzes of Hebrân were by far the most ruffianly-looking set we had seen in the Hauran, but they were civil to us. I almost shuddered to think of the treatment an enemy would meet in that fastness.

The women were not civil, and they looked even more villanous than the men.

From the village we descended a very steep hill, passed great dams of yellow water, caught from the winter rain, and proceeded through a pathless, stony plain, with abundance of grass growing among the stones. In some of the fields I counted over one hundred storks. We passed the village Schewet el-Khudr on our left. Khudr is the Arabic name of St. George, who was put to death, under Diocletian, at Lydda(?), and whose bones repose in the Church of St. George at Ezr'a (?). The saint is held in the highest veneration by Moslems as well as by Christians. They all make pilgrimages to his shrine here, and on the 23rd of May they sacrifice a lamb on the threshold of the chapel of St. George.

On our right, over against Schewet el-Khudr, is an extinct volcano, called Tell Miriam — the Mound of Mary. The evening shadow lay black on the mouth of the crater, and brought out its character very distinctly. Here, in a lonely spot, we met five armed Druzes, who deployed in the most skilful manner as we approached, and yet their action was so quiet and natural that one could hardly believe they were preparing for defence. One remained with the horses, and the others took up positions among the rocks, from which it would have been extremely difficult to dislodge them.

We pushed on straight for Ormân, but from the time we came opposite Sulkhad we entered among high-walled gardens. The walls still stood very high, but the gardens were uncultivated. For days we had been exploring the secret recesses of untenanted houses, but now we entered among well-fenced gardens that for ages had known no cultivator. For miles and miles we saw the gardens and vineyards, from which the vine had disappeared, and the silence and desolation were as oppressive as among the homeless houses of the deserted cities of the Lejah.

I have often said to myself, as I wandered from chamber to chamber of some deserted palace, "This was once, probably, the home of some chief, looked up to by his neighbours, whose footstep was listened for by wife and children, and there were here the thousand domestic ties that bind a man to place." But now we were passing through desolate vineyards from which joy had been taken away, and we saw how literally the judgments pronounced by Jeremiah had been here fulfilled: "And joy and gladness is taken from the plentiful field, and from the land of Moab; and I have caused wine to fail from the winepresses: none shall tread with shouting" (Jer. xlviii. 33).

We have now reached the place where I must fulfil my promise, and speak of the object and uses of the round towers that we meet with throughout the Hauran; and the place is most fitting, for here every garden has its tower, some small, some large, according to the size of the gardens.

In investigating the unknown, we should always proceed from the known. The question then is, Have we anything known at present corresponding to these towers, and have we any written notice of such towers? I think I may answer these questions in the affirmative. I believe that these towers corresponded exactly, in use and object, to the *mantaras*, or watch-towers, now raised in the plain of Damascus, and elsewhere, wherever crops are raised.

In the plain of Damascus, for instance, four long poles are planted firmly in the ground in the form of a square. Near their tops sticks are fastened across from pole to pole, and a large cage is made and covered over, from which one or two men watch the crops and keep off robbers.

For such uses were the towers at Ormân; but they were built of stone, the material which was most abundant, and such were nearly all the towers in the Hauran.

The round tower near Khubab, of which I gave a picture, stood not far from a well, and the land around it had once been cultivated, and it was doubtless the *mantara* for the bits of garden watered from the well, and for the fields round about.

But the chief key to unlock the secret of these mysterious towers may be found in the parable where our blessed Lord speaks of a " householder which planted a vineyard, and hedged it round about and digged a wine-press in it, and *built a tower*, and let it out to husbandmen " (Matt. xxi. 33). To-day, in Syria, every vineyard and garden has its tower, bearing the same relation to the permanent structures of the past as does everything modern in the land.

A few round towers were *mantaras* for beacon lights, such as the Kasr Mabroom above Kanawât, and the towers on the hills along the road from Damascus to Aleppo. Some square towers, where Palmyra influence prevailed, were for the bodies of the dead; but nearly all the towers in the land clearly correspond in use and object to the tower mentioned in the parable.

In the neighbourhood of Damascus men sit in these *mantaras* all day, watching a few roods of melon, or a field of maize, or a vineyard, and they sleep in them during the night; and no doubt these high towers of the Hauran were slept in during the summer, and were used as refuges in times of danger; but most of those that exist now were originally intended as watch-towers.

But if so, why so many together, as at Kanawât? From

their position at Kanawât, they were intended to command the plain and the vineyards on the opposite hill, which shows signs of terraced cultivation, and from the spot where the towers are the watchmen could have a bird's-eye view of every vine on the hill. Each man who had a vineyard on the hill would have a tower from which to watch it; and doubtless he and his family slept there during the summer months. As we entered Ormân, enormous flocks of sheep were converging to the village from all sides.

We received a welcome, unusually hearty, from the sheikh, Ibrahîm Nejm el-Atrash, and the other Druzes who remembered my previous visits. The sheikh was a splendid-looking, big, dark man, about two hundred and eighty pounds' weight. He was also a mighty man of valour, and it was believed that bullets could not pierce him. He occupied one of the outposts of the Druzes, and had to bear the first shock of Arab invasion. He had a large body of Druzes under his command, and they were all well armed, and nearly all well mounted.

In the autumn of 1810, Burckhardt visited Ormân and found it uninhabited. At the time of my visit it had a large Druze population, chiefly made up of men who had been civilized off the Lebanon, and whose interest it is to be far from the government; and Nejm el-Atrash ruled as supremely in this cave of Adullam, over his outlaws, as David did over his wild following.

The sheikh and his son, and their retainers, visited us in our tent after dinner. They examined all our books, and for hours we read to them portions of the New Testament. We were much impressed with their intelligence, and especially with their knowledge of foreign politics.

Next morning we returned the visit, and found the sheikh sitting in the gate, surrounded by all his followers. The news that disturbed the Druzes on our path had arrived, and a council of war was being held. The sheikh rose and met us, and took us to the guest-chamber, a large, low-roofed house, once a church, erected from material rifled from other buildings.

The roof was supported on two sets of heavy arches, and stone rafters laid across from arch to arch formed the roof. Light was admitted only by the chimney and door, and served to make the darkness visible. The roof was ebon black, ebon stalactites seemed to hang from the rafters, and the chamber was sombre in the extreme. Crowds of Druzes sat around in the thick darkness. Two Christian altars, with Christian emblems and inscriptions, stood in the middle of the floor, having probably never been removed from the building since the time it was a Christian church. We had first, as in all other places, to go through the ordeal of waiting for and drinking coffee, in a becoming manner.

The ceremony was worthy of a sketch, especially as modern civilization had never yet affected the stereotyped customs of this remote village. My companion was deciphering a Greek inscription on one of the altars in the floor, so that I was able to take accurate notes of the coffee-making, the Druzes thinking that I was writing the inscription to dictation.

The operator, a thick-lipped Abyssinian, sat down, evidently deeply impressed with the importance of the operation he was about to commence.

He first took a handful of small green coffee-berries from a sooty bag, and put them in an iron pan with a long iron handle, which he held over the fire in the middle of the floor, stirring the berries till they were brown (not black). Then he put them into a wooden mortar, beautifully carved, and with a long wooden similarly-carved pestle he pounded them to the tune of rat-e-tat-tat. The music was so impressive that every one listened in deep silence, and with fallen under lip. He broke the berries fine, but did not pound them into dust, and he emptied them into a very grimy pot, which he placed on the fire in the centre of the chamber.

When the coffee had boiled a little, he took six cups, poured a little water into one of them, and held it, with his fingers outside the cup and his thumb inside, and dexterously turning it rubbed the bottom all round with his thumb. He then poured the water out of the cup into another, and so on till the last.

Then he emptied a little coffee into the first cup, rinsed it, and emptied it into the second, and so on till he rinsed with coffee all the cups. These rinsings are not thrown away, but poured back into a pot of second-quality coffee for the common guests. He had now reached the climax, when he solemnly poured out a little coffee into cup number one, and bravely drank it off, to show it was not poisoned. He then filled the six little cups, which were as large as egg cups, about half full, and they were gravely handed round.

When we had finished, we handed our cups back unto a brass tray, and the slave instantly covered them with his hand, that no one might know whether we trusted our host by drinking or only pretending to drink; and we, having laid down our cups, made graceful bows to our host, accompanied with our sweetest smiles and a stereotyped expression.

Before the coffee ceremony was over, we had become so accustomed to the darkness that we could see the outlines of the Druzes, who sat in concentric circles around the room. And what a thrilling picture might have been made of the dark room by the genius of a Rembrandt!

The sheikh, who had never learned the art of "honeying at the whisper of a lord," and who feared no potentate, publicly announced to us the cause of the excitement.

The government of the Hauran had resolved to levy a new tax on the Hauran. The governor had assembled the sheikhs of the villages and proceeded to value the land. The people had risen in their wrath and slain two of the sheikhs, and the governor had saved himself by flight. The people then wreaked their vengeance on any emblems of Ottoman rule they could find. They tore down fourteen miles of the telegraphic wires, and all the officials fled for their lives. The government had ordered up cannon and troops, and threatened vengeance, and the

Hauranees replied that on the 14th of April they would leave the Hauran *en masse.*

The sheikh then pointed to the messenger who had brought the report, and wound up a calm statement of facts by a few impassioned, burning sentences: "The quarrel of the Hauran is our quarrel. If they tax them, they will also tax us. The government does nothing for us — does not defend us from the Bedawîn — does not make roads for us; and having driven us from our fathers' homes in Lebanon, they now follow us into this desert, that we have reclaimed by our industry and defend with our lives. Shall our children be as cruelly wronged as we have been? No, my children! We will unite with our suffering brethren in the Hauran. We must meet the enemy on the threshold before he enters our harems. With a righteous cause, and God on our side, we are invincible." We required no preternatural perception to see that the sheikh spoke the sentiments of every one present.

Of all who heard the sheikh's declaration we were, perhaps, the most annoyed, for we had resolved to return home through the district that had become disturbed, and offer our books at every village. At Ormân I met a Druze teacher from Mount Hermon, who long ago came to me and professed to be a Christian. He gave me an autobiography, showing by what processes of thought and education he had become a Christian. Chiefly through the influence of this man we were enabled to sell more books in Ormân than at any other village.

Ormân is the *Ultima Thule* of travellers in the Hauran, but most of them wisely content themselves by looking at it from the castle of Sulkhâd. It was with no ordinary pleasure and surprise that we heard there was an inhabited city two hours east of Ormân in the desert. We rejoiced that the "Handbook" knew nothing of the city, and we resolved to become discoverers ourselves, whatever might be the result.

We sprang to our horses with some of the feelings of Columbus when he started on his great voyage of discovery. We brought with us a mule, with luncheon and books, — all good generals think of the commissariat, — but we soon vanished from the sight of the muleteer, riding into the unknown desert, and we did the whole distance in half the prescribed time.

The morning mirage lay all about, exaggerating every little ruin into "giant cities" and "donjon-keeps," and we felt the spirit of exaggeration creeping upon ourselves — that spirit which generally enters into a man in the Hauran. On our right, on distant hills that bordered the horizon, were many ruins, and a few on our left also. We stopped occasionally in our headlong career "*to take a round of angles*," but it was only for a moment, for we had ceased tamely to follow in the footsteps of others, and we had become discoverers ourselves. Our pace for the future would only be "a hand gallop," and woe betide any luckless Arab tribe that might cross our track!

At last a town rose up before us, in the mirage larger

than Palmyra. On we spurred fiercely, and five high towers (like those at Palmyra) came safely out of the mirage and stood majestically around on the city walls. The walls were high, but there were breaches in them here and there; and there was much apparent bustle about the city, and over twenty yoke of oxen were ploughing in the suburbs. The name of the place proved to be Melah es-Sarrâr.

STONE DOOR (HAURAN).

COIN OF BOSRA.

CHAPTER XXVIII.

WE completed our exploration of Melah es-Sarrâr in a spirit of high-wrought enthusiasm. We found it an irregular square, surrounded by high walls partly in ruins, with great towers in the walls, in some places grouped two and two, and over sixty feet high. They resembled the towers of Palmyra, but contained no *loculi* for bodies. Five of these high towers were in a good state of preservation, three more were in a tolerable state, and there were foundations of several others in different quarters.

The ruins were wonderfully crushed together, and "battered by the shocks of doom." Some of the ruins had very lofty doors, and there were a number of very high arches standing among the ruins, the object of which it is difficult to conjecture. On many of the lintels we saw Greek crosses, and we copied eight Greek inscriptions, one of them dedicated to Dusares, a deity much worshipped in Bashan.

The town stands in the midst of a large cultivated plain, which, when looked at horizontally, seems one flat of grey stones, but when you ride through it you find that all the stones are loose, and that the soil among them is all cultivated. Owing to the altitude of the plain, they were still ploughing and sowing a little on the 11th of April. From one of the towers of Melah es-Sarrâr we counted fourteen other ruins in sight, and most of them inhabited. On the top of a hill, due east, stands a very conspicuous ruin, Deir en-Nasara, the convent of the Christians, which is said, I hope truly, to be the last ruin in that direction.

A large number of Druzes and some Christians burrowed among the ruins of Melah es-Sarrâr. Their sheikh was Husein Abu Muhammed, a son of Nejm, sheikh of Ormân. Husein was not so big as his father, but resembled him very much, and was exceedingly handsome and gentlemanly. From him we learned that the ruin was visited three years previously. We conjectured rightly that it must have been by the indefatigable Waddington, but we were very much chagrined when we found that we could not have even this little corner beyond the bounds of civilization exclusively for our own exploration. Immediately the glory began to fade from colossal tower and massive ruin, and we put the whole thing down as late Roman — in fact, Byzantine.[1]

[1] The coins we found were Byzantine, and one of Bosra, with the name Dusaria.

And rightly, too, for one of the Greek inscriptions dates from the middle of the seventh century; and the names of places, such as Deir en-Nasara and Imtan el-Khudr, show that the region attained to eminence during the time that Christianity, victorious, was becoming degenerate.

While we were seated in the guest-chamber with the sheikh and his people, two Arabs arrived, who were a wonderful contrast to the Druzes. They had on them the left-off habiliments of the Jebusites, and they entered the chamber as if going to execution. They cast quick, furtive glances at everybody, without being able to meet any one's look in return. Their voices, a kind of glugging bark, seemed borrowed from the camel, and appeared to sound up out of their boots. They were salt-smugglers from the Jowf.

There are fine beds of salt at Jerûd and Palmyra; but a few years ago the Turks declared the salt to be government property, and forbade any one to carry it away on pain of severe punishment. They did not, however, bring it to the cities themselves, and so the price of salt rose enormously without any one gaining advantage from the high price; and so, while enormous piles of salt, like a frozen sea, lay uselessly at Jerûd, a day's journey from Damascus, these creatures were engaged in smuggling it from the distant Jowf. They entered in the most thievish and sheepish manner, and as soon as they were seated they were presented with a bronze basin of water, of which they drank enormously. The Druzes seemed to look upon these Arab guests with good-natured contempt; and I have no doubt the aristocrats of the desert look down in turn upon the Druzes as upon a plebeian race.

We returned past Ormân, where we waved an adieu to the sheikh *en passant*, and, joining some men who were waiting for our protection on the road, we proceeded through a fenced country to Sulkhâd, where we pitched our tent for the night.

Sulkhâd is doubtless the Salchah of the Bible, one of the northern boundaries (Deut. iii. 10) of the kingdom of Og. We found the name in a Nabathean inscription on the front of a church now used as a dwelling-house, but the Arabic name is sufficient of itself to settle the identification of the place.

Sulkhâd is a large Druze village containing, according to Burckhardt, eight hundred houses. The town is situated on the south-eastern base of a conical hill which was once a volcano. A magnificent castle now stands on the very crater of the volcano, and the scoriæ, or volcanic cinders, are lying about. The castle is Saracenic, and the walls are full of Greek inscriptions rifled from other buildings.

The chief building in Sulkhâd is the mosque, which is made up of beautiful odds and ends from temple and church and shop.

The roof is supported by nineteen arches, which rest on buttresses built of square stones. Light is admitted through windows of beautiful patterns worked in stone, and the roof is composed of long stone rafters, reaching from arch to arch.

Five of the arches in a corner are walled off for the secret meeting-place of the Druzes. It must be a sombre assembly-room, for it has no windows, except a few pigeon-holes among the stones. Across the court from the mosque,

LEBANON DRUZES.

there is a beautiful minaret, standing alone, with a belt of white stone round it about half-way up, and on the belt a Kufic inscription, dating from A.D. 1224.

Streets of shops lie open and unused, but show many signs of wear and occupation. A large number of houses in the village have been repaired, and are now occupied. The place was almost unoccupied when visited by Burckhardt; but the tax-gatherers, and the money-lenders, and other civilizing agencies have driven whole colonies of the Druzes from the Lebanon to these distant and congenial regions.

The Sheikh Muhammed el-Atrash was absent, for troublous times had arrived, and the turbulent spirits were up and moving. I shall never, however, forget the circumstances under which he received us on my first visit to Sulkhâd. We arrived after dark, and pitched our tent in a tempest of rain. The sheikh sent for us, and when we entered his large guest-chamber, we found it packed full of Bedawîn. They were the Isai, who had made an onslaught that day on the Ma'ajal, and had been victorious.

We had at last before us an Arab army, and an Arab army flushed with victory. Their spears were yet red, and they had the trophies of war with them,—thirteen mares, ninety camels, and forty guns. The rain had driven them to seek shelter in the sheikh's house, and he was preparing them a feast. A great fire was blazing in the middle of the floor, and tongues of flame licked the stone ceiling. The smoke was thick and bitter, but we bore it for sake of the heat, as our clothes were drenched through and through.

The dinner could not have been much more savage, and

CASTLE OF SALCHAH.

yet there was order. A brass tray, seven feet in diameter, was carried in by four men, and placed in the middle of the floor. On the tray was a great heap of *burgal* — crushed wheat, boiled. A number of sheep had been cooked together outside in a large cauldron, and two men carried in a pot full of gravy, which very much resembled coal-tar, and poured it over the heap of *burgal*. My friend naively suggested, " That is the snowy pyramid we read of in the guide-book"; and we held our breath for fear we should be invited to begin.

The animals were torn up, each into four pieces, and built up round the " snowy pyramid."

The sheikh, when everything was ready, mounted a Christian altar, which stood in the corner of the room, and calling out rapidly twenty or thirty names, the men rushed forward as they heard their names and attacked the pyramid. Each caught up a handful of *burgal*, and, rolling it up in a ball, put it into his mouth, and then, tearing a handful of the flesh from some quivering limb, put that in also. When these had fed noisily for about five minutes, they suddenly fell back into the outer darkness, and another relay advanced at the word of command, with bare, black arms and hungry eyes.

There seems to be this broad difference between an Arab feast and a civilized feast: with civilized people there are courses of dishes, but with the Arabs the men form the courses. And so they advanced, course after course, at the word of command, till, with the seventh course, my muleteers advanced, according to their rank, and fell with great fury — for it was Lent, and they had been fasting — on a great heap of bare bones and greasy *burgal*. There was a course lower still; to the last the guests advanced with the same hungry look of desperate determination. When the men had all feasted the remains of the feast were carried off and thrown in a heap for the women.

We left Sulkhâd for Kureiyeh by the Roman road, and after a short time, fearing that we had missed the turning to the right, some of our party rode off in search of it, and thus our cavalcade got divided. We soon grew nervous for the safety of our companions, who were strangers in the country, and started off to look for them, and so we wandered about looking for each other in vain; nor was our anxiety diminished by the fact that armed bands of wild-looking men were riding through the land, and firing off their guns. Our muleteers, who had been stealing some growing wheat for their mules, came up breathless, having been chased by "fourteen men" with guns, — perhaps there were four!

At last, weary of climbing over the billows of a rocky ocean, we left our errant companions to their fate, and struck right across the hills for Kureiyeh. About one-third of the soil was under cultivation, with the stones piled up in cairns. We started a very small black hare and two foxes, and we saw swarms of partridges and storks. The small birds were chiefly wheatears and Persian larks, which screamed a great deal, but had little music. The ground was covered with hyacinths, white daisies, and beautiful dark irises.

We hurried on and reached the brow of a hill, and to our inexpressible relief saw our lost party riding up before us into Kureiyeh. We had crossed each other, but how, we could not explain; no doubt we went up the furrow of one wave, and they came down the furrow of another.

We entered Kureiyeh in company with a shepherd, and found that Ibrahîm el-Atrash and most of the important Druzes of the place had gone off to Damascus to try to ward off the coming struggle. We made a hasty survey of the place, and passed on to Bosra.

At first the ground was very stony. By-and-by the stones were gathered out of the fields, and gave place to cultivation; and the latter part of our way was through a broad wavy sea of wheat, with ruins standing up here and there like black islands. The ruins of Bosra stood up massively before us, and we entered the city, passed a large tank built of cut stones, just as the setting sun flung back a golden good-bye to capital and spire of Grecian column and Saracenic minaret.

Bosra was just what we expected it to be, a splendid city in ruins,—palaces, castles, theatres, baths, temples, colonnades, triumphal arches, churches, and mosques, all magnificent, and all in ruins. Bosra was the greatest city in Bashan at the period when Roman rule was leaving its impress upon the land. From the castle we could see the true evidences of Bosra's greatness in the numerous Roman roads that converged to the city from north, south, east, and west. In whatever direction we looked, we saw these roads narrowing in the distance, until they ended in a fine point on the distant horizon.

Bosra proper lies nearly foursquare, its greatest length being east and west, and each side of the rectangular figure is over a mile. It stands in the open plain, but was

BOSRA.

surrounded by strong walls, and it has a magnificent castle. The outer walls of the castle are Saracenic, and some parts of them are built almost entirely of columns squared, and

COLUMNS AT BOSRA.

placed in the walls with the ends out. They also contain numerous Greek and Latin inscriptions, generally placed with the wrong side of the inscriptions uppermost. The walls of the castle, however, were built round a Roman structure, probably a similar castle, as they contain a Roman theatre in a good state of preservation. "Smith" was busy in Bosra, and he has left engraven on stone over four hundred lines of Greek and Latin inscriptions, the earliest of which date from the second century of our era. In one of these we find that the worship of Dusares, whose name we met elsewhere, was still practised in the middle of the sixth century. On a marble column in the great mosque there is one most interesting Greek inscription, contained within two circular lines. It begins thus: "In the name of our Saviour Christ," etc. It is not without pain that one thus meets the name of Christ as one among many deities of a bygone worship.

In the mosque of Bosra, which Burckhardt says "is certainly coeval with the first era of Mohammedanism," we see a characteristic specimen of Moslem architecture in its palmiest days; and in front of the mosque there are the *dakakîn*, or little arched shops, which the Moslems built on the sites of Roman boulevards, and in which they squatted beside their piles of wares, and swore and cheated as they do to-day in Damascus.

By the side of this specimen of Moslem architecture there are fragments of architecture from the best days of the Roman dominion. There are columns towering above the ruins to a height of forty-five feet, and, in particular, there are "the four large Corinthian columns" referred to by Burckhardt as "equalling in beauty of execution the finest of those at Baalbec or Palmyra."

To show a fine cultivated taste, we should say here, as at Baalbec, Palmyra, and elsewhere, " Yes, yes, very fine, but too florid for correct taste!"

Evidently we have not yet acquired correct taste, for to us these columns, in the wilderness of ruins, seem wonderfully perfect and surpassingly lovely. What adds to the marvellous effect of the columns is the *negligé* manner in which they are placed. They stand at irregular distances from each other, and it does not *appear*, from anything we can see, that they have ever had any connection with any other building.

The cathedral church of Bosra,[1] which was built early in the sixth century, is a fine specimen of Christian architecture.

It has a general resemblance to the church of St. George in Zerá, but is much larger and finer. A few traces of fresco are still seen on the walls, but there is sufficient to show the idolatrous character of Christianity in Bosra in the sixth century. It would be an instructive chapter that would show how the corruptions of the Christian church prepared the way for the triumphs of Islam.

We spent the first night in Bosra in trying to keep the

[1] This is the church of the monk Boheira, who was believed to have coached up Muhammed in Biblical history.

THEATRE AND CASTLE.

RUINS OF BOSRA.

tent over us, for a terrible hurricane swept over the plain, and seemed to mingle heaven and earth in one great dust cloud. The sand was blown into every place, into our mouths and noses and down our throats, and when we attempted a tea breakfast we had to hold the palms of our hands on the mouths of the cups to keep out the dirt.

Sunday morning broke red and lowering through the dust cloud, reminding me of a morning in the Mediterranean after a tempestuous night. The city enjoyed its Sabbath. Doubtless, once there was the roar of Sabbath desecration in this great centre, but at the time of our visit it was as quiet as the grave, — in fact, it was the huge grave of a great, proud, luxurious city.

The captain of the garrison in the castle, spying our tent among the ruins, sent us word that we must remove our tent into the castle, as the country was in such a disturbed state that he could not be accountable for our safety beyond the walls of the castle. We felt that to erect our tent in the castle would entirely interfere with our chief object, and so, resolving to look out for our own safety, we pitched it in a green field, sheltered by a large building with a curiously-arched roof.

We proceeded, however, to the castle, where we found the captain, a handsome young Syrian, drilling his men, and preparing for defence. He had two guns drawn up at the entrance, where there was a guard sufficient to prevent a surprise, and in case of the approach of a large force, to close the huge door. At all the weak points he had sentinels, and watchers on the high towers.

The captain conducted us to the commandant, whom we found still in bed. He was a typical little Turk, with bandy legs, and a nose like the scabbard of a Persian scimitar. He occupied a little ruinous chamber at the highest corner of the castle, near the flagstaff. Over the chinks and holes in the walls bits of the *Illustrated London News* had been pasted, serving as windows, but the violence of the storm had blown them all away.

On a straw mat in the corner, this little Turkish officer had his "shake-down," consisting of a few sheepskins and two *leehafs* or quilts stuffed with wool or cotton.

Contrary to our wishes, we were obliged to enter the room before the little man had got into his enormous trousers; but without betraying any secrets of the chamber of rest, I am free to express my opinion that such sleeping arrangements ought to be conducive to early rising. The little man was delighted to see us, and a letter from the Wali, which I presented to him, he placed on his head, to show his reverence for the authority behind it; but he was in a most uncomfortable state of mind, for the people of the Hauran had threatened to abandon their homes on the morrow, if the government persisted in their demands.

He declared that they were in a state of siege, and that for the last two weeks all their letters to and from Damascus had been intercepted, and he feared that the people of the Hauran might converge on the Turkish garrison at Bosra. He said he would not be surprised to see thirty thousand or fifty thousand armed men appear around the castle at any moment.

RUINS OF BOSRA.

We asked if he would be able to defend himself, and if the garrison would be able to hold out, and he only answered with Turkish passivity and helplessness, "Allah karîm" (God is honourable).

In contrast with the commandant, the captain was full of confidence and energy. He had been indefatigable the last fortnight in trying to make soldiers of the garrison, and now he was waiting watchfully for the shock. A battle was expected that day at Mezareeb, and they were listening for the sound of the guns. The wildest rumours were afloat, and the officers assured us that we must not think of leaving for three or four days, as a hundred horsemen could not guard us beyond the walls of the city. This news was most disappointing, for we had resolved to strike across the desert by Um el-Jemâl (Beth-Gamul) to Es-Salt, but the disturbances rendered such an enterprise out of the question.

We spent an uncomfortable day at Bosra, and wandered over miles of ruins as far as Bab el-Howa, the Gate of the Wind. Wherever we went, we were dogged by tall, sooty-looking men, with long hair and big clubs. We kept our eyes upon them, and they kept at a respectful distance from us. Beyond the walls of the city proper, the suburbs extended far into the plain, as may be seen from the numerous foundations; but the houses seemed to have been very small, and the streets very narrow, both within and without the walls.

We spent a long and peaceful time in the ruined mosque, which had only one entrance, and we felt assured that no one could enter unseen by us. Evidently our followers had lost our scent, for we were left undisturbed. At last a native Christian entered the mosque, made a casual remark, and slipped away.

It was time for us to be moving once more, for that Christian had been sent to *explore* us. And indeed for all such business in the Hauran, Christians are employed. At Schwet el-Khudr, Hebrân, and Ormân, we had met

BAB EL-HOWA, THE GATE OF THE WIND.

Christians bearing the "fiery cross" through the land for their local masters.

As we left the mosque a drumming sound at a little distance attracted our attention. I saw that an attack was about to be made upon us, and I directed my companion to slip quietly down a back way to our camp, and leave me to deal with the mob. As I approached the angle near the four columns, I saw a crowd of eight or ten stalwarts hurrying to intercept me, and, as I could not run past them, I husbanded all my strength to meet them.

They quickly surrounded me, and demanded my money. I told them who I was, not an ordinary traveller, but a missionary, and that I had books for them, if they would come to my tent; that I had no money to give away, and that I would not give them any if I had.

I was standing on a high bank, with my back to a wall, and they were all below me, and thus I kept them at bay for a few minutes. At last the leader of the party seized me by the throat, but instantly he fell rolling like a bundle to the bottom of the bank. The thing was so instantaneous that the whole party seemed stunned and paralyzed, and I walked quietly away. I moved off in such a manner that I could see the mob, without seeming to do so, as the eye takes in a wide angle. As I turned the corner of a ruin, I saw that they had collected their thoughts, and were gathering stones and starting in pursuit of me. Having got round the corner, I ran straight for the tent, and with more than my old college pace, I was soon clear of my pursuers.

The Turkish officers visited our tent in the evening, and the watchers were still looking towards the west from the towers. Two or three alarms had been given during the day, when a band of Arabs hove in sight on the horizon; but through the long day of suspense no trustworthy news had reached them.

They urged us to remain, as it was impossible to depart in safety; and when we assured them that we would go if there were fifty battles being fought, they insisted that we should take twelve men as a guard, led by one of themselves.

I verily believed that the little Turk wanted to escape with us to Damascus. We protested in vain, and twelve men were told off to accompany us in the morning. We spent another sleepless night in Bosra, disturbed, however, by no sound except that of the horses crumping their barley, and my companion quoting again and again the Homeric couplet, as rendered by Tennyson, —

> "And champing golden grain, the horses stood
> Hard by their chariots, waiting for the dawn."

The dawn at last came, and while the morning star "blazed in the forehead of the morning sky," we gave the soldiers the slip, and started for the Druze mountain.

On the previous year we went straight from 'Ary to Mezareeb, through a wondrous plain of wheat. On our left, behind and before, the sea of wheat stretched away to the distant hills. When, a few days before, we had looked down from Jebel el-Kuleib we saw what seemed to be little lakes of blood among the wheat.

We concluded it was some phenomenon produced by the setting sun and the mirage, but as we passed along we found that wherever there was a break in the wheat the ground was all ablaze with scarlet poppies.

In working our way over the hill to Kefr el-Laha, we were in doubt about the way, and I struck off to the right to look for the road. Passing over a little hill, a solitary Druze saw me, and rushed straight at me. He had an ox-goad — a long pole tipped with an iron spike — in his right hand, and as he came up close to me he snatched a dagger out of his belt.

According to this man's idea, the battle of Mezareeb had been fought, and the Turks had been beaten, and I was one of the Turkish officers escaped thus far, — a fugitive to be promptly despatched. I had a good idea of what these men are, on their native mountains, when their blood is up. With head thrown back, and eyes flashing, he bounded up to me like a strong bull of Bashan. He was confounded by my laughing at him.

"Don't you see I am an Inglizi?" I said to him, with a laugh.

His whole demeanour instantly changed, and from being one of the most heroic of men, he became a quiet-looking old patriarch, about sixty years of age or more. He inquired eagerly if I had heard how the battle went; but he was incoherent, and so confused that he sent us on the wrong way. At last we entered Kefr el-Laha at a sharp gallop, and the sound of our horses' feet brought the Druzes out of their assembly-room, swarming like wasps when their nest is touched.

Nothing worse happened than a kiss from the sheikh. We rushed at each other, placed our two hands on the front of each other's shoulders, and reached our heads over each other's shoulders as if we were kissing some one behind each other's backs. Thus we did not in reality kiss, we only fell on each other's necks.

From Kefr el-Laha we might have proceeded by a direct route to Damascus. In a few hours we should have reached Shuhba, the ancient Philippopolis, a city which gave to Rome the Emperor Philip the Arabian, and gave to the Druzes the princely Koreish dynasty of Shehâb. Shuhba contains many evidences of its former greatness. Temples and columns and ruins of palatial

SHÛHBA, ROMAN BATH.

buildings abound, and on the ridge is a theatre well preserved. The place is well deserving of a visit, and on the straight way to Damascus there are many other interesting scenes and ruins; but I had been over the route previously, and so we proceeded to Rimet el-Lohf with intent to cross the Lejah from east to west.

COIN OF PHILIP STRUCK AT PHILOPPOPOLIS.

CHAPTER XXIX.

AT Rimet el-Lohf we found the Druzes as usual in conclave in their dark assembly-room. Sheikh Akhzîn accompanied us round the town, and pointed out to us all the antiquities of the place. These comprise a Christian church in ruins, a square mortuary tower about twenty feet high, and a number of inscriptions in Greek, Latin, and Nabathean.

The sheikh, after having shown us all he had to show, returned to his assembled brethren, and I started for a more thorough exploration of the village alone. As I passed the two reservoirs of the village I asked a drink from some Druze women, who were filling their jars, and they immediately became very talkative, and asked questions much faster than I could answer them. The first question generally asked by the women is, —

"*Have you entered the world?*" which means, "Are you married?"[1]

---

[1] The wailers at the funeral of an unmarried man make this their bitterest plaint, "Ma dakhal ed dunya" ("He had never entered the world").

Then they ran me through my catechism, about the colour of my wife's skin, whether or not she wore rings in her nose, and if she had any boys, the question nearest the hearts of these Spartan mothers. When they asked if it was true that with us the women ruled the men, I gave an evasive answer, and passed on from my horned catechisers.

While exploring an extensive private ruin, I dropped down through a break in the stone roof, and found to my astonishment that I had frightened a family from their supper. Fancy a man dropping through your ceiling when you are all at supper, and you will not be surprised to hear that I was received with a stony stare. I said all the apologies that I was acquainted with in Arabic, suitable to the circumstances, and immediately they were all delighted to see me, and no excuse would save me from partaking of their food. At last I consented on condition of every one returning to the place which he occupied previous to my unceremonious descent.

I had seen the patriarchal and lordly feast given by the sheikh again and again, always with the same dignified courtesy on the part of the host, and I was glad of an opportunity of joining with a poor family at their ordinary evening meal.

The family consisted of the father and mother, three plain girls, and a spoiled boy. They all squatted on a hair cloth round a little straw tray, on which was spread some barley bread, and in the centre of the bread stood a large

DRUZE SHEIKHS AT 'AHIRY.

earthenware bowl filled with *kishk*. The *kishk* has a smell like sauerkraut; it is made of *laban* (sour milk) and *burgal* (crushed wheat), which are mixed together and left standing until the whole mass is rotten. Then it is dried in the sun, and served up in many ways.

Our feast consisted of *kishk*, with a little greasy water poured over it, and well stirred up with a spoon. The women withdrew their veils, exposing mouths and chins horribly tattooed. The father of the family leant forward, and with a " Bismilla " (In the name of God) took a handful of the *kishk*, rolled it up in a ball, and threw it into his mouth. The others did accordingly. I confined myself exclusively to the black bread and brass bowl of water, which was handed round.

The smell of the *kishk* was sickening, and the bread, which was baked with cow's dung, had too much of the flavour of the fuel. The boy bullied his sisters and mother, patronized me, and contradicted his father on grave points of history, archæology, and domestic economy. The father seemed to enjoy his son's triumphs over himself.

One of the reasons why this boy assumed such airs with his father, was that he was one of the *ukkal*, or initiated in the higher mysteries of the Druze religion, a rank to which his father could not attain, as he would not abstain from swearing and smoking, and so he remained among the *jahhâl*, or ignorant, while his precocious boy of twelve was received into the highest rank.

When the maidens had each disposed of four or five balls apiece of *kishk*, about the size of a pigeon's egg, they started up and fell back one by one. This is the rule; no one waits for another at table. They feed rapidly and silently, and each one withdraws when he has done.

Leaving my hospitable entertainers, I proceeded to the square tower at the west of the village. It is a great tomb built in imitation of the Palmyra towers, with *loculi* round the walls for the reception of bodies. It has a fine Greek inscription over the entrance.

While copying an inscription in a garden wall close by the tower a tall, venerable Druze issued from a hole in a ruin, which appeared to be only an irregular heap of stones, and approaching took up a position beside me. He told me many wonderful stories, for the Druze people have an amazing faculty for believing the incredible.

The sheikh had taken a fancy to me, I was so good a listener, and invited me to his den. I refused to accompany him, urging the lateness of the hour, but being actually afraid of this strange old man, whom I saw heaving with inspiration in the glow of the setting sun.

When I rose to depart he seized my arm with a force that I did not think was in him, and began to drag me towards the ruin which he called his house. I went quietly along with him till just at the door, when, feeling his grasp relax, I plucked my arm out of his hand, and, jumping over a low wall, turned at a distance of ten or twelve yards to apologize.

As I hurried back to the tent I met the whole Druze population, who had been to our camp to see my wonderful gun, which my muleteers had informed them "has only to be wound up, and it will blaze away as long as you like without missing."

On April the 15th we were early working our way over the execrable path between Lohf and 'Ahiry. The grim appearance of the basalt was here relieved by the glancing green of the *butm* trees that grow among the stones. In about an hour we approached two beautiful *tells*, or conical hills, with fields of waving wheat sweeping round their bases, and surging up their sides, but not reaching to the top. 'Ahiry is at the base of the second *tell*, which is named Tell 'Ammâr.

This town is distinguished from all the towns of the Lejah in having a perennial supply of water. Among the numerous inscriptions that abound here we find the names of Aumos and Agenes, ancient deities of the Hauran.

On every side we saw Roman remains and Greek inscriptions, and from the *tell* we saw the abiding traces of the Roman dominion, in the road, stretching away in straight lines through the stony wilderness.

Sheikh Hussein pressed us much to stay for breakfast, but time pressed us still more to move, as we wished to cut right through the Lejah, and far out into the plain at the other side, during the day. The crowd that gathered round us here was of the usual character.

The Druzes, in person and dress, differ from the Moslems and Christians, who are pretty much alike. The tub-like turban [1] of the Druzes gives them a top-heavy

[1] The Druze turban consists of a white felt cap, which is covered by the red fez, and this is swathed about with calico until it assumes the

appearance; and indeed, heaviness, I might say grossness, in limb and feature, is their general characteristic. They are often very fair, have blue eyes, and are generally fat and ruddy. They are always well clothed, and are seldom met with barefooted.

The Moslems and Christians who live among the Druzes are, as a rule, lean and lithe, have black hair, dark, piercing eyes, and olive complexions. They wear a handkerchief over the head, fastened there with a hair-rope, and hanging down over the shoulders. They wear also a kind of cotton gown, with a sack-like garment thrown over it, and they are constantly met barefooted. They are "the hewers of wood and drawers of water" to the Hauran Druzes.

We struck once more into the Lejah in the direction of Dama, without guide or guard, as usual, though everybody assured us that the Arabs were in our path. I had been over the road once before, and we were, in fact, becoming sceptical about the ferocity of the Arabs. Besides, I had previous lessons in the Hauran on the value of guides and guards.

Once when reconnoitring the country with a view to future operations, we became excited at Khubab in reading the description of the wondrous approach of Dama. "Lofty, impending cliffs," "deep gullies and ravines," "a wild labyrinth that none but the Arabs can penetrate," are scenes rarely within one's reach, and too

dimensions of a tub about eight inches deep and eighteen inches in diameter.

tempting to be passed without a visit. A spice of danger was added to the wondrous bill of fare; for if we showed paper and pencil, which we certainly would do, we would be taken for magicians, and set upon by lawless vagabonds with clubs and stones. We had hitherto found everything tamer than we had expected, and our faces were at once set to go to Dama.

My companion had a magnificent rifle, which was safely packed up at the bottom of a box, and he carried a breech-loading fowling-piece — so much *improved* that it could hardly be fired at all. Our Arab guide had a *dabbous*; but then, we might calculate that he would be on the wrong side with this murderous weapon. Our guard, a Kurdish soldier, carried a little howitzer with a flint lock, but the arm had not been fired for a quarter of a century, nor was it ever loaded during our whole tour. My servant had also tied himself to a tremendous pistol; but he fired it for the first and last time as we were entering Damascus on our return, and it burst in the most becoming manner, blowing the lock into the air and injuring his hand.

Thus formidably equipped, and with a supply of sticking-plaster, we entered the Lejah on our perilous adventure. For the first hour we had to trace out our own way, as neither guide nor guard appeared, but at last they overtook us, and still urged us to go back.

We had set our lives upon a cast, and we would stand the hazard of the die! At last we reached Dama, and just as we came up to the entrance of the town, three women rushed up out of a deep pit where they had been filling skins with water. They raised a wild scream, and notwithstanding I cried, " We are not enemies, O sisters," the sisters rushed over the ruins like tigresses, screaming, and disappeared.

They were tremendous women, Amazons of the Hauran, the only remains of the giants that I feel certain about having seen in the whole district. " Now, we are in for it," we both uttered in the same instant, " for the women will bring the town upon us." My friend looked round to give a parting salute to the retreating guard, but he was nowhere to be seen. In fact, our whole party had discovered something extremely interesting in the rear, and did not join us for nearly an hour.

After waiting like Bob Acres, with our valour oozing out at our fingers' ends, and no infuriated mob coming to attack us, we picked up courage and entered the town *vi et armis*. The women had evidently hidden among the ruins, for the only human beings we saw in the place were three most savage-looking men, armed with *dabbouses*. These men kept away from us a distance of about four hundred yards, and we could not induce them to approach us, or to wait till we should approach them.

We wandered at will through the ruins, descended into vaults, and ascended into dormitories, and rambled over suites of apartments, and copied inscriptions, and shot partridges, and neither gave nor received injury. Neither did we see the " impending cliffs " nor " deep ravines."

The inscriptions proved to be of little value, and Dama

did not seem to have ever been of any great importance. It contains the ruins of one large building, the gate of which is adorned with vines and grapes, similar to what we saw at Kanawât. The houses were good, solid structures, *à la* Hauran, but they were all in a ruinous state. The town, which stood in one of the most dismal spots of the great lava bed, had neither spring nor fountain, as far as we could ascertain; but the rocks beyond the walls were full of excavated cisterns, the sides of which were plastered with cement, and in most of the houses we saw "broken cisterns" half filled with their stone roofs, which had fallen in. In subterranean chambers the winter rains were preserved for summer use.

In this dreary and deserted region we came upon patches of the most wonderful colouring. Wherever the soil remained among the rocks, "we scarce could see the ground for flowers." Crimson poppies, and white daisies, and yellow rape, and green grass, made a strikingly lovely picture, set in a rigid frame of black basalt.

Should any one accuse us of foolhardiness for going through the Hauran in those times without a guard, the foregoing experiences are our justification for dispensing with such impedimenta, especially as one's guards always bully the weak, cringe to the strong, and abuse the hospitality of one's hosts generally. The one great use of guards — to bear home the news in case you should be killed — we did not take deeply into consideration, and so, guardless and alone, we crossed the Lejah at 'Ahiry and made straight for Dama.

At first we found the country rough, but generally cut up into fields, many of which were cultivated. The stones had been gathered into heaps, and built up in fences, as is done in the mountainous parts of Ireland and Scotland. As we penetrated further, the cultivation increased, and extended up nearly to Dama.

As we passed Deir Dama on our right, two tall Arabs came in sight, on our path before us, and just as they saw us one of them deliberately stooped for a stone, which he held in his hand under his garments. They were thoroughly armed, and they came up to us in a very defiant manner, and the one who picked up the stone — a tall, desperate-looking character — came up in front of my companion's horse and stopped it. I kept at a distance behind, to one side, and ready for any emergency; and the Arabs, after measuring our strength, and concluding that the balance of chances was against them, stood sullenly aside, and let us pass.

Our servants, however, urged us never to let the Arabs come so close to us. They pointed out that they were armed with swords and clubs, and as one of them had a large stone in his hand, the battle would have been over before we could have had time to begin. It seems we should challenge at a distance all Arabs we met.

We were greatly surprised at the amount of arable land which we found in the heart of the Lejah. We turned off the ordinary track at Dama to go to Harrân, and wandered for a long time out of the beaten path, and we came fully to comprehend the secret of the numerous towns and cities contained in Argob.

Almost the whole country had once been under cultivation, and the little fields, when not now under cultivation, are green with soft, rich grass.

South-west of Dama, also, about one-third of the fields contained wheat and barley. As we approached Jêdâl the cultivated ground became more rare, but everywhere we saw traces of former cultivation.

Again from Jêdâl the cultivation extended with occasional interruptions up to the rugged margin of the Lejah. Burckhardt, when writing of this part of the country, speaks of "the number of small patches of meadow, which afford excellent pasture for the cattle of the Arabs," but we were utterly taken by surprise to find such an amount of arable land cultivated, and non-cultivated, as exists in these parts. The land is also of a very good quality and easily worked, like all soil in basaltic regions.

West of Jêdâl, we met several flocks of goats, and as our servants had been vainly looking out for water all day, we called a halt in order that we might get some milk. The first goatherd we met was a little boy whose only garment was a single piece of white calico, which was hung round his neck like a scarf, and fell down on each side, partially covering him. It was with great difficulty that we could get him to understand what we wanted. Soon a second boy, dressed like the former, but a little older, came forth like a fairy from among the rocks. He was very zealous to strike a bargain with us. We promised him a piaster for the full of a copper basin which he carried with him, but he insisted on having his money in advance. We produced a silver piece which was one-eighth more than a piaster, but he firmly declared that he must have a piaster, and that he would take neither more nor less.

While we were lying in the grass, drinking the milk, two great tall Arabs issued from the rocks, and eyed us from a distance. They then approached one of the muleteers, who was feeding his mule on the wheat at a distance from us, and asked him if we would surrender.

He replied, "Not if there were two thousand of you instead of two; for the Khawajât have guns that fire thirty shots a minute, and five thousand an hour." The logic was conclusive, for the Arabs said, "W'alla," and came up to us at once.

One of them was over six feet two inches high, but looked much taller. His dress consisted of a single coarse calico shirt, and a leathern girdle round his waist, from which a dagger was suspended. He had nothing on his enormous black head, and his buttered and plaited locks hung down his shoulders. He was barefooted, and his right arm, which was tattooed with figures of camels in the most archaic style, was bare to the shoulder, exhibiting muscular development in the highest perfection.

This, and the Arab who crossed our path in the morning, were the finest specimens of their race, physically, I had yet met, and I doubt if I have ever seen a man so powerfully built as that almost naked savage.

On coming up, he assured us, in a somewhat grand manner, that he was a Selût Arab; but seeing that we were not mightily impressed with the information, he overwhelmed us with the additional fact that Abu Suliman, whom all dread, was his sheikh. We assured him that we were greatly delighted to know that he was a Selût Arab, and that his sheikh was Abu Suliman, but that we wanted another piaster's worth of milk; whereupon his highness stooped down, caught a little goat, and provided us with what we wanted, taking care, however, to get paid in full, and a little more.

By-and-by, another little Arab, in the same undress as the former, issued from among the rocks, and the three stood timorously watching all our movements. The tall Arabs were very greedy, and asked us for everything we had, like children.

The little boys were more easily satisfied, and seemed filled with delight on receiving a few percussion caps. They had never heard of Adam, or David the shepherd, or the other Good Shepherd who gave His life for the sheep. They were wild and hardy as the goats and sheep they were tending, a little higher intellectually, and not so well clad or cared for. They all assured us that no one in their tribe could read, and so they had no use for our books.

As we approached Zobeir, the ground became more wavy, and as we had to go along the hollows and had no steady object in view, we kept moving about for a time almost in a circle. We all hurried up to an elevated point, believing that we had almost reached the village, when, to our surprise, we discovered it behind us, and that we had been going further from it, instead of approaching closer to it. As we thus wandered about, we had additional opportunities of seeing the capabilities of the land, and of forming an idea of the high state of perfection to which it must have been brought, for almost everywhere, even on the bare rocks, we saw traces of former cultivation, and we ceased to wonder that so many ruins existed among the sable waves of the Lejah.

By keeping our eye fixed on the highest rock in the line of our march, we at last got free of the mazy waves among which we were entangled, and soon we emerged once more on the open plain at Khubab.

As we cast our eye along the black rocky coastline, we thought of the striking appropriateness of the Hebrew word *Hebel*, always applied to Argob in the Bible, whether that word means a rope, in reference to its "sharply defined border," or whether, as would be equally appropriate, the word signifies *a wave*.

We now proceeded north-west for more than an hour, through an unbroken flat of level wheat, in which we passed an enormous flock of gazelles, and reached Buseir at the going down of the sun. We soon discovered that the inhabitants of the place were Christians, by their curiosity and activity. They swarmed about us, bringing antiquities, and eggs and milk, unasked, and showed much eagerness to make bargains with us.

The people, having finished the ploughing and sow-

THE HAJJ LEAVING DAMASCUS.

ing, were all busily engaged in dressing mill-stones, and we were shown eight which were purchased on the day of our arrival, by a merchant from Akka, for forty napoleons. We passed an uncomfortable night at Buseir, and though the rain poured down upon us, we were obliged to pay for water for ourselves and horses.

On April 16th we started early for Damascus. Our path lay through a stony, cultivated plain, in which hundreds of storks were marching up and down the wheat in straight lines, and partridges were shouting from rock to rock. As we approached the Hajj road we saw enormous flocks of vultures, soaring and wheeling, and filling the air before us. We soon learned the cause. "Where the carcass is, there will the *vultures* be gathered together."

The great caravan of pilgrims from Mekka had passed that way the day before, and had left their track strewed with horses, and mules, and camels, dead and dying. Apparently no officer from the Society for Prevention of Cruelty to Animals accompanies the Hajj, and so the holy men ride on their animals till the saddles sink into the bones, and when they can force them along no further, they abandon them to die of their wounds and thirst.

The vultures come along a day in the rear of the pilgrims, and strip the quivering flesh off the animals ere they are quite dead. They all fall upon a carcass together, and when they have stripped it bare, they rise like a mighty whirlwind into the air, and ascend and soar round and round for a few minutes, until one of them, espying a new victim, strikes off at a tangent from the huge, revolving vulture cloud, and draws the rest after it in the form of a comet, of which it is the nucleus.

Down, down they come swooping on their prey, and they cover the animal until nothing is seen but a struggling heap of vultures; and so intent are they on the feast, that you might run in among them and knock them down with a stick. All the vultures of Arabia seemed to be gathered together in this one great army, and they were so confident that they stood red in talon and beak and watched us from a few yards' distance as we passed.

We halted at Kesweh,[1] a town on the 'Awaj, where the river has made a little paradise among the bare red fields. The pilgrims had abandoned the place a few hours previous to our arrival, and everything was abominably filthy, except the little stream of running water.

We approached Damascus, bringing up the rear of the Hajj, but it being Wednesday, an unlucky day, the caravan could not officially enter the Holy City. Some of the pilgrims of the worldly sort pushed on straight to their

---

[1] "The accurate Burckhardt" sometimes takes one's breath away. He says, El-Kesweh is a considerable village situated on the river 'Awaj, or the Crooked, which flows from the neighbourhood of Hasbeya, and waters the plain of Djolan ("Travels in Syria and the Holy Land," p. 53). He would have little trouble in making a "stream meander level with its fount," who could bring the 'Awaj over Mount Hermon from Hasbeya or carry it over Joulan.

homes; but the devout ones were sitting outside the walls, quarrelling and swearing, and plying the instruments of King James' luxury, their nails; and when their wives and children came out to meet them after a long absence, they did not rise to receive their welcome or show any sign of gladness at meeting them once more. We met crowds coming out of the city to kiss the hands and beards of these holy pilgrims, and their blessing was eagerly sought.[1] Keating would have been useful.

As we entered the "pearly Damascus" in its emerald setting, after a weary ride through an uninteresting country, we could thoroughly sympathize with the extravagant manner in which the Arabs speak of "the *Pleasant*," "the *Honourable*," "the *Holy*," "the *Blessed*" Damascus.

I have thus endeavoured to present a simple picture of Bashan, its people and ruins, as I saw them. No doubt the picture is only a sketchy outline, but it is an outline of all the important parts.

Moreover, in the disposition of light and shade I have had no theory to support, and therefore I have had no inducement to distort facts to give colour to my own preconceived opinions. I have sought truth for its own sake, without any attempt to champion Scripture history, or prophecy, believing, as I do, that simple facts in every department of human research best illustrate the Divine Word.

[1] The prophet said, "God pardons the pilgrim, and him for whom the pilgrim prays." Hence, on meeting the pilgrim, the people say, "Pray for pardon for me," to which the pilgrim replies, "Allah, pardon him."

No one need be discouraged because the picture is poor in mechanical evidence of the pre-Israelitish inhabitants of Bashan, when he remembers how many thousand years the spoilers have been within her borders; that the Romans, who reconstructed her cities, pulled down to build up; and above all, when he remembers what destruction a few centuries of misrule have been able to accomplish in the splendid cities of Syria.[1]

And is not the light shed on the Sacred Record by simple facts, of a nature to satisfy the most utilitarian investigator? That Bashan contained an enormous number of towns is a fact proved beyond all cavil.[2]

The ruins of "the towns of Jair, which are in Bashan, threescore cities" (Josh. xiii. 30), are there to this day, some of them unchanged even in name, and we have seen, from the tokens of a former cultivation, that these cities had extensive resources in their own strange land.

But with the picture, I wish to present a plea on behalf of the inhabitants of Bashan. We are the hereditary friends of the Druzes. They look on us as their protectors, and welcome us among them as their bene-

[1] In digging the foundation of the Presbyterian church in Damascus, Roman remains were found to a depth of fifteen feet; thus the floors of the houses in the Damascus of to-day occupy nearly the same position as did the roofs of the houses in the Damascus of Augustus.

[2] Burckhardt, during two brief tours in Bashan in 1812, discovered one hundred and seventy-one ruins. Since then, Porter, Waddington, and others have brought important ruins to light which were unnoticed by Burckhardt. I have in my note-book over two hundred names of places in Bashan, all of considerable importance. A rich harvest still awaits the patient archæologist in that wonderful land.

factors; but have we ever done anything for them? For a few individuals, yes. For the Druze people, no. Bashan as a mission field has never been occupied, nor are there in existence within its borders any really serious direct missionary operations.

And yet there is no more attractive mission field for a missionary of manly piety than among the chivalrous Druzes of the Hauran.

Nor have we any reason to consider a mission to the Druzes hopeless, for they who believed, through the preaching of Dorazy, in the incarnation of the mad Fatimite, El-Hakem, would surely be brought, through the preaching of the Gospel, which is the Power of God, to believe in the incarnation of Jesus, who is the Wisdom of God.

And let me add, without presumption, that whatever church or people attempts mission work in the Hauran, should send their best man to the work, one of themselves, who will carry the living sympathy of his people with him; for a mere hireling, or adventurer, will be as impotent for good as the prophet's servant when laying a lifeless stick on the face of a dead child.

INDEX.

Abana, 235.
Abanias, 236.
Abraham, 9.
Abu Ali, 329.
Abu el-Fawaris, 97, 139, 181.
Abu Muraj, 243.
Abu Rebâh, 34, 35.
Abu Sahil, 60, 80, 90.
Abu Suliman, 379.
Adraa, 284.
Adra'at, 284, 286, 287.
Agrippa, 64, 312.
'Ahiry, 371.
'Ain el-Wu'ul, 40, 54, 141, 184, 200.
'Ain Mousa, 328.
Akka, 275, 383.
Alath, 106.
Alemanni, 150.
Aleppo, 105, 141.
Alexandria, 133.
'Alliasha, 90.
Amelius, 133.
Ammonius Saccas, 133.
'Amour Bedawîn, 33, 178, 185.
Anazi Bedawîn, 208.
Ancyra, 140.
Anti-Lebanon, 5.
Antioch, 118, 141, 142, 147.
Antony, Mark, 103, 104, 110.
Apamea, 148.
Arab curiosity, 269.
Arab romancers, 124.
Archæological fever, 195, 196.
Arethusa, 148.
Argob, 247, 271, 377.
Armenians, 132.
Ashtaroth, 289.
Asia Minor, 140, 153, 154.
Asîleh, 199.
Athens, 133.
Athila, 319, 320.
Atîl, 320.

'Atny, 191.
Atrash, 325.
Attack of guard, 198.
Augustus, 137.
Aurelian, 67, 104, 140, 145, 146 ; to Zenobia, 157 ; his triumph, 164.
'Awaj, 234, 235, 384.
Azzab, 179.

Baalatga, 90.
Bab el-Howa, 359.
Bab es-Shurki, 193, 225.
Bab Tûma, 5.
Babîla, 232.
Bagdad donkeys, 49 ; post, 3.
Baldwin III., 226.
Ballista, 118, 120.
Barada, 236.
Bârady, 42.
Barri, 141.
Bashan, 223, 250, 315 ; reapers, 30 ; threescore cities, 386.
Bathaniyeh, 252.
Bath-Zabbai, 73, 127.
Battle of Immae, 145.
Beaufort, Miss, 63.
Bedawîn, 22, 23, 26, 29.
Bedawi raids, 3, 20, 171, 206 ; attack, 172, 186.
Beilan Pass, 142.
Belkis, Lady, 33.
Ben Hadad, 239.
Beni Samayda, 124.
Berkeley, Hon. C. F. P., and wife, 4.
Bible Society, 224.
Bible testimony, 1.
Birch, Dr., 88, 89.
Blackmail, 190, 254.
Blight of Islam, 170, 332.
Blood-mare, 199.
Blunt, Lady Anne, 53.
Bosphorus, 140.
Bosra, 105, 284, 349, 350, 354 ; robbers, 361.

390 INDEX.

"Brandy Bob," 41, 42, 172, 176, 180, 183.
Brandy used, 203.
British Museum, 88.
Broomfield, W., 231.
Buckle, 230.
Bukha, 16.
Burâk, 240, 247, 252.
Burckhardt, 254, 263, 313, 334.
Burton, 74.
Burzeh, 6.
Busr el-Hariry, 296.
Bustard, 263.
Byzantium, 164.

CAIUS CASSIUS, 135.
Callistus, 118, 120.
Camels, 224.
Capitolias, 284.
Cappadocia, 116.
Captive's song, 47.
Captive Syrian girl, 46.
Caravan, 185.
Carchemish, 105.
Cassius Chærea, 135.
Cassius Longinus, 133, 142, 148.
Castle of Palmyra, 98.
Ceionius Bassus, 163.
Celtic legions, 149.
Cemeteries, 226.
Chalcedon, 164, 252.
Chaldæan monarch, 91.
Challenge, 207, 216.
Chased, 201.
Chester, Rev. Greville, 88.
Choosing workmen, 79.
Christian inscriptions, 353.
Christian spies, 360.
Church at Ezrá, 293.
Cilicia, 118.
Circesium, 111.
Claudius, 136.
Cleopatra, 123, 132.
Coffee making, 336.
Coins, 136, 155, 194, 284, 300.
College at Beyrout, 59.
Colportage, 276.
Conference, 218.
Constantia, 252.
Consul, 301.
Convent of Saidenâya, 10.
Corinthian capitals, 63, 283.
Cornelius Capitolinus, 132.
Cotesworth, Mr., 84.
Crawford, Dr., 216.
Cruelty to animals, 383.
Crusaders, 226.
Ctesiphon, 121.
Cuckoo, 330.
Curlew, 56.

DABBOUS, 150, 215.
Dalmatian cavalry, 149.
Dama, 372, 373.
Damascus, 5, 6, 9, 192, 220; massacre, 226; rivers, 236.
Danava, 111.
Danube, 117.
Daphne, 147.
David's trick, 183.
Dawara range, 60, 98.
Dawoud, Khalîl, 224, 231.
Decius, 117.
Deir 'Atîyeh, 22, 23, 187.
Deir en-Nasara, 343.
Derá, 286.
Deyr, 160.
Digby, Lady, 231.
Dilly, 288.
Diocletian, 169.
Diomede, 293.
Dionysias, 326.
Disillusioning, 196.
Disraeli, 46, 219.
Dorazy, 387.
Druzes, 12, 223, 251, 254, 298; excited, 335; guerilla, 363; horns, 306; mission, 387; song, 93; speech, 338; women, 306, 317, 327, 365.
Dusares, 341, 353.

EDESSA, 117.
Edrei, 284, 291.
Egypt, 123, 136.
El-Hakem, 387.
El-Kra, 314.
El-Kufr, 329.
El-Kutifeh, 192.
Ellenborough, Lady, 110.
Emesa, 120, 133, 141, 147, 152.
Encounter with Arabs, 217.
English engineers, 9, 80.
English travellers, 224.
English workmen, 6.
Ephca fountain, 95, 152, 155.
Ethiopia, 89.
Eth-thunîyeh, 192.
Et-Tell, 10.
Euphrates, 23, 98, 103, 111, 116, 159, 185.
Europe, 137.
Eusebius, 145, 284.
Excavators, 130.
Ezrá, 280, 293.

FAMINE, 20.
Faris, gipsy guide, 41.
Father of ladders, 77.
Fendy Abu' Fakhr, 297.
Feride, 276.
Florentinus, 315.

INDEX. 391

Fox, 33.
Frazer, Rev. J., 230.
GALLIENUS, 120, 121, 161.
Gaza, 104.
Gazâwy, 24, 175.
Gazelle traps, 42.
Gazzo, 22.
Gergesa, 19.
Giath Bedawîn, 33.
Gichos, 83.
Gideon, 313.
Gilead, 313.
Gladstone, 219.
Goths, 115, 123, 140, 150.
Greek Catholic convent, 13.
Greek inscriptions, 16, 32, 34, 282, 296, 326, 365.
Greville Chester, Rev., 88.
Grouse, 263.
Guide, 24.
Gunthur, 32, 33.

HABIBA, 274.
Hadrian, 64, 106, 107, 111.
Hadrianopolis, 111.
Hafr, 25.
Hair, 271.
Hairan, 115.
Hajj, 383.
Halet Pasha, 187.
Hamah, 25, 141, 219.
Hamam, 141.
Hamnets, William, 230.
Handcuffs, 13.
Hare, 33.
Harper, Professor A., 223.
Harrân, 376.
Hauran, 240, 318; Towers, 279.
Hawarîn, 30, 31, 32, 141.
Hazar-enan, 37.
Hebel, 380.
Hebrân, 330.
Helbon wine, 14.
Heliogabalus, 135.
Hell (Sheol), 91.
Heraclianus, 136.
Hermon, 6, 221, 232, 234, 277, 289.
Herod the Great, 318.
Heshbon, 284.
Hierocles, 253.
History, 1.
Hittites, 25.
Hittite inscriptions, 220.
Holy of Holies, 68.
Hospitality, 257.
Hums, 6, 25, 149, 151.
Hunger, 21.
Husein Abu Muhammed, 342.

IAMLICHOS, 83.
Ibex, 48; hunters, 49.
Ibrahîm Pasha, 21, 254.
Ibrahîm el-Atrash, 325.
Ibrahîm Nejm el-Atrash, 334.
Idumeans, 318.
Immae, 145.
Imperator, 137.
Imprisoned, 92.
Imtan el-Khudr, 343.
Isaiah, 91.
Isai Bedawîn, 346.
Ishmaelites, 4, 49, 189.

JAIR, 386.
Jambrouda, 18.
Jân, 110.
Jaral, 141.
Jebel ed-Druze, 314.
Jebel el-'Aleib, 101.
Jebel el-Aswad, 233.
Jebel el-Kuleib, 295, 362.
Jebel el-Mantar, 60, 95.
Jebel Kalamoun, 3, 5, 6.
Jêdâl, 377.
Jeremiah, 332.
Jerûd, 192, 343.
Jisr et-Taiyebeh, 285.
Jogbehah, 313.
Jordan, 313.
Josephus, 312, 318.
Jowf, 343.
Jub-'Adîn, 16.
Jupiter Capitolinus, 164.
Justinian, 169.

KADISHEH, 199.
Kalamoun, 3, 5, 6, 25.
Kanath, 313.
Kanatha, 315.
Kanawât, 308, 311, 312, 314, 319, 333.
Kara, 25.
Karak, 4, 105.
Karrhæ, 105.
Karyetein, 3, 30, 31, 36, 37, 141, 184, 188, 211.
Kasr el-Hazûn, 101.
Kasr el-Hiyar, 43, 51, 141.
Kasr eth-Thunîyeh, 84.
Kasr Mabroom, 311, 333.
Kefr el-Laha, 362, 364.
Kefr Howar, 234.
Kerbela, 48.
Kesweh, 384.
Khaled, 193, 226.
Khubab, 272, 274, 333.
Khuderîyeh, 42.
King James' luxury, 385.
Kishk, 369.
Koradæa, 37.

Koran, 16, 296.
Kufeiley, 177, 178.
Kuleib, 328.
Kurds, 17.
Kureiyeh, 348, 349.

LABAN, 297.
Ladders, 74.
Larissa, 148.
Latin inscriptions, 234, 365.
Lava, 271.
Lebanon, 5, 101.
Lejah, 247, 250, 258, 297.
Lent, 348.
Levant Herald, 30, 185, 190.
Longinus, 103, 124, 134, 158, 162.
Lord Amadhon, 272, 273.
Lullaby, 47.

MADDER ROOT, 20.
Magrabi woman, 320.
Máloula, 10, 13, 16, 17.
Manasseh, 289, 313.
Mantar, 60, 95.
Mâraba, 9.
Marbat 'Antar, 140, 141.
Mar Theckla, 14.
Maundrell, 11.
Mediterranean, 116.
Mejdel, 301, 302.
Mekka Pilgrims, 383.
Melah es-Sarrâr, 340, 341, 342.
Melihat Hezkîn, 279.
Menin, 10.
Mesopotamia, 111, 116, 121.
Midianites, 313.
Mission school, 52.
Mommsen, 111, 152, 161.
Monks, 13.
Muaddamiyeh, 192.
Muhejjeh, 282.
Muhîn, 26, 141.
Mule, 77.
Mummies, 194.
Musmeih, 253, 268.
Mysians, 149.

NAAMAN, 235.
Nabathean inscriptions, 344, 365.
Naked soldier, 213.
Nazala, 37.
Nazareth, 20.
Nebk, 10, 21, 24, 187.
Nehala, 37.
Nejha, 234.
Nejrân, 297, 301.
Nero, 135.
Nice, Council of, 18.
Nicomachus, 158.

Nile, 103, 138.
Nisibis, 121.
Nobah, 313.
Noricum, 149.
Nuthatches, 15.

ODAINATHUS, 73, 103, 115, 117, 119, 121; victorious, 119, 120; murdered, 122.
Og, 284, 289, 290, 300.
Og's Edrei identified, 291.
Omar Bey, 35, 50.
Orientals, 119.
Origines, 133.
Ormân, 331, 332, 334, 338.
Orontes, 140, 149.
Ottoman rule, 337.

PALESTINIANS, 149, 150.
Palmyra twice visited, 3; castle, 55, 98; mountains, 98; name, 101; cavalry, 146.
Palmyrene inscriptions, 89, 110.
Paonians, 149.
Parthia, 103.
Parthians, 66, 154.
Partridges, 33, 51, 255.
Paul, 226.
Peaceful Arabs, 49.
Penuel, 313.
Persian larks, 25; greyhound, 54.
Persians, 112, 132.
Petra, 4, 104.
Peutinger Itinerary, 37, 284.
Phæna, 253, 265, 267.
Pharpar, 6, 234, 235, 239.
Phœnicians, 149.
Philip, 266.
Philip the Arabian, 364.
Philippopolis, 364.
Phronto, 133.
Picture, 11.
Pliny, 104, 110.
Plunder, 186, 187.
Pompeiopolis, 118.
Porphyry, 134.
Porter, 254, 294.
Princess, 46.
Probatus, 136.
Probus, 137.
Prussian Sisters, Beyrout, 276.
Ptolemies, 124.

RAHA, 328.
Rahibeh, 187.
Ransacking the tombs, 80.
Ras el-'Ain, 37.
Ras el-Kowz, 18.
Recruits, 13.
Rhœtium, 149.
Rhubarb, 21.

INDEX.   393

Rimet el-Lohf, 364, 365.
River scenery, 10.
Roman arms, 103; purple, 103; historians, 110; legions, 111, 135; cavalry, 146, 149; triumph, 169; road, 105, 283, 307, 323.
Rufinus, 115.
Ruse, 203.
Rustan, 46.
Ruth-like gleaners, 29.

SAFA, 232.
Saidenâya, 10, 11, 12, 13, 23; miracle, 11 12.
Saladin, 9.
Salcah, 289.
Salimîyeh, 141.
Salmalath, 106.
Salt, 343.
Sapor, 116, 117, 118, 119.
Saracens, 193.
Sasa, 234.
Scalpers, 271.
Schewet el-Khudr, 330, 331.
Scott, Rev. Jas. Orr, 223, 230.
Scythopolis, 313.
Seleucidæ, 25.
Selût Arab, 379.
Septimia Zenobia, 73.
Septimius Odainathus, 73.
Severus, 111, 112.
Shehâb, 364.
Sheikh Abu Shahîn, 307.
Sheikh Dabbous, 30, 185.
Sheikh Hasimeh, 301, 302.
Sheikh Hezkîn, 280.
Sheikh Hussein, 371.
Shems, 106.
Sheol, 91.
Shepherds robbed, 3.
Shuhba, 364.
Shukra, 283.
Shunning the camp, 200.
Sihon, 289.
Skulls, 87, 93, 194.
Soada, 326.
Solemus, 252.
Solomon, 1, 33, 35, 102, 124.
Solomon's Baths, 32.
St. Elias, 292.
St. George, 292, 293, 330.
St. Luke, 10.
Stanley, 24.
Statues, 124.
Stone doors, etc., 250.
Storks, 233.
Strabo, 89.
Straight Street, 5, 224.
Strange lady, 298.
"Strip!" 216.
Subhi Pasha, 148, 187, 219.

Succoth, 313.
Sudud, 25, 26, 27.
Suez, 230.
Suleib Arabs, 48; donkeys, 52; beauty, 53.
Suleim, 307, 311.
Sulkhad, 331, 344.
Sunday at Bosra, 355; at Khubab, 276.
Suweideh, 323, 324.
Syriac spoken, 16.
Syrian maps, 5; roads, 9.

TADMOR, 23; ruins, 1; artists, 67; belles, 83; name, 101; origin of, 102; prosperity of, 104; cavalry, 129; besieged, 152.
Tamerlane, 236.
Taura, 6, 239.
Tax gatherers, 80, 255.
Teleky, Countess, 230.
Tell 'Ammâr, 371.
Tell Ash'areh, 290.
Tell Ashtarah, 290.
Tell Karak, 289, 290.
Tell Sheehân, 307.
Terra-cotta tablets, 194.
Temple of the King's Mother, 64, 107.
Temple of the Sun, 17, 61, 107, 163, 165, 170.
Teutonic chivalry, 23.
Theandrias, 320.
Thomson, Dr., 285.
Tibny, 282.
Tigris, 98.
Timagenes, 137.
Tirhakah, 88, 89.
Tomb towers, 81, 82, 86, 110.
Towers, 279, 333.
Trachonitis, 247.
Trade routes to India, 104.
Trebellius Pollio, 109, 119, 136.
Turkish officials, 179, 187, 190; soldiers, 355
Turks, 21, 32, 177.
Tyana, 141.
Tyanians, 149.

UMBRELLA HANDLE, 195.
Um el-Jemâl, 359.
Underground tomb, 91.
Unpleasant companions, 215.

VALERIAN, 116, 117.
Via recta, 225.
Victors' feast, 346.
Vopiscus, 109, 158, 161.
Vultures, 383.

WA'AL, 48.
Waddington, 253, 315, 342.
Wady Barbar, 239.
Wady Zeidy, 285.
Wah-ballath, 115, 195.

Waked el-Hamdân, 324, 325, 327.
Walnuts, 10.
Warm fountain, 96.
Wasm, 35.
Water-carriers, 50.
Weedy horses, 179.
Wetzstein, Dr., 288.
Wheat pits, 275.
Wood and Dawkins, 83.
Wounded, 210.

YABROUD, 10, 17, 18, 19, 21; people, 19.

ZABBAI, 127.
Zabdas, 127. 136, 147.

Zabdeathus, 105.
Zedad, 25.
Zeinab, 72, 109.
Zenobia, home of, 1; jewels of, 68; palace of, 72; Tadmor of, 87; kinship of, 123, 131; head of, 128; described, 131; a linguist, 133; army of, 142; in arms, 147, 149; defence of, 156; letter to Aurelian, 157; flight of, 159; captured, 160; a captive, 164.
Zobeir, 379.
Zobeireh, 274.
Zorava, 292.
Zosimus, 109, 142, 147, 149, 156, 168.
Zulmeh Hills, 289.